Sheryl & Mel London's CREATIVE COOKING WITH GRAINS & PASTA

Other Books by Sheryl and Mel London

The Fish-Lovers' Cookbook
(Rodale Press, 1980)

By Sheryl London

Eggplant and Squash: A Versatile Feast
(Atheneum, 1976)

Making the Most of Your Freezer
(Rodale Press, 1978)

By Mel London

Getting into Film
(Ballantine, 1977)

Bread Winners
(Rodale Press, 1979)

Easy Going
(Rodale Press, 1981)

Second Spring
(Rodale Press, 1982)

Sheryl & Mel London's CREATIVE COOKING WITH GRAINS & PASTA

Editor: Charles Gerras

Book Design: Merole Berger

Book Layout: Daniel M. Guest

Illustrations: Susan Rosenberger

Color Photography: Carl Doney, Mitchell T. Mandel, Sally Ann Shenk, and Margaret Smyser

Black and White Photography: Mitchell T. Mandel, Pat Seip, and Christie Tito

Food Stylist: Laura Hendry Reifsnyder

Rodale Press, Emmaus, Pa.

Printed in the United States of America on recycled paper, containing a high percentage of de-inked fiber.

Library of Congress Cataloging in Publication Data

London, Sheryl.
    Sheryl and Mel London's Creative cooking with grains and pasta.

    Includes index.
    1. Cookery (Cereals) 2. Cookery (Macaroni)
I. London, Mel. II. Gerras, Charles.
III. Title. IV. Title: Creative cooking
with grains and pasta.
TX808.L66 1982   641.6'31   82-9155
ISBN 0-87857-413-1   hardcover   AACR2

2 4 6 8 10 9 7 5 3 1   hardcover

For Carole
Who showed us all what courage means.

Contents

Contents

viii

Acknowledgments

In the development and the writing of any cookbook, its authors will tell you that at some point in the process, there is a feeling that it is one continual, nonstop, perpetual succession of testing, tasting, and tinkering. There is a nagging suspicion that there is no other room in the entire house except the kitchen and that you might never be released from the chains of the measuring cup, the pots and pans, and the range and oven. But, at the same time, there *is* a light—the realization that you are not alone, that somewhere there is support and encouragement and help. And as triumphant recipes take their place atop the pile that grows each day, you begin to hear a silent cheer from those who have helped so very much.

Throughout the testing of our cookbooks for Rodale Press, we have been delighted, encouraged, and very grateful for the support given us by the Rodale Test Kitchen personnel—Tom Ney, Anita Hirsch, JoAnn Coponi, Karen Haas, Deborah Deis, Sally Zahradnik, and Pat Singley.

In the writing of this book in particular, they gave of their help unstintingly in retesting our recipes and serving them to willing Rodale employees for evaluation. In the areas of unusual grains such as amaranth, their knowledge was especially important to us in developing an entirely new cuisine.

To our delightful editor, Charles Gerras, who has once again put up with our questions, our tendency to provide too many recipes to fit the limited space of a book, and the fact that we never do anything in sequence, our deepest thanks. To Camille Bucci, who managed to collate the blizzard of paper that went by messenger from New York to Emmaus, and who checked through every recipe for consistency and accuracy, a special note of gratitude for her care and efficiency.

Our thanks go out to Tina Gonzalez, not only for her research and her typing (and retyping), but for making amaranth her own personal challenge. And to Jackie Hickey, for her good-natured and impressive work on the homemade pasta section of the book. And to our friends at the farms, mills, distributors, and co-operatives all across the country, we admit humbly that we could not have done it without your gracious help.

And finally, a nod to all our Fire Island neighbors who so willingly partook of our tested recipes for almost two years. To all who were our guests at breakfast, lunch, or dinner, usually with only five minutes notice, since we never knew when a dish would be ready—or, indeed, if it would be a triumph or a failure—we thank you one and all. At least, you do know now that whole grains are good for you!

x

Introduction

These past two years devoted to a grains cookbook have evolved into a remarkable adventure for us. In the writing of our four previous cookbooks, and in testing the recipes for them, the guidelines were more obvious. The generations that preceded us had left fairly explicit instructions about the qualities and the handling of fresh-grown vegetables or the baking of bread, and even for the preparation of fish that carried a thousand different names and came from a hundred different sources. We assumed, naively, that the literature and the cookbooks on the subject of grains would be as helpful to us; we even thought that, possibly, a book such as the one we had in mind had been done before.

After all, we were dealing with one of the oldest forms of food energy in the history of mankind. Anthropological and culinary studies brought images of grain-harvesting Assyrians and Aztecs and ancient Chinese dancing through our heads. In our minds we saw the romantic pictures of American pioneers standing waist-deep in fields of grain, the chaff of the wheat wafting downwind in a golden-yellow blizzard. Surely, the women of those days had left their secret and tasty recipes for future generations to savor. If we were at first naive, we were soon to find that we were, more often than not, *wrong!*

Here was a remarkable and varied roster of foods—some of them with familiar names like wheat and rye, corn and oats and rice. Others were common to cultures in other lands on other continents, but were sorely underutilized or totally ignored by most American cooks: millet, for example, and to a lesser extent bulgur and buckwheat. One had only recently been developed (triticale), and we were still experimenting with its characteristics. And still others, however ancient their history, were new to us—sorghum (milo) and amaranth, that remarkably nutritious grain, prized all over the world since the time of the Aztecs, but virtually unknown in the United States.

To our complete surprise, we found that reliable instructions for the basic preparation and cooking of most of these exceptional foods were not available. Directions given by the "experts," as well as by the growers and the marketers (not to mention the so-called "instructions" on the packages), were rampant with misinformation. The recipes themselves generally reflected the prejudices (oats as breakfast cereal, rice with Oriental dishes, and such) that have kept so many of us away from an extraordinary and versatile source of nutrition and taste.

We set out to learn more about grains, America's most underrated, underutilized treasure. The shelves of our Fire Island kitchen now bulge with small jars, all of them filled with golden and brown and white and yellow grains in all their glorious forms. Neat labels designate their family tree, the type of milling process, and geographic source. We haunted the natural foods stores and supermarket aisles, discovering names and farm sources we had not known to exist, and wondering just what a cook might do with all of those grains. On occasion, we found the name of a grain form that was new to us, and then could not locate it in our local store. This started a hunt across the country, contacting friends at the grain-growing farms—Arrowhead, Hereford, Texas; Shiloh, Sulphur Springs, Arkansas; El Molino, City of Industry, California; Walnut Acres, Penns Creek, Pennsylvania; and even down in Kutztown, Pennsylvania, at our own beloved Rodale Research Center, where most of our research on amaranth was done.

The grain collection grew. On the shelves were Bulgur #1 (Fine), Bulgur #2 (Medium), and Bulgur #3 (Coarse), all set next to a jar labeled Bulgur Whole. There were Rice Flakes, Rice Cream, Rice Flour, Wild Rice, Short and Long Grain Brown Rice. We had grains that had been ground into meal, into flour, and into flakes. We had kernels, and we had puffs. *Frumento* (Italian) bore a subhead *Kuta* (African), though both are basically the same hulled wheat berries. Triticale, with which we had become familiar during the testing of the recipes for *Bread Winners,* took its own shelf space with textures that ranged the gamut from flour to flakes.

We may have been presumptuous, but we decided that, once and for all time, we would attempt to take the mystique out of the subject of grains. We would try to be more explicit and comprehensive than any who have preceded us in this realm of detailing what should be simple and wholesome gastronomy. And so, it took two years of testing and creating, of investigating and questioning to produce this book. And—not the least of all—it also involved two years of cooking and eating whole grains almost every day for nearly every meal and sometimes through every course from appetizer and soup to entree and dessert, and, of course, bread.

If you are already one of us, if grains are already a part of your regular daily diet, we think that you will discover, as we did, that there are still a thousand new doors waiting to be opened in a world of innovation with familiar friends. If, on the other hand, whole grains are new to you, you are joining a long overdue renaissance in America. You are one of many who would like to reduce their dependence on meat for protein and cut back on their intake of the saturated fats in meat and the processed chemicals that typify the packaged supermarket fare. And if you are interested in stretching the budget dollar in these days of high inflation—while adding limitless nutrition and pleasure to the diet of your family—then the best is yet to come. In the process, you will come very far from porridge (or is it pottage?) and cornmeal (or is it mush?) and grits and groats (or are they gruel?).

Sheryl & Mel London
Fire Island, New York

Part I
Getting Acquainted with Grains

The Chronicles of Grain

Food of History, Legend, and Tradition

Both of us are avid readers of our daily newspaper, not only the headlined items but also the one-inch "fillers." They give us all the necessary information and statistics guaranteed to make us thoroughly boring dinner company, should anyone dare to invite us. These fillers frequently turn out to be more interesting and certainly less aggravating than the political and international headlines.

This morning, another interesting story surfaced. The headline informed us that the antibiotic tetracycline had been found in the bones of the ancient Sudanese people who had lived along the Nile River about 14 centuries ago. Had tetracycline been invented at that time, this would have been no real revelation. We merely would have passed it off with the guess that the Sudanese doctors had overmedicated their patients as our own physicians often do today. In this case, the University of Massachusetts research group theorized, the bacteria that comprises the drug had grown spontaneously in the mud bins of grain—the wheat, the millet, and the barley stored for future use. Not surprisingly, therefore, the researchers found that Sudanese who lived in that area between the years of A.D. 350 and A.D. 550 had a low rate of infectious disease.

In one way or another, the history of grain appears again and again in today's news. How could it be otherwise, when grains are so closely involved with human life? It's no accident that garlands of wheat, for example, have been the symbols of power and bounty since before the time of the Romans. For the ancients, the harvest was a buffer against starvation, and as far back as 9000 B.C. the villages formed near the fields of wild wheat and barley so that these people of the neolithic period would be close by for the few days when the crop was ripe for gathering. Though the grain was easy to store for the winter, it was impossible to carry it for a long distance—and the wheel had not yet been invented.

In *Food in History* by Reay Tannahill (Briarcliff Manor: Stein & Day, 1973), a remarkable and fascinating book, grain appears frequently as the main character in the development of man's food chain—from the prehistoric world to the present. And it is no wonder, for in the history of the world, *no single major civilization has ever developed in the absence of a basic cereal grain!*

Archeologists have uncovered silos of maize in the excavations of Mayan ruins here in North America. The Aztecs were cultivating high-yield amaranth—today's "food of the future"—when the Spaniards came to the New World. For the ancient Chinese, rice was the designated sustainer of life. The Japanese god that symbolizes prosperity and plenty is known as the Great Grain Spirit. The Incas celebrated maize as the Child of the Sun, and the Babylonians venerated wheat. Rome kept its population content with bread and circuses, and right up to the present day, our own "America, the Beautiful" celebrates our "amber waves of grain." It is by no means an accident.

It is fascinating to see that grain sometimes surfaces as a political football. In our own century, the sale of grain to the Soviet Union sets off loud debates between the members of Congress and the farming community. The story is not new. Even ancient Rome ran into severe problems when it levied tribute in the form of grain on the territories it had conquered. So much grain poured into the port of Ostia that the local farmers stopped raising it because they could not compete, and, eventually, the Empire became completely dependent upon outside sources of food.

That certain cultures came to depend upon specific species of grain was largely an accident of climate. Simply put, if the temperature, the winds, and the precipitation were best for oats or millet or maize, these grains were planted and harvested by the people in that part of the world. Before the fourteenth century, for example, Iceland was a cultivator of grain, but when the weather turned frigid, the dependence on fish became the prime factor in the food chain.

In some cases, grains were imported to their current fields. Rice, for example, came to Europe with the Saracens and found acceptance and a place to grow in Italy. Other grains did not fare as well. Columbus brought back maize from the New World, but Europe, in general, is still not a major producer of corn, while the United States measures its bounty in millions of metric tons.

The paddy fields of Asia, California, and Texas, the terraced, flooded beds of the Philippines, and the wet Po Valley in Italy are perfect for the cultivation of rice. Subtropical China and Africa give us sorghum and millet, while chilly Russia and Eastern Europe offer buckwheat, and Scotland and Ireland are noted for their oats. Wheat, barley, and rye flourish in the temperate zones such as our own Great Plains, the Canadian prairies, and Central Russia, and corn is at home almost all across America.

Understandably, the cuisine of any nation or area reflects its most abundant grain crop—the barley paste, *tsampa,* of Tibet, the oatmeal of Scotland, the *polenta* of Italy, the mealie porridge of Africa, the Johnnycakes of the United States, and the *chapatis* of India.

What surprises and disturbs us most is that today grains are almost generally ignored as a prime food source in our own country. Our grandmothers were much more familiar with the use and the values of whole grains than we are. Their knowledge has been lost somehow in the blizzard of colorful packaging, overprocessing, and the changes in diet that have given us the gift of a fast-food culture.

Whereas the ancients and our own grandparents used grains as a large part of the complete diet, we have relegated this remarkable food source to a few predictable appearances in breads, cakes, pastas, or breakfast cereals. Most of this so-called "fuel of civilization" grown in America is used to feed animals! We have almost totally written off the potential in grains.

Grains and Nutrition

Merit, Myths, and Misconceptions

Over dinner in a Chinese restaurant, we mention to a friend that we are currently working on a book about whole grains. "Boy! Will you get fat!" is the reaction. A walk on a sunny day near the ocean and we meet one of our neighbors, a doctor who generally has progressive and refreshing ideas about medicine and holistic health. "Grains?" he comments, "You must be awfully constipated!" Another friend laughs, interrupting her snack of peanut butter and jelly on white bread, and mumbles, "How can you write a whole book about *breakfast?*"

The comments no longer surprise us. We have learned in these few years that the public myths and misconceptions about whole grains are superceded only by an appalling lack of knowledge and a wealth of distorted information disseminated by those we trust to teach us about eating healthfully. Our family doctors, so ready to help in an acute emergency, have studied the subject of nutrition for only a few hours in medical school. The teachers of our children have graduated from college without taking a single course on the subject. The food industry is certainly the last place we'd want to turn for advice on eating wisely. We say this, fully aware that an executive of one of America's huge processed-foods conglomerates roared, "If *we* make it, *it's got to be good!"* when a group attacked them for foisting nutritionless garbage on the unsuspecting public.

In our fantasies, we see the doctor, the teacher, and the executive all meeting for lunch over a Big Mac (560 calories, mostly fat), or a Whopper (630 calories, mostly fat), or a batter-coated, quick-fried chicken dinner with mashed potatoes, coleslaw and white rolls (830 calories, also mostly saturated, fattening fat).

More than one writer interested in the subject of health and nutrition has commented that we are a nation of fat-eaters and that this fat mania is fast becoming a plague. In addition, we have what amounts to the greatest "sugar fix" in recorded history, and the statistics are astounding. The average individual sugar consumption in this country is over *100 pounds a year.*

On an average, we also consume about the same amount of grain foods, but almost all of it is eaten *indirectly*—in the chickens, the hogs, and the beef cattle who are fed huge amounts of grain, and give back to us only a small percentage of the energy contained in the original food. Only a small proportion, as little as one pound of wheat per year per person, is consumed *directly,* the way we benefit most from whole grains.

When we were young, we would eagerly read details of the coming heavyweight fights—it was the time of Joe Louis and Max Baer and other immortals who will never be replaced in our minds. Avidly, we read the sports pages until the day of the bout, and we never failed to note that the last meal before the main event was *steak.* A large, well-marbled, thick-cut, blood-red slab of Western beef. Protein for energy, animal fat for endurance, calories to be burned in the arena. The stories were generally accompanied by photographs. Then our mothers forced the same diet on us in order to make us strong like Maxie Baer.

Can you imagine our dismay if we had known then that these superb athletes might have done just as well by eating chicken, a slab of cheese, some eggs—or a combination of *legumes and grains*—and that in doing so they might have been better off in terms of health? In those days—and until quite recently—carbohydrate was a dirty word. Carbohydrates made you fat. Everyone knew that. Nowadays the picture story in the daily newspaper features the latest marathon run instead of a boxing match. The heroes are pictured in their homes devouring the last meal before they meet the thousands of others over a 26-mile course that will take its grueling toll. And what are they pictured eating, these modern gladiators of the running world? Certainly not a thick slab of well-marbled beef. They are eating plates of *pasta!*

What ever happened to the fabled steak, that rich repository of protein? Well, it is really the much-maligned *carbohydrates,* not protein, that your body uses to provide fuel and energy, in the form of blood sugar glucose. The "complex" carbohydrates contained in bread and

pasta (and other grain foods), fruits, vegetables, and nonfat dairy products, are composed of "chains" of energy, providing the body with an adequate supply over a longer period of time. Sugar, of course, is a carbohydrate, but it is known as a "simple" one, and it is quickly used by the body as a rapid energy source, leaving you more enervated than before you consumed it.

Certainly, we need our proteins, particularly in our early years when they help the body build its structure and the connective tissues that layer our muscles. We also need more protein after a serious illness, for example, when there is a need to rebuild muscle tissue. The protein requirements are substantially higher for pregnant or lactating women too. However, once the extra needs for a specific situation are met, most adults have about the same basic protein requirements for maintaining healthy tissue, depending upon their normal weight.

But there is a still more important point that can be made for reassessing our dietary balance to include more of the complex carbohydrates in place of such a high intake of proteins. Most of the high-protein foods we eat come with far more calories in fat than do the natural carbohydrate-rich foods, such as grains, pasta, legumes, or even potatoes. This is especially true if the major source of that protein is processed foods. The *fat* puts weight on us about twice as fast as either protein or carbohydrates. For example, a baked potato has about 110 calories, less than 1 percent of them in fat. A ten-ounce steak has almost 1,000 calories, 80 percent of them in fat.

There is an additional advantage to a diet that stresses the complex carbohydrates, which are rich in fiber. In these two years of testing our grain recipes, we have required much less food than ever before. We are satisfied with smaller portions of each dish, be it appetizer, entree, or dessert. The reason is that fiber-rich, carbohydrate-filled grains contain greater amounts of bulk and satisfy us faster and longer than protein-rich foods. And, since fiber speeds the food through the digestive tract, we absorb fewer calories.

We have read story after story about the protective effect of a high-carbohydrate, high-fiber diet against everything from bowel cancer to minor digestive irregularity. Our background hardly qualifies us to comment on these claims. We can, however, attest to one thing with certainty after our two-year experiment with grains: Grains do *not* constipate. Our doctor friend (and all our other friends) turned out to be woefully misinformed on that point. Many of our readers may well find that with increased grain consumption they are more regular in their bowel habits than ever before.

Certainly, grains, vegetables, and fruits are not, by themselves, perfect foods. They do not contain all of the amino acids needed by the body and thus are labeled "incomplete protein" foods. Nevertheless, they are so remarkable in their nutritional values that it takes but a small amount of other protein sources to round out their contribution to the complete nutritional needs of the body. The whole grains, plus a few ounces of meat, poultry, fish, or dairy products, or the addition of legumes, will make your daily diet "complete." The most popular and common combination of foods, found in hundreds of cultures throughout the world, is the mixture of grains and legumes—rice and beans, for example.

What surprises us is that it took so long for our modern, science-based society to discover what our forebears seemed to know about diet instinctively. It is equally surprising to us that even as we unearth new and innovative facts about our diets, the myths and the misconceptions about grains continued unabated. There is still the nagging feeling among our friends that all of this grains-eating will make us fat. Yet, a Michigan State University study by Dr. Olaf Mickelsen proved that eating even a great amount of *bread*—particularly whole grain bread—can result in weight loss. The participants in his study ate 12 slices a bread a day for eight weeks. Those who ate high-fiber bread lost an average of 19.4 pounds during the period; even those who ate refined bread lost 13.7 pounds!

If we do not reduce their nutritional values by the contemporary tendency to overprocess, whole grains give to us a food supply incredibly rich in carbohydrates, proteins, unsaturated fats, vitamins, and minerals. Used wisely and combined with small amounts of other nutrients, they open a new world of cuisine. As we learn to utilize their vast potential of tastes and forms, they also provide us with an economical, healthful energy source.

In spite of what one of our friends thought, a book about whole grains is *not* a book that is entirely devoted to the ritual (or nonritual) of breakfast. There was a time when corn and wheat, rye and oats, served well as the basis for the first meal of the day, and also as important ingredients for luncheon and dinner. Those days, unfortunately, are mostly gone, and except for an occasional slice of whole wheat bread or an accompanying side dish of rice at dinner, whole grains are relegated mainly to the image of "breakfast cereals" by our current misconceptions.

Certainly, grains *are* breakfast fare, and we are happy to see the new awareness of their value for the first meal of the day. But grains are also incredibly versatile at the other meals and in varieties of preparation that will amaze you. In the recipe sections of this book, we attempt to make amends for the near absence of these natural, wholesome, and tasty ingredients in our daily fare. You will find a whole range of dishes for every course at every meal of the day, and even for snacks and hors d'oeuvres.

For this moment, though, we would like to speak of the steaming bowl of oats that grandmother or mother, little knowing about complex carbohydrates, forced us to eat on those cold winter mornings, totally convinced that it was "good for us." For many of us, it was our introduction to whole grains; nowadays even this token attempt at good nutrition has all but disappeared from the scene. There are several contemporary villains in the scenario, over and above our own responsibility for the radical change in our breakfast diets.

The pace of life has increased in recent decades so that most of us—particularly the city dwellers—seem to have no time to prepare or to consume the kind of food our parents knew was "good for us." The average breakfast in America today is no breakfast at all—a hurried cup of coffee, accompanied by a sweet roll, followed by a second cup of coffee when the blood sugar sags at about ten o'clock in the morning. The

The *not so* Great American Breakfast

Going against the Grain

alternative is the breakfast that most of our business people consume on the road—either at a long buffet table, with food set out to become stale and cold within the hour, or a meal ordered from a waitress who presents the same menu printed for nearly every restaurant in the country. The meal is predictable: bacon or sausage, two or three eggs fried in saturated fat (if they are not precooked, powdered scrambled eggs), white toast, a sweet roll, and coffee with three teaspoons of sugar and nondairy chemical creamer.

The first brick in the road to Froot Loops and Sugar Pops, Apple Jacks, Cocoa Pebbles, Count Chocula, and Orange Quangaroos was set in the nineteenth century by John Harvey Kellogg. This young medical student, living in a cramped and uncomfortable boarding house, begrudged the time and the effort that it took him to prepare oats and wheat and corn bought by the pound. "It often occurred to me that it should be possible to purchase cereals at groceries already cooked and ready to eat," he wrote.

Two years later, along with his brother, Will, Dr. Kellogg finally developed what he described as ". . . the first Battle Creek health food, which I called Granola." Eventually, the Kellogg brothers developed a method of flaking wheat and corn kernels, and the first "corn flakes" were with us to stay.

The rest, of course, is history, and fortunes were made—and are still being made—on the vast array of "ready-to-eat," processed dry cereals that fill the shelves. To the list have been added the countless brands and forms of cereal grains that are to be served hot. They move downward from normal cooking time to "quick" to "instant," and in the transformation lose most of the nutrition that the grains offered in the first place.

Ready-to-eat breakfast cereals lose most of their vitamins and minerals as the grains are refined. The protein quality declines. Sugar is added to almost every brand. Chemical preservatives are put in to increase shelf life. Flavor enhancers make certain that we never taste the original essence of the grain. All of it destroys the wonderful idea of Kellogg—a man ahead of his time.

The criticisms of the cereal industry have gone on for years and will probably continue to do so for a long time, for the public is, we hope,

becoming more aware of the "hype" that has been foisted on it. The industry says that it is only 'giving the public what it wants." Why, then, does the industry spend well over *200 million dollars a year* to advertise a product we are already crying for!

The Berkeley Co-operative of Richmond, California, has published several editions of their own superb analysis of breakfast cereals in a newsletter cleverly entitled, *"Cereals: Champion of Breakfasts?"* In addition to recommending both the best of the whole grain hot cereals and whole grain ready-to-eat cereals, they compare the costs of whole grains used as cereals and the packaged processed brands. Without exception, the cost per pound of the bulk or packaged oats, corn, rice, rye, triticale, and wheat is from *50 percent to 90 percent less* than that of the packaged, high-sugar, "enriched," "fortified," popped-from-a-gun, American breakfast fare!

Certainly, there are new areas where modern technology has been of some help to us. And, added to that, new ideas about food preparation suggest the diversity of dishes waiting to be served. These are not the days of grandmother, and we can return to the heritage of whole grains without accepting the burden of impossibly sticky pots, long hours of cooking and simmering, or misconceptions that grains have to be brown and they have to be tasteless. This book brings families back to a healthful and tasty diet without the concomitant kitchen drudgery, and with a view toward innovation and freshness.

The very first place to change our American eating habits is at breakfast. There are ways to prepare granola and have it ready for instant service (see Index), but rest assured that *your* granola will be better than *their* granola—just as your rice and your wheat and your corn products will be better than theirs.

We have yet another fantasy that occurs from time to time. We think that Dr. Kellogg, seeing what has become of his ingenious idea for a ready-to-eat breakfast cereal, and seeing the distortion of his beloved corn flake, might very well go back to that small burner in his cramped room and gladly take the time to prepare his breakfast in the same way that his mother used to make it.

The World's One and Only Corn Palace

It is an extraordinary building and its home is Mitchell, South Dakota. The first Corn Palace was built before the turn of the century in 1892 and then rebuilt further down the street. Since then, it's become an institution in Mitchell, and it has grown into a wonderland of minarets and towers, complete with an exhibition hall, an auditorium that seats 4,500 people for sporting events, and an annual redecoration of the exterior panels with materials consisting entirely of local grains and grasses. Each year, the theme changes, and a new display unfolds for the visitors who come in late September for the annual Corn Palace Festival.

Starting in July, the old corn and grain are removed in preparation for the new crop, the scaffolding goes up, and the panels are redone in an entirely different theme. For many years, the designs were created by Oscar Howe, a Sioux Indian, professor of art, and one of the foremost artists in the area. Many were on the subject of ecology, the unnecessary slaughter of the buffalo, the pollution of the cities, and the emotional frustration he felt in the treatment of the Indian nations.

The corn is not dyed or colored in any way — the red corn is Bloody Butcher, the speckled corn Calico or Indian, and the nearly black corn is Blue Flint. The yellow and white colors are made from regular field corn. The "grain artists" also use oats, grain sorghum (milo), sudan grass, barley, and burdock (sour dock, a local weed) to complete their designs. By the time the new panels are finished, about 2,000 bushels of corn have been used.

This is one of those places on our list of "We must get there some day." With all of our travels around the globe, we somehow have missed one of the most unusual buildings in the world, the One and Only Corn Palace. However, we have been carrying a full-color brochure in our files for about ten years in anticipation of our trip there. Even though we have not visited the Palace personally, it certainly deserves an honored place in a book devoted to whole grains.

About 600,000 visitors pass through the Corn Palace each year. If you happen to be near Mitchell, remember that the Palace is open from June 1st until right after Labor Day, when it closes for two weeks in preparation for the annual festival.

The Gamut of Guidelines for Grains

Buying Grains

We remember, a long time ago, when Mel first became interested in cooking Chinese food, the Asian markets in New York became our new horizons of adventure, our Saturday afternoon cornucopia of wonder, as we wandered down the aisles feeling, looking, squeezing, and gaping. So much to see and to try, and yet we knew so little about it.

Mel picked up a package of oval-shaped, hard-as-a-rock, flat, yellow objects and brought it to the counter. There were, of course, absolutely no instructions on the package, and even if there had been, the language would have been Cantonese or Mandarin.

"What are these?" he asked the clerk.

"They are for cooking," came the flat, disinterested reply.

"How do you prepare them?"

"You soak them," the clerk answered.

"How long?"

"Until they are soft." By this time, the inscrutable East was becoming bored with the unstoppable West.

Mel plunged on. "How long do you cook them?"

"Until they are done!" And the clerk turned to wait on a customer who didn't ask so many questions about so obvious a product. We returned home and soaked them, but they never softened. It was not until two years later that we discovered that they were to be immersed in water for up to 36 hours!

The story is not much different from the experience of the shopper or the cook who approaches the marketplace to buy whole grains for the first time, anxious to find out just what they are and how to use them properly. Breaking the bonds of "instant oatmeal" and "Cream of Wheat" can sometimes be confusing and frustrating. We have not only many different varieties of grain, but each one can be broken down into a vast array of classifications and forms, all with different properties. There are 200 varieties of barley, for example, and the strain used for beer is different from the strain used for baking bread. The rye used for bread and that used for whiskey differ considerably. One type of corn is used for succotash, another type for tortillas, another for corn-on-the-cob, and still other varieties for the good old American standby, popcorn.

Some packages of grain sitting on the shelves of our supermarkets and natural foods stores carry no instructions; others give details that might just as well be in Chinese. Some packages do, indeed, give a recipe for using that particular grain form, but they omit the basic preparation information. Asking a clerk at the store just how you might prepare the "mystery product" inside the plastic bag or openly displayed in a bin, elicits either a shrug, an uninformative mumble, or a suggestion that you write to the farmer listed on the label. If it were not that we, too, have had to travel a long and exciting road of learning about grains, we might be amazed at the fact that a country so familiar with the cuts of steak on a menu or in a butcher shop is so ignorant in the area of a basic, nutritious, ancient food.

Knowing what the problems are, then, and having gone through an intense learning process over these past two years, we are able to give specific detailed information about each grain as we begin its section in the book. There you will find the grain forms, from groats to grits to flour to popped grain, cracked grain, and flaked grain. In addition, we describe the basic methods of cooking the various forms, with some tips based on what we've discovered in testing these hundreds of recipes. We feel that if they know more about grains, many of our readers will include them in their diet more often just as we have done.

If You Are Buying Packaged Grains: Toasted grain will have a longer shelf life, but much of the vitamin and mineral content will have been lost in the heating process. This is especially true for packaged, dry, flaked cereals, no matter what the manufacturer tells you. The raw whole groat (or berry) preserves most of the nutrition originally put there by nature. We are reminded of the wonderful J. I. Rodale statement about processed foods, "Never eat anything that has been through a factory!"

The word "natural" on a package label, as we've mentioned, means little or nothing to a health-conscious shopper, for sugar and salt are both in that category. At the end of the book, we give the names of farms and the labels we prefer in buying grain products. They are all quite reliable.

If You Are Buying Your Grain Products in Bulk: Take a good look at how they are stored. Make sure your market or natural foods store or food co-operative uses covered bins, and that the grains are kept in a cool place. Buying in bulk is cheaper than purchasing the packaged grain forms, but storage is more difficult. Of course, you can buy in small amounts at first and store them as we suggest later on in this section. As you discover your new favorites, you can increase the amounts gradually.

If Grains Are Not Available in a Variety of Forms: We list some mail-order sources at the back of the book. All of them are gracious, willing, and ready to ship everything from grits to graham flour. We have purchased many of our own grains from these organic farms and mills, and in the process, we have become friends with many of their owners. If you are looking for a source near you, we suggest that you check the phone book for a co-operative food source, market, or warehouse in your area. We have found some excellent resources in the Midwest, in California (the Berkeley Co-operative is probably the best known), and in the Southwest. More and more families are becoming informed about the costs of processed foods and their paucity of nutrients, and local consumer groups are forming co-operatives all around the country. It is a good sign.

Cleaning Grains

Most of the packaged grains, especially the ones that are shipped to your local outlet by the reliable growers and mills—Arrowhead, Shiloh, Walnut Acres, El Molino, just to name a few—are quite clean, having been picked over at their source. They are, however, generally more expensive than the grains purchased in bulk from bins or barrels.

Remember, if you purchase grains in bulk, as we generally do, you are dealing with food right from the fields or the mills, and in some cases, you will find little bits of chaff or weed seeds or tiny pebbles among the grains. They are generally quite easy to see, and they should be removed by hand before you cook the grain.

The first rule is: *Don't wash the grains!* They have a tendency to stick together when they're wet, and they'll be quick to get moldy when you store them. Keep grains dry; lay them out on a piece of white paper or on a jelly-roll pan. Then, under a bright light, push them aside, bit by bit, removing the particles of foreign matter. Repeat the process a second time, making sure you've removed all the unwanted bits and pieces.

Storing Grains

Almost ten years ago, Paul Hawken, who was then president of Erewhon Trading Company, wrote a letter to one of the executives at Rodale Press, in which he stated, "We have a farmer in North Dakota who has wheat which is ten years old and it still has a 97 percent germination rate. Good grain can last an incredibly long time under proper storage conditions."

For those of us who use whole grains at home, the same statement is true. It follows that such long-lasting grain can take up a lot of space for a long time! Of course, over these past two years, we would like to have had more space in which to store the countless varieties and forms of grains that have decorated our kitchen. However, the cry for "more space, more space!" is one that is heard often throughout our land, especially from the apartment dweller or the large family living in an average-size house with an average-size refrigerator or freezer.

There are some simple rules for keeping grains fresh and available without having to make way for an inundation of bulky packages, jars, or sacks. If you live in a small apartment, buy your grains in small amounts and use one-quart glass jars with tight seals in which to store them. They make colorful decoration for the kitchen cabinet or top shelves, and they are easy to label so they can be identified in an instant.

Grains should be stored in a dry, cool place,

and in summer you may want to refrigerate them. Remember that the germ of whole grains contains an oil that may turn rancid after a week or so, if the grains are left in a warm spot. Under refrigeration, they will keep for months.

If, on the other hand, you share the problem of moderate refrigeration space with us, limit the amount of grains that you purchase at any one time, so that storage problems will be minimal.

For the prepackaged grains, most of the reliable farms and mills try to keep their storage bins cool, and, generally, they mill their grains as close to shipping time as possible. No matter how carefully the grains are cleaned or cared for at the point of origin, however, one or two insect eggs can easily slip by, and you may find that incorrectly stored grains will develop a webby cocoon if they are left in a warm, humid spot. We have avoided such problems by remembering to store the grains as recommended—small glass jars, tight seals, cool spot.

Grinding Grains

We have always had a fascination with old mills, and, obviously, we are not alone, judging by the summer crowds that fill the windmill and water-mill restorations that we visit. Some years ago, we very nearly purchased an old, run-down water mill in New Hampshire, right on the roaring Little Sugar River, but finances and a lack of vision kept us from achieving a childhood dream. What we do remember most about the mill, however, was the fact that the original grinding stones had been left intact on the top floor of the building, a perfect centerpiece for what might have become the living room of a vacation home. Even today, we carry with us that romantic picture of the old mills, and we manage to stop along the highway at any time a restored mill is offered as a tourist attraction.

Today's milling methods are much improved over the days of the old water mill, the windmill, the treadmill, and the donkey mill. But amazingly enough, the basic principle for grinding grains between stones has remained unchanged since primitive times. In fact, a common phrase based on the craft remains with us to this day.

[*Continued on page 14*]

The Lure of the Old Mills

We discovered with some delight that there is actually a Society for the Preservation of Old Mills, plus a growing interest in these restored historical buildings, and thousands of people just like us who love to stop along the roadside to crawl through them to admire their solid construction. Many of them are still operating today, just like the windmill at Prescott Farm in Middletown, Rhode Island.

We visited Prescott on our way to the Johnnycake Festival on a beautiful autumn day. The windmill, originally built in 1812, still grinds cornmeal when the wind is right—producing five to six bushels an hour—and whatever is produced is sold at the adjacent country store.

The most interesting thing about the mill, however, is the fact that it still grinds flint corn, the type thought to be just like the corn found growing in North America in 1607. It is said by purists to be the best corn for Johnnycakes, while the more ordinary and common dent corn has replaced it as a high-yield crop throughout America, both for animal feed and for cornmeal.

If you're traveling through the area, the mill is only a few miles north of Newport, and it's open to the public for guided tours.

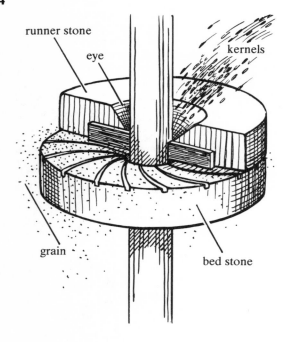

runner stone

eye

kernels

grain

bed stone

"Keep your nose to the grindstone" can be traced to the miller who leaned forward to see if he could detect the smell of granite coming from the grinding stones, an indication that the stones were too close and had to be adjusted.

Even with the advent of high-speed roller milling, hammer mills, and steel-plate mills, the stone-ground method remains ideal for achieving a product rich in both nutrition and flavor. With stone grinding, the slow rubbing with slotted granite stones distributes the germ oil evenly through the flour, leaving no concentration of oily flakes to become rancid as they oxidize. On the other hand, the steel rollers most commonly used by commercial processors create small oily masses, which turn rancid more quickly under conditions of warmth or extreme humidity. The obvious solution for the large commercial processors, therefore, is to remove the germ, and with it, of course, the basic nutrition it contains. Certainly, the degermed flour will last longer, but it is inferior to the stone-ground product in almost every other respect.

Some people grind their own grains right at home, and in the back of the book we suggest

some hand and electric home mills that might be worth looking into. However, you may not want to go to the expense of buying one and the effort involved in using it, preferring to depend — as we do — upon the organic suppliers and local stores you have come to trust.

Aside from the milling of flour, the grinding of grains may have other benefits for some of our readers. Young children as well as adults with chewing problems will find the ground grains easier to chew and to digest. In addition, your cooking time will be reduced.

If you do not own a mill and if you have no intention of purchasing one, you can grind small amounts in a blender, electric coffee grinder, or spice grinder. Food processors, however, do not always work well. Softer grains can even be ground in small amounts using an ordinary mortar and pestle. But for the growing number of people who want to grind larger amounts of grain, there are two choices.

The Hand Mill: You can choose from two basic types—steel grinding burrs or stone grinding burrs—and either type will require a fair amount of effort. The average bread recipe calls for about 2½ pounds of grain, a chore that will take from 15 to 50 minutes of your time, depending upon the mill you've chosen and the type of grain to be milled. It might take most of the day to mill enough flour for an ovenful of bread! We do admit, however, that the idea is romantic, however impractical for busy people. Mills range in price from $50 to just under $300.

Electric Mills: No matter which type of mill you choose, electric or hand operated, you will have to make the choice between stone grinding and steel-blade mills. Remember that the stones should not be washed, and cleaning them may be a difficult process. If there is any flour left on the stones, it has a tendency to turn rancid and you'll taste it in your future grindings. Steel-blade electric mills are much easier to clean. Basically, it all comes down to how much you want to spend and what kind of grains you will be milling most often (oats are better with steel, wheat with stone). A new process now being incorporated in grain mills uses microatomization as a method of exploding the grains into tiny particles, using neither stones nor steel rollers in the milling. Electric mills cost between $200 and $300.

Before You Buy: As with any expensive piece of kitchen equipment, the high cost of a mill should lead you to investigate, ask questions, and confer with friends who own mills in order to get preliminary recommendations. It is not always possible to see and to test a particular type of mill before you make your purchase, though this is the best way to determine your choice. Here are some other points to consider:

- How much grain does it grind? Does it take a reasonable time to grind the amount of flour you'll need for one loaf of bread? For six loaves?
- How noisy is it? The grinding process, whether achieved commercially or right in your kitchen, is a noisy one at best. It is difficult to determine the noise level of a particular model from the advertising copy.
- Is it easy to clean? Are all the parts accessible, easy to remove? This is an important consideration for both hand mills and electric machines.
- Does the mill have to be assembled by you or some other member of your family who is adept with tools and can follow instructions? If it is already assembled, it might be more expensive, but worth it to those of us who have difficulty using a screwdriver and furniture glue.
- As with the purchase of any equipment, automobile, television set, or appliance, it's a good idea to check the warranty and any other guarantees offered by the manufacturer.
- Don't be taken in by the manufacturer's claims about how much money you'll save by owning your own mill. Unless you grind a large amount of grain, the savings will not be the major reason that you make your investment.

The reasons for owning a mill always come back to three things: nutrition, convenience, and flavor. You will have freshly milled flour, rich in vitamins, fiber, and minerals, available whenever you want to cook or bake; access to a variety of flours from amaranth to buckwheat, rye, or oats; and the inner satisfaction that comes with returning to the basic tradition of "doing your own thing." We've researched the available mills, and suppliers of them can be found in the Mail-Order Sources. Just select the one that seems to meet your own personal needs.

How to Cook Grains Easily

If this were *Larousse Gastronomique* or a publication of Cordon Bleu, what follows might be called the *batterie de cuisine*—put more simply for something as fundamental as grains, the list of *basic kitchen equipment* that will make it convenient to cook the recipes compiled in this book.

The Magic Pot: The objection to cooking whole grains that we hear most often is that they stick to the pot, making it a mess to clean up afterward. This may have been a legitimate complaint in the days of grandmother's cast-iron pot on the wood-burning stove. Even our mothers, when they cooked whole grains, found scorched pot bottoms impossible to scrape, so that cooking vessels were set in the sink to soak for hours. However, if modern space technology has brought us nothing else, it has given to us an ingenious development that we call "The Magic Pot."

We rarely recommend a specific utensil or product by name, unless it is so unusual and so necessary to our cooking procedures that we know of no alternative. All of our recipes in this book utilized the nonstick SilverStone-lined five-quart pot, with a wide, flat base, made by Wear-Ever. It has a heavyweight bottom and a tight-fitting lid, and as recently as this morning, Mel was blessing the genius who invented it as he whisked the pot clean after a breakfast of cooked whole grits.

For your bread, muffins, and cupcakes, Baker's Secret cookware will do the same thing. In both cases, you'll be able to cut down on your use of butter or oil, since neither type of cookware

[*Continued on page 18*]

Grains Cooking Chart

Form of Grain	Dry Amount Grain	Approx. Amount Liquid	Method of Cooking	Approx. Cooking Time	Approx. Yield
Amaranth					
whole	1 cup	3 cups	Bring water and grain to a boil together.	25 minutes	2½ cups
Barley					
hulled or pearled	1 cup	4 cups	Add to boiling water.	45 minutes	4 cups
flakes (rolled)	1½ cups	4½ cups	Add to boiling water.	25 minutes	6 servings
grits	1 cup	4 cups	Add to boiling water.	15 minutes	4 cups
Buckwheat (unroasted)					
groats	1 cup	2 cups	Add to boiling water.	10-15 minutes	4 cups
grits	1 cup	5 cups	Add to boiling water.	10 minutes	4 cups
Kasha (roasted buckwheat)					
groats	1 cup	2 cups	Mix with beaten egg and add boiling water.	10-15 minutes	4 cups
coarse	1 cup	2 cups	(same as groats)	10-15 minutes	4 cups
medium	1 cup	2 cups	(same as groats)	8 minutes	4 cups
fine	1 cup	2 cups	(same as groats)	5 minutes	4 cups
Bulgur					
whole	1 cup	3 cups	Add boiling water to bulgur and *SOAK*. DO NOT COOK.	2 hours*	3 cups
#3 coarse	1 cup	3 cups	(same as whole bulgur)	1 hour*	3 cups
#2 medium	1 cup	3 cups	(same as whole bulgur)	1 hour*	3 cups
#1 fine	1 cup	3 cups	(same as whole bulgur)	1 hour*	3 cups
Corn					
meal	1 cup	1 cup cold water + 3 cups boiling water	Mix meal with cold water and add to boiling water.	5-10 minutes	6 servings
whole hominy	1 pound	water to cover + 5 cups	Soak overnight, then drain, and bring to boil slowly in 5 cups water.	2½-3 hours	6 servings
hominy grits	1 cup	4 cups	Add to boiling water.	25-30 minutes	3 cups
Millet					
whole	1 cup	2 cups	I. Toast grain in skillet, boil water in saucepan, and add grain to water.	25-30 minutes	4 cups
(same)	1 cup	2½ cups	II. Add to boiling water.	25-30 minutes	4 cups

*NOTE: These are soaking times, not cooking times.

Grains Cooking Chart—*Continued*

Form of Grain	Dry Amount Grain	Approx. Amount Liquid	Method of Cooking	Approx. Cooking Time	Approx. Yield
Oats					
whole groats	1 cup	3 cups	Soak overnight in water, then bring to a boil, and cook.	25 minutes	6 servings
steel-cut	1 cup	4 cups	Add to boiling water.	15 minutes	6 servings
rolled	2 cups	3 cups	Stir into boiling water, remove from heat, and let stand.	8-10 minutes	6 servings
Rice					
long grain	2 cups	5 cups	Add to boiling water.	45 minutes	8 cups
short grain	2 cups	5 cups	(same as long grain rice)	45 minutes	7 cups
rice cream	1 cup	4 cups	Toast in saucepan, add cold water, bring to a boil, and cook.	4-5 minutes	6 servings
Rye					
groats	1 cup	2½ cups	Clean grain, soak overnight, then add to boiling water, and cook.	45 minutes	2¼ cups
flakes	1 cup	3 cups	Toast flakes in butter or oil, add to boiling water, and simmer, covered.	15 minutes	3 cups
Triticale					
berries (groats)	1 cup	2¼ cups	Clean grain, soak overnight, then add to boiling water, and simmer, covered.	40 minutes	2½ cups
cracked berries	1 cup	2¼ cups	(same as groats)	20-25 minutes	2½ cups
flakes	1⅓ cups	2½ cups	Add to boiling water, stirring, cover, and simmer. Let stand before serving.	10 minutes	4 cups
Wheat					
whole berries	1 cup	3½ cups	Toast grain in skillet, soak overnight, then simmer.	1 hour	2¾ cups
whole hulled berries	1 cup	3½ cups	Soak overnight, then simmer.	1 hour 10 minutes	2¾ cups
cracked	1 cup	2½ cups	Toast grain, add boiling water, stir and cook, covered.	15 minutes	3¾ cups
flakes	1⅓ cups	4 cups	Boil water, slowly add flakes, and cook, covered.	20 minutes	6 servings
Wild Rice					
extra fancy long or medium	4 ounces	2¼ cups	Pick grain clean, rinse and bring water to boil, add rice, and bring to boil again. Lower heat and simmer; let stand until dry.	45 minutes	2 cups
(same)	6 ounces	3 cups	(same as 4 ounces)	45 minutes	3½ cups

needs any lubrication at all to prevent the end product from sticking.

The rest of your needs will generally be found right in your kitchen, since there are very few special utensils involved in the preparation of whole grain dishes. Here is a list of the equipment, cooking utensils, and tools that we found valuable during these two years of testing. If you can't find them in your local store, most are available by mail order from the sources listed in the back of the book.

Pots, Pans, and Other Cooking Vessels

- Nonstick griddle.
- Heavy, black cast-iron skillet.
- Various baking pans—round, square, and springform.
- Heavy, oval, enamel-covered cast-iron casseroles that can go from top of stove to oven to broiler to table.

- Souffle dishes for baking.
- Sesame seed and spice toaster (available in stores that sell Japanese items).

Equipment and Tools

- Food processor (handy, but of course, not necessary).
- Electric coffee grinder or spice grinder.
- Blender.
- Electric hand mixer.
- Egg beater.
- Wire whisks (including tiny bar whisk).
- Wire racks for cooling.
- Fat separator.
- Tools for paring citrus and removing rind.
- Rubber and metal spatulas.
- Slotted spoon.
- Chinese strainer.
- Wooden spoons, measuring cups.

Chick-peas, split peas, black-eyed peas, pinto beans, black beans, red and white kidney beans, soybeans, marrow beans, navy beans, pea beans, and Great Northern beans, and all their cousins and relatives have been, historically, the perfect accompaniment to traditional grain dishes around the world. As we know, grains are lacking in certain essential amino acids, while legumes have these and lack some of the others. But put them together and a more perfect nutritional match can't be found.

No book about grains would be complete, then, without some word about these remarkable partners of whole grains. Long before we had ever thought of writing an entire book about grains, and before we were aware of the logic and the ingenuity of grain-legume combinations, we had tasted of the black beans in Brazil, the lentils in India, the chick-peas in the Middle East, the split peas in Holland, and the refried beans in Mexico—all of them accompanied by some type of grain such as rice or corn.

"Bean Appetit!"

Legumes: Perfect Partners for Grains

A Who's Who of Legumes

Basically, a legume is what is inside the hanging pods attached to plants—from peanuts to beans. (Little did we realize as children that Jack's beanstalk was actually a legume.) By using the *fresh* varieties during their growing season, and switching to the multitude of *dried* legumes at other times of the year, we're guaranteed a nutritious, economical supply.

Fresh or "Green" Beans: These are wax beans, string and pole beans, snap beans, fresh peas, lima beans, fava beans, and butter beans.

Dried Legumes: The vast varieties are always available. Collect as many as you can and keep them in glass jars; they will add beauty and color to the kitchen. They need no refrigeration, and their diversity of size, appearance, and texture allows us to use them not only for traditional grain-legume recipes, but also for our own original cooking combinations:

- Navy beans, pea beans, Great Northern beans, marrow beans, and cannellini (or white kidney beans) are all white and come in various shapes and sizes.
- Pinto beans, pink beans, red kidney beans, chili beans, and cranberry beans all have a reddish or pink color, and some are speckled.
- Blackeye beans (or cowpeas) and yelloweye beans have black dots that distinguish them, and in the South they're all called "peas."
- Black beans (or turtle beans) are oval, black on the outside, lighter inside.
- Chick-peas—also called garbanzo beans or ceci-peas.
- Lima beans. The larger beans have a strong, distinctive flavor, the baby limas are milder.
- Green flageolet and dried haricot are the most expensive, since they are usually imported from France or Belgium.
- Whole green peas, green split peas, whole yellow peas, yellow split peas, cowpeas and pigeon peas.
- Soybeans.
- Green lentils, orange lentils, brown lentils. Lentils are the fastest cooking of the legumes, but they don't hold their shape well.

General Cooking Instructions

The amount of water and the length of cooking time for preparing legumes will vary. However, as a general rule, *each cup* of dried legumes will expand to *three cups* as the legumes absorb water during the cooking process. The following list provides some suggested cooking times, with the legumes simmered on the top of the stove using low heat.

Some people suffer from intestinal gas (flatulence) after they consume legumes, and many avoid these foods for that reason. There are three ways to handle the problem:

- Eat very small amounts of legumes at first, until your body becomes adapted to them.
- Try our Basic Cooking Method for Legumes. It will let you digest them more easily, and our friends report that it does, indeed, reduce or eliminate flatulence. Try it.
- Sprout the legumes first (see page 24), and then combine them with grains.

Some Handy Tips

Soaking Tips

- Lentils, split peas, and black-eyed peas do not require any presoaking before you cook them.
- Dried large white beans and brown fava beans, because of their size, require lengthy soaking.
- When soaking soybeans during warm weather, refrigerate them, since they have a tendency to ferment easily.

Cooking Tips

- The pot should never be more than three-quarters full of water.
- If you grease the rim of your pot, the water will not boil over.
- Never use a pressure cooker for soybeans—The vents will clog up.
- In any case, pressure cooking beans is pure guesswork. You may end up with a puree rather than whole beans. We prefer to see what's cooking.
- Hard water will lengthen the cooking time.
- To make certain the skins do not burst, legumes should be simmered gently and stirred only occasionally while cooking.
- Soybeans, large lima beans, and black beans tend to foam up while cooking. To avoid this, add one tablespoon of oil to the water while they're simmering.
- We never use salt in our recipes, but if you feel you absolutely must, never add salt while cooking legumes. It inhibits the tenderizing process.

Our Basic Cooking Method for Legumes

Yields about 6½ cups—can serve 8 to 10 people

1   pound dried beans
      (about 2¼ cups)
7 to 8   cups water

Pick over dried beans, removing any foreign matter. Wash them several times under cold water, discarding anything that floats to the surface. Add fresh water to the beans, covering them with about 3 inches to spare and let them soak for several hours, or overnight if you wish.

When ready to cook, discard the soaking liquid and add fresh water to the beans. Bring to a boil, then lower heat and simmer, covered, for 30 minutes. Drain and discard the cooking liquid. Cover the beans with 7 to 8 cups of fresh water and bring to a boil for a second time, then lower heat. Cover the pot and simmer until beans are soft and most of the liquid has been absorbed.

The size of the bean dictates the length of cooking time (See Legumes Cooking Chart). When done, the beans should be tender but should still retain their shape. During the cooking, stir occasionally (not often, or the skins might burst), and add water if needed. Beans should be covered with liquid at all times. We keep the lid of the pot slightly ajar to prevent boil-overs. We also save the drained liquid for soup stocks.

After the beans are cooked, they may be baked with other ingredients, or added to soups and stews. Some recipes in other books recommend adding the legumes to soups and stews dry and unsoaked. If you use that method, you'll find that hours of cooking time are required and the beans will absorb great amounts of liquid. We suggest the presoak-precook method instead.

Legumes Cooking Chart

Legume	Cooking Time	Legume	Cooking Time
Black Beans	1½-2 hours	Navy Beans	1½-2 hours
Black-Eyed Peas	30 minutes	Pink Beans	45 minutes
Brown Beans	1-1½ hours	Pinto Beans	1½-2 hours
Chick-Peas	1-1½ hours	Red Beans	1½-2 hours
Great Northern Beans	1-1½ hours	Small Lima Beans	45 minutes
Kidney Beans	1½-2 hours	Soybeans	1½-2 hours
Large Lima Beans	1-1½ hours	Split Peas	30 minutes
Lentils	30 minutes	Whole Peas	1-1½ hours

- Some recipes call for the addition of baking soda for antiflatulence, since it breaks down the carbohydrates (and it also reduces the cooking time). Keep in mind that baking soda also destroys some of the vitamin content of the legumes.
- Small yellow and red lentils cook and disintegrate quickly. Yellow split peas and chick-peas never disintegrate.
- If any acid ingredient is called for in the recipe—vinegar, tomatoes, or lemon juice, for example—add it toward the end of the cooking time, since such ingredients delay tenderizing the beans. In fact, a good general rule for cooking legumes is: soak, simmer—and then flavor.
- Legumes are done when they are soft to the touch. They should look plump and shapely. Bite into one to test.

After-Cooking Tip

- Drain and cool, then refrigerate or freeze. Thrifty, energy-saving cooks always keep legumes on hand along with their grains for quick combination dishes.

A Chinese emperor was writing about the sprouting of mung beans almost 5,000 years ago, and the Sumerians were sprouting barley for beer shortly thereafter. Why has it taken the American family so long to discover both the taste and the added nutrition of these home-grown, remarkably fast-acting grains and legumes? From a dormant, silent seed, in three to five days (for most sprouts), hundreds of live, nutritious little plants are ready for the dinner table. At any given time, both our island home and our New York apartment have from two to four jars of sprouting grains or legumes—wheat, rye, barley, lentils, and mung beans—in various stages of growth, and we use them in much of our cooking, as well as in our bread baking and salads.

The nutritional information is quite astounding. Sprouted oats, for example, have 13 times as much riboflavin (vitamin B_2) and $1\frac{1}{2}$ to 2 times as much protein as the seeds themselves. Soybeans contain 5 times as much vitamin C after only three days of sprouting. As the little plants grow—whether of wheat or beans—almost every mineral and vitamin multiplies in its nutritional strength. Sprouts are low in calories, they're tasty even when eaten raw (to which we can attest, for we are constantly nibbling on them as they begin to sprout), and they're incredibly economical, for as they grow, they expand their potential as they pamper the pocketbook.

Most important of all, they're very easy to grow.

The Sprouting Jar

There are various methods and a great number of special sprouting jars on the market. However, there's no need to invest in anything but a large jar, preferably one that is not round, so that it will not roll off the kitchen counter as you pass. For a cover, use a piece of cheesecloth and a strong rubber band with which to fasten the cheesecloth to the mouth of the jar. It's that simple.

Sprouting Grains and Legumes

A Home Garden of Edible Houseplants

23

The Sprouting Method

1. Remove the foreign matter from your grains or legumes.
2. Put between one and four tablespoons of the seeds in the jar and fill three-quarters full of lukewarm water. Cover with cheesecloth and place a rubber band around the mouth to hold in place. Shake a few times and then drain the water. Fill partially again with fresh water and soak overnight with the jar in upright position. The seeds will begin to swell.
3. Next day, drain the water and rinse well, swishing the seeds around in fresh lukewarm water. Repeat two or three times and then drain.
4. Place the jar on its side and keep it in a warm place (about 70°F.), preferably in a dark place. Repeat this rinsing process two or three times each day. We keep our jars near the sink for easy access and we cover them with a towel. Just make sure to leave the cheesecloth end open for ventilation.
5. Repeat the process for about three to five days, or until the sprouts are developed (about 1½ to 2 inches long). With most seeds, you will begin to see the results at about the third day. Other seeds may take even less time.
6. When the sprouts are the proper length, place the jar in direct light for the last few hours in order to develop a bit of green chlorophyll.
7. Remove the sprouts from the growing jar, place them in a plastic container, and refrigerate. They store well for several days.

Some Handy Tips

- Don't worry about the hulls of the seeds. They provide fiber in your diet.
- Use the rinse water for soups—or feed it to your houseplants.
- Sprouts are kept in darkness until the last few hours because they tend to turn bitter when grown in direct light.
- To keep your precious crop from failing, make sure the water is thoroughly drained each time you rinse the sprouts. We keep our jars at a 45-degree angle pointing mouth down in order to drain excess water.
- You will probably have some extra seeds left over after measuring off the amount you want to sprout. These will keep well in sealed containers in a cool, dry place.
- Don't try to accelerate the sprouting process by using hot water or by trying to grow sprouts in a hot place; 60° to 70°F. is quite perfect.

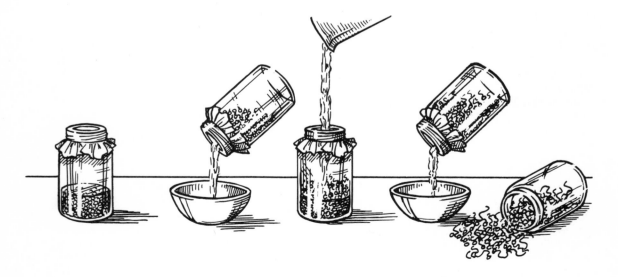

"A recipe," it has been said, "is like sheet music. It instructs you on how to get beautiful effects, but you can't fully appreciate a tune until it has been played, or an apple pie until it has been baked." In our household, we learned through this joyous time that grains can be beautiful, original, and truly appealing—in addition to providing sustenance at every course of every meal, from appetizer to dessert.

Our testing began to take on a pattern, both in terms of nutritional attitude and in practicality of handling, cooking, and serving. We had set out to write a book that was totally in keeping with today's move toward lighter and fresher ingredients, and we began to discover new uses for our country's vast reservoir of fresh fruits, vegetables, and herbs. In fact, we discovered so many possibilities and combinations along the way that we could have written a complete cookbook about *each* grain, and we still would have had recipes left over for a book entitled *Son of Grains.*

We found along the way that grain dishes are eminently satisfying and quite filling, thus requiring much smaller portions at the lunch or dinner table, without making us feel deprived or the least bit hungry between meals. When whole grains are a regular part of your diet, you will find that there's no need to even think of a mid-morning snack or something to pick up the afternoon letdown. For the first time in his life, while working on this book, Mel finished breakfast and worked straight through to lunch without his usual wandering past our refrigerator to see what there was to fill the gaping hole of hunger that he attributes to being "a growing boy!"

In terms of kitchen economics, the results are fascinating to study at a time when the food budget is taking up a larger portion of our weekly income. When using grains, only small additions of other ingredients are needed to create a meal that is complete in proteins and all the essential amino acids.

And Finally: The Recipes

After Two Years of Testing . . .

- In many of the dishes that follow, instead of the accent being on meat, we have developed grain and pasta dishes that use only small amounts of meat as an accent for the basic grains.
- Many of our dishes use legumes and grains. These dishes will appeal not only to the complete vegetarian, but to everyone looking for a refreshing change from the standard high-fat American diet.
- We have also designed our recipes to maintain the integrity of each grain, so that the texture and the flavor of that grain will be the primary essence in each dish. However, some grains do complement one another, and we have included a section on mixed grains. Sheryl, an artist by training, uses her own analogy of kitchen philosophy. "After all," she states, "it's necessary in art to know what a true red and a true blue look like before you mix them to get purple!"

About Some Other Ingredients

Sweeteners: We do not use sugar in any of our recipes, and this has been a standard that we've followed through all of the books written for Rodale Press. In all of our recipes, you'll find one of five sweeteners suggested:

- Mild, clear, golden honey—use a gentle honey that doesn't fight with the other flavors.
- Light molasses.
- Pure, unprocessed maple syrup, without preservatives.
- Date sugar—It sometimes tends to lump, so we suggest that you grind it in an electric coffee mill first.
- Fruit and vegetable juices—fresh or frozen concentrate, and apple cider.

Fresh Ingredients

- We used fresh fruits, nuts, vegetables, and legumes for the best nutrition and for the best taste.

- We use hot peppers to perk up flavors, but if the amounts seem too strong for your palate, cut them down by all means.
- Wherever possible, we used fresh herbs right from our summer island garden and our winter apartment windowsill garden. We find that if they're fresh, they're quite consistent in flavor, and that fresh parsley, chives, chervil, and leaf coriander have an integrity of taste that is lacking in the dried herbs. We realize, however, that dried herbs will sometimes be used out of necessity. Just keep in mind that the flavor is usually more concentrated than that of the fresh herbs, and you must use a smaller amount in the recipe. Also, store dried herbs out of the heat and light, and purchase them in small amounts. The longer they are stored, the more they lose their zing or develop an off-taste.
- You will notice an extensive use of fresh citrus: the juice, the pulp, and the peel of oranges, lemons, and limes. As we discovered when we wrote our book about fish cookery, citrus is one of the most versatile replacements for salt.

Oils and Fats: We call for sweet butter in some recipes, and polyunsaturated fats wherever possible. Put very simply, the decisions were made because of flavor considerations or the way in which the oils handle during cooking. For example, safflower oil is light, but it burns at high temperatures. On the other hand, corn and sunflower oils are excellent for frying because they can reach high temperatures without smoking. Peanut and sesame oils go well with Oriental dishes and olive oil with salads and stronger-flavored foods from areas like the Mediterranean.

The Pastas: We deal with three types of whole grain pasta: "Store-bought" Italian, homemade pastas and noodles, and international noodles.

We have been eating the standard, yellow, semolina flour pastas for so many years that most of us carry an unfounded prejudice against whole grain pastas and noodles. As with all products, some are superb and some are not as tasty or easy to handle. We give some general recommendations, based upon our own experience. Whereas only a few years ago there were hardly any whole grain pastas on the market, the variety of brand names has mushroomed within a very short time. We also offer a range of sauces that were developed especially to suit the shapes of the pastas you choose, and we give some special tips on choosing the cheese and oil to be used for Italian pastas. The "homemade" section is completely devoted to making your own whole grain, light, fresh pastas from corn, buckwheat, whole wheat, and vegetables. And finally, lest we forget that our friends around the world are also users of pasta—though they call them noodles—you'll find a number of international recipes for your enjoyment.

Aha!
Where's the Salt?

There is no salt. So much has already been written on the subject of salt and hypertension and high blood pressure, sodium in processed foods, salt-free solutions, and confessions of "sodium addicts" that there is no need for us to add to the flood of print from magazines, newspapers, and the Food and Drug Administration.

To paraphrase a bit, "One person's salt is another person's poison." We have seen dinner guests reach for the saltshaker almost as soon as the steaming dishes were put down on the table, even before they tasted them. It is a universal habit—but we do believe that it is a damaging one, and we have devised as many substitutes as possible for those who agree with us.

Those who have been forced to give up sodium, and those who have chosen to do so, have discovered new flavor sensations in their cooking, a perception of natural tastes that have long been camouflaged by large doses of salt. Along with sugar, salt has created an American (and Japanese) addiction, for it appears in gross amounts in most of our packaged foods. We have found that the "salt junkies," just as the "sugar freaks," can give it up if they really want to.

Mel found it easy some years ago to ignore the saltshaker on the table completely, while Sheryl's "withdrawal" took longer. We try, therefore, to wean our readers from sodium (if they want to be weaned) in as painless a way as possible (see Appendix). Personal preferences vary, and as Bob Rodale once said so wisely (and we have quoted him on this before): "Remember, the saltshaker is in *your* hand."

Part II
Great Grains and Great Recipes

Amaranth: Grain of the Past, Grain of the Future

When the Spanish conquistadors invaded the land we know as Mexico, they found that the native Aztecs grew a grain crop with which the conquerors were totally unfamiliar. It was a grain that dated back almost 8,000 years to the Tehuacan cave dwellers in Mexico. By the time of the Spanish conquest about five centuries ago, this grain had become a staple in the daily diet of the Aztecs, and it was also revered by these people as a religious symbol.

The Aztecs fashioned statues of their war gods and fire gods from the grain, mixing it with honey and a measure of sacrificial human blood to form a paste called *zoale*. The images were worshipped and then eaten by the Indians. The Spanish, in spite of their reputation as one of history's most bloodthirsty conquerors, were so horrified by what they considered a pagan travesty of the Eucharist that in the early sixteenth century they banned the grain. Amaranth was lost to much of civilization, to resurface only recently as a "grain of the future."

In a world where only 12 crop species stand between civilization and starvation, amaranth is a potential supercrop. The plant grows vigorously under the most adverse conditions, especially in areas that are plagued by drought. Amaranth grows quickly and abundantly, and both the leaves and the seeds offer unusually high quality protein. In fact, when the grain is mixed with whole wheat, the protein of that combination comes very close to that recommended for optimum human nutrition. Amaranth is higher in fiber than wheat, corn, rice, or soybeans. It has a long shelf life and an unusual, nutty flavor, and it works remarkably well in a vast range of recipes.

The world is always slow to accept something "new"—and even though amaranth has been on our doorstep for so many years, it exists now only in a few places in the world, such as in the *alegria* candies of Mexico, made from popped amaranth and honey. In parts of Asia, the leaves

30

are eaten as a vegetable, and the seeds are parched and milled and made into a flat bread. And, because of the experimentation now taking place at the Rodale Research Center, amaranth is just beginning to gain a new popularity as a staple food grain. Cornell University is researching it, and so is the U.S. Department of Agriculture. Almost 15,000 people throughout the 50 states are voluntarily growing amaranth in their back-yards and sending reports to the Research Center. Possibly it is a grain whose time has come.

The agricultural world seems to concentrate on crops that must be grown on huge farms, harvested by machine, and then shipped to California or to New York to feed the population. The energy emergencies and the vast problems of the developing nations make amaranth, which can be grown anywhere and is easily harvested by hand, the perfect grain for local farming communities, and for the more labor-intensive countries around the world who desperately need a high-yield, high-nutrition grain.

In its own peculiar way, it is very "new," this amaranth. As a result, you will not yet find it on the supermarket shelves or even at the natural foods store. You may have to grow it yourself (and seeds are available). We write this chapter as a prelude, as a look to the near future, we hope. Even as we write about and cook with amaranth, some of the major food suppliers and processors in the United States are visiting the Rodale Research Center with an eye toward growing, processing, and marketing amaranth.

We have spent many hours at the Center, we have tasted of amaranth, and we have cooked with it. Curious as to just how easy it would be for someone else to handle, we asked our assistant, Tina Gonzalez (shown below), to experiment with amaranth. We took her to visit with the researchers in Kutztown, and commissioned her to develop recipes that might easily be duplicated by our readers. What follows is her report.

Adventures in Amaranth

The fact that the amaranth recipes in this book were developed in my kitchen with almost no failures is not so much a testimony to my ability as it is to the marvelous versatility of amaranth as a food ingredient. The grain cooks easily and quickly, and it always retains its shape. It never gets soft or mushy, the hulls stay firm and chewy, and the golden variety of amaranth has an unusual peppery/spice flavor.

When the grain is ground into flour, it behaves best in combination with wheat flours, since it has a low gluten content. And it retains its spicy flavor. The whole grain can also be popped and eaten like popcorn, and it can then be sweetened with honey or molasses, very much as the traditional Mexican *alegria.*

Experimentation is still going on at the Research Center, much of it in conjunction with the Rodale Test Kitchen, under the direction of Tom Ney. In one study, for example, 56 varieties of amaranth grain were examined. The aim was to identify the characteristics of each grain type and to analyze the properties in baking, absorption, popping, and taste. Flavors vary from sweet and mild to peppery and assertive, and there is even a variety that tastes very much like corn.

At this time, you can purchase amaranth grain and flour from Walnut Acres (see Mail-Order Sources), or you can grow your own amaranth, just as 15,000 volunteer families are now doing in all 50 states. If you'd like further information about amaranth, write to:

Rodale Research Center
P.O. Box 323, R.D. 1
Kutztown, PA 19530

If you do grow your own, the Rodale research and development people have come up with a simple-to-construct piece of equipment to facilitate the processing of homegrown grain. They've developed a machine that will winnow these tiny seeds, making the cleaning process a simple procedure.

If you use your own coffee or spice grinder, you can make an excellent amaranth *meal* from the whole grain. However, for *flour,* you'll have to use a professional mill, or you can grind *popped* amaranth in your little spice grinder for an adequate substitute flour.

How to Pop Amaranth

Since the entire subject of amaranth is an adventure, methods of using the grain and popping the grain are still being worked out. At some future date, no doubt, commercially popped amaranth will be available in the marketplace. Here are two methods of popping amaranth, the first one used by the Rodale Test Kitchen and a second one, worked out in my own small kitchen, that seems to be an easier method. In either case, pop just enough amaranth to use immediately. Though the grain has tremendous keeping power in its natural state, it turns rancid rather quickly after it's popped.

The Rodale Test Kitchen Method: Use a wok or heavy skillet; heat the utensil *dry* until it is very hot, and then add approximately one tablespoon of amaranth seeds. A few of the seeds will pop immediately. Using a small pastry brush, keep the seeds moving to keep them from burning. When all of the seeds have popped, remove the wok or skillet from the heat and empty the popped seeds into a bowl. Repeat until the desired yield is achieved. One cup of seeds will give approximately three to four cups of popped amaranth. It has a toasted, nutty flavor.

The Gonzalez Small Kitchen Method: Use a Japanese sesame seed toaster (available from Katagiri—see Mail-Order Sources), and add one teaspoon of amaranth grain. Hold the toaster about two to three inches above the heat source, and the seeds will begin to pop in a few seconds.

All my recipes are experiments that actually worked! I encourage you to try them. Because the grain is so new (in spite of its history with the Aztecs), you will not find the recipes in any other cookbook.

Basic Amaranth Grains

Yields 2½ cups

1 cup amaranth
3 cups cold water

Clean amaranth thoroughly! This can be an extremely labor intensive project without some of the basic equipment. It can, of course, be done by patient picking, all of which is very worthwhile since the grains' flavor and texture won't have to compete with the grit.

Amaranth is very easy to cook, using the same basic principles you use to cook almost any other grain. The principal difference is that amaranth grains never get very soft—they retain a chewy texture. Amaranth also has a much more assertive flavor than most other grains, almost spicy or peppery.

Combine amaranth and water in a SilverStone-lined saucepan with a tight-fitting lid. Bring to a boil, cover, lower heat, and let simmer for about 25 minutes. Grains will absorb the water and bind together, but still retain their shape. Use immediately, or store in the refrigerator for up to a week.

Main Dish

Mixed Vegetables Stuffed with Amaranth and Mushrooms
Serves 6 as a main course or 12 as a side dish

Filling:

2 tablespoons butter
⅔ cup finely chopped
    scallions
⅔ cup finely chopped celery
2 cups coarsely chopped
    mushrooms
1 tablespoon finely chopped
    chives
½ teaspoon dried tarragon
    freshly ground black
      pepper to taste
1 cup cooked amaranth grain
½ cup grated cheddar cheese
    (or any sharp, firm
    cheese)

Melt butter in a medium skillet and saute the scallions, celery, and mushrooms until wilted. Add chives, tarragon, pepper, and amaranth and combine well. Remove from heat, let cool, and stir in grated cheese. Set aside while preparing vegetables for stuffing.

Vegetables:

6 small cigarlike zucchini
    (to total no more than
    2 pounds)
3 medium-size tomatoes
3 medium-size green peppers
1 to 2 cups Chicken Stock (see
    Index)

Preheat oven to 350°F. Cut about ½ inch from each end of the zucchini and reserve. Using a zucchini corer or a long-handled iced-tea spoon, scoop out the pulp, leaving ¼-inch-thick shells.

Cut about a ⅓-inch slice from top of each tomato and reserve. Scoop out seeds, leaving shells about ¼ inch thick. (Reserve the pulp of the tomatoes and zucchini for another use.)

Cut about a ⅓-inch slice from stem end of each pepper and reserve. Remove and discard seeds.

Stuff the zucchini and replace ends. Stuff the tomatoes and peppers and recap with top slices. Place all vegetables in a baking dish or two so that they fit comfortably in a single layer. Pour enough stock around vegetables to reach about 1 inch up the sides of the tomatoes and peppers but not to cover the zucchini. Bake for 1 hour. Arrange vegetables on a large platter and serve warm.

Amaranth Tempura

Yields about 1 cup batter

Amaranth flour makes a spicy, light, and airy tempura batter.

Batter:

- 1 cup popped amaranth flour
- 1 teaspoon baking powder
- 1/8 teaspoon cayenne pepper
- 1 tablespoon olive oil
- 2 eggs
- 3/4 cup ice water
- peanut oil for frying

Vegetables:

- sweet potatoes, onions, and turnips, peeled and cut into paper-thin slices
- eggplant, peeled and cut into 1/4-inch-thick slices
- parsley sprigs, left whole
- broccoli and cauliflower florets, broken into bite-size pieces
- okra, 1- to 2-inch size (remove thin slice from top)

In a medium-size bowl, combine flour, baking powder, and cayenne. Make a well in the center and add olive oil and eggs and mix well. Gradually add ice water until mixture has consistency of heavy cream. Let stand for 1 hour before using.

Prepare the following vegetables by washing and drying thoroughly. (Any water left on vegetables can cause dangerous splattering of hot oil.)

When ready to prepare, heat oil in a deep saucepan to 375°F. Dip prepared pieces of vegetables into batter and then into frying oil. Don't fry too many at once, since doing so will lower the frying temperature and make for soggy tempura. Serve immediately with tamari soy sauce and lemon wedges.

Eggplant-Amaranth-Garlic Marinade

Yields about 2 cups

- 1 large eggplant (about 1 pound)
- 3 cloves garlic, finely minced
- 3 tablespoons olive oil
- 1 tablespoon lemon juice
- pinch of cayenne pepper
- 1/8 teaspoon black pepper
- 3/4 cup cooked amaranth grains

Preheat oven to 350°F. Wash eggplant and puncture all around with a fork, place on a piece of aluminum foil in the oven, and bake until very soft (about 1½ hours). Let cool completely.

Cut eggplant in half. Scoop out pulp and place in a medium-size bowl. Discard skin. Add the remaining ingredients to the eggplant pulp. Mix and then let flavors blend for at least 1 hour before serving. Serve chilled or at room temperature with crackers, or as a side dish with rice.

Bread

Amaranth Date Nut Bread
Makes 1 loaf

I shared a slice of this bread with a friend who has a notorious sweet tooth. He devoured it and clamored for more. He could not believe it was made without white sugar and white flour.

2 eggs
½ cup mild honey
¼ cup butter, melted
2 cups whole wheat flour
1 cup chopped dates, soaked
   in ¾ cup boiling water
1 teaspoon baking powder
½ teaspoon baking soda
1 cup cooked amaranth grain
1 cup chopped walnuts
1 teaspoon vanilla extract

Preheat oven to 350°F. and butter a 9 × 5 × 3-inch loaf pan. In a large mixing bowl, beat eggs well. Add honey and melted butter and beat again. Stir in flour and then half the dates and half the soaking water. Add all remaining ingredients and the rest of the dates and soaking water and blend well. Pour into prepared loaf pan and bake for 1 hour and 15 minutes, or until cake tester inserted in center comes out clean. Let cool for 10 minutes on a wire rack before removing from pan and then cool completely on rack before slicing.

Dessert

No-Bake Amaranth Cashew Chicks
Makes 12 chicks

⅔ cup toasted popped
   amaranth flour
3 tablespoons mild honey
4 tablespoons cashew butter
12 whole roasted, unsalted
   cashews
¼ cup grated coconut

Blend flour, honey, and cashew butter in a medium-size bowl until well combined. Wet hands and wrap half of each cashew (the fat bulb end) with a tablespoonful of mixture, allowing hook end of cashew to protrude from ball. Roll formed cashew balls in coconut and refrigerate until ready to serve.

Variation: Try wrapping the dough around pitted date halves and rolling them in popped amaranth. For a different texture, these same balls can be baked at 350°F. for about 10 minutes.

Note: To toast popped amaranth flour, heat a heavy skillet until very hot. Add the flour and stir it around until a nutty aroma is apparent (about 2 to 3 minutes). Take care not to let it burn.

Cock-a-Leekie Soup   For this recipe, see page 44

Corn-Bread Ring with Sausage and Red Peppers   For this recipe, see page 89

When barley was first brought to this country by the colonists, it was more valued for its brewing properties than for its taste and nutrition. It is no wonder that most of us know about John Barleycorn, made famous by Robert Burns in the eighteenth century, while too few of us have discovered the other remarkable properties offered by this ancient grain. (About 10 percent of the barley we grow is used for human food, and the balance fed to animals or kept for making beer.)

The Eastern civilizations have long used barley as a substantial food source. The Chinese grind barley flour with lentils or beans to make bread, and in Tibet, there is a fermented barley flour bread that is raised overnight and spreads out into a large, round shape when it's baked. Its name describes it well: Prayer Wheel Bread. The Buddhist monks in Tibet also make a porridge called *tsampa* by mixing barley flour with yak butter and the recipe is quite simple if you happen to have a yak grazing in your backyard:

There's More to Barley Than Beer

Tsampa

⅔ cup barley
2 cups boiling tea
   fermented yak butter

Toast grains and grind into flour. Mix with boiling tea and simmer for 15 minutes. Pour yak butter over it and serve.

The Japanese also use barley as an accompaniment to the main courses of fish or meat, very much as they use rice, while the Koreans make an excellent tea called *bori cha,* and the main ingredient is roasted barley.

However underutilized barley is in the Western world — used only as an occasional porridge, pilaf, drink, or coffee substitute — it nonetheless was one of the earliest crops cultivated by mankind. The Bible speaks of David's army being given rations of barley, and long before biblical times—as far back as 5000 B.C.—the grain was used as food in Egypt and in China soon afterward. The Sumerians used barley as the basis for a measuring system for almost 2,000 years, and the ancient writings of Babylon and the Code of Hammurabi speak of barley as a form of payment, the basis of a simple monetary system.

Unfortunately, the most common form of barley available here in the United States is the hulled variety, called pearled barley. The lost outer bran is an excellent source of vitamin B, and milling also reduces the calcium content and the nutritive value of the grain. However, the protein content of the milled barley and the pearled barley is almost identical, since most of the essential amino acids are in the endosperm of the grain, not the husk. You can generally get the whole barley in your local natural foods store or by mail order (see Mail-Order Sources).

Basic Whole Hulled Barley

Yields 4 cups

1 cup whole hulled or
  pearled barley
4 cups water

Bring water to a rolling boil and slowly add the barley without disturbing the boil. Cover pot, lower heat, and simmer for 45 minutes, or until all liquid is absorbed. Bite-test a grain or two to see if done. Fluff with a fork. Remove from heat and place 2 thicknesses of paper towels between the pot and the lid to absorb any excess moisture and to insure separation of grains. Let stand for 10 minutes in this manner before serving.

Note: Pearled barley may take a bit less cooking time. Bite-test after 40 minutes.

Basic Barley Flakes

Serves 6

This makes an excellent breakfast and a nice change from rolled oats. The pressed grain saves 20 minutes of cooking time.

4½ cups water
1½ cups barley flakes (rolled
  barley)

Bring water to a rapid boil and slowly add the barley flakes without disturbing the boil. Stir, then lower the heat, cover pot, and simmer for 25 minutes, or until water is absorbed. The flakes fluff up and can be used in soups and stews.

Note: For a delicious treat, stir in ½ cup of diced mixed dried fruit for the last 5 minutes of cooking. Serve with fresh milk or cream. Honey can be added if you like sweet hot cereal.

The Forms of Barley

Natural Unhulled Brown Barley: Used for cooking and for sprouting. It is generally available only in natural foods stores or by mail.

Whole Hulled Barley: A natural white barley with only the *outermost* chaff or hull removed. This is not the variety called "pearled," and it can be cooked unground, added to soups and casseroles, or used as a whole grain cereal.

Barley Flakes or Rolled Barley: Barley rolled or pressed in the same way as rolled oats, then used as a cereal or toasted and used as a thickening agent in soups, stews, and baked goods. Because of the processing, it cooks more quickly than the complete grain form. The flakes make a chewy, hearty breakfast cereal.

Pearled Barley: The most common commercial variety. If you cannot get the natural forms of the grain, pearled barley is quite all right to use in the recipes that follow. It generally comes in fine, medium, or coarse grains.

Barley Grits: Whole, hulled barley, toasted and cracked into six to eight separate pieces. It is excellent for use as a meat extender in dishes such as meat loaf.

Barley Flour: A finely ground, hulled barley for blending with other flours, usually with a high-gluten flour that lightens the loaf in breads, cakes, and muffins. It is also used as a thickening agent and is sometimes recommended for people on wheat-restricted diets. Some people prefer to grind their own flour from the unhulled natural barley—it's easy to make right in your own coffee grinder, spice grinder, or blender.

Basic Barley Grits

Yields 4 cups

1 cup whole barley
4 cups water or milk

Toast whole barley lightly in a dry skillet, shaking the pan to prevent burning. Cool and crack coarsely in a blender or grain mill. You now have barley grits. (Sometimes you may be able to find cracked barley grits at your local health food store.) Boil water or milk (milk makes a creamier version), slowly add barley grits, cover, lower heat, and simmer, stirring occasionally, for 15 minutes.

Note: The grits can also be ground very fine in a blender, almost to a coarse flour consistency, before cooking. This grind makes a particularly digestible cereal for people who have problems chewing and for babies without teeth. Cooked fruit, honey, maple syrup, or grated orange rind can be added for flavor; or try a mashed banana and cinnamon.

Appetizer _____

Sprouted Barley, Mushroom, and Walnut Balls
Makes 12 or 13 balls

A most unusual and tasty hors d'oeuvre for any festive gathering. See if your guests can guess even a few of the ingredients, especially the subtle, evasive flavor of the sprouted barley.

½ cup finely chopped walnuts
1 medium-size onion, quartered
2 large mushrooms
1 cup sprouted barley
1 cup dry fine whole wheat bread crumbs
¼ teaspoon dried thyme
¼ teaspoon ground cumin
⅛ teaspoon black pepper
pinch of cayenne pepper
few drops of lemon juice
2 tablespoons finely minced parsley
1 egg, beaten
1 tablespoon milk
peanut oil for frying
wedges of lemon for garnish

In a food processor, grind walnuts. Then add onion, mushrooms, and sprouted barley and continue to process until fine. Turn out into a bowl and add all remaining ingredients except peanut oil and lemon wedges. Wet hands and form mixture into walnut-size balls. Place on waxed paper and chill for 10 minutes. Heat oil in a large skillet and fry the balls, turning to brown on all sides. Drain on paper towels and serve hot with lemon wedges.

Note: Unhulled barley for sprouting looks like a longer, browner kernel of rice, and it can be bought in natural foods stores. Two tablespoons of barley kernels make about 1 cup of sprouts.

Momma's Dried Lima Bean, Barley, and Mushroom Soup
Serves 6 to 8

As a child, Sheryl's mother lived in a small village on the Polish-Austrian border during troubled times. From day to day, that border town was occupied alternately by Austrian or Polish soldiers who came to keep order. This required her to speak German one day and Polish the next. Of course, it did little to develop a feeling of identity or security for a young child. One day, while reminiscing about this period in her life, she said that the only comfort was this favorite soup, which her grandmother made for the family. Unlike the Polish-Austrian border, it has never changed.

3 or 4   beef marrow bones, sawed in 2-inch pieces and washed (any chicken backs, necks, and giblets are a welcome addition also)

10   cups water

1   large onion, peeled

1   clove garlic, peeled

⅓   cup dried baby lima beans

½   cup fine or medium pearled barley

1   ounce dried mushrooms, preferably imported from Poland

1   tablespoon rolled oats

½   teaspoon paprika

½   teaspoon white pepper

2   large carrots, quartered

2   stalks celery with leaves, cut in half

1   small turnip, peeled

1   small parsnip, peeled

1   parsley root

1   leek

6   sprigs parsley

2   sprigs dillweed

In a large pot, place bones and water. Bring to a boil and skim foam from surface of soup. Add the onion, garlic, lima beans, and barley. Cover pot and simmer for 30 minutes.

Meanwhile, soak the mushrooms in enough boiling water to cover for 20 minutes. Strain liquid through a fine sieve and reserve. Rinse mushrooms under cold water and then cut into small pieces. Set aside.

Add the oats, paprika, and pepper to the pot along with the carrots, celery, turnip, parsnip, and parsley root. Cook for 10 minutes more, then add the reserved mushrooms and mushroom liquid, and continue to cook for 30 minutes more.

Meanwhile, tie the leek, parsley, and dillweed together and add to the pot. Continue to simmer for 45 minutes more. Before serving, lift out and discard the onion and garlic, the celery, turnip, parsnip, and parsley root, the leek and herb bouquet, and the bones. Reheat slowly before serving.

Note: Parsley roots are sometimes difficult to find. If you do not have parsley root, just add several more sprigs of fresh parsley to the herb bouquet.

Tanabour—Armenian Beef, Barley, and Yogurt Soup
Serves 6 to 8

3	tablespoons butter
1	medium-size onion, finely chopped
1	small clove garlic, finely minced
½	pound lean ground beef
1	teaspoon ground cumin
½	teaspoon ground allspice

¼	teaspoon white pepper
	about 6 scallions, thinly sliced
2	tablespoons chopped mint, or 1 tablespoon dried crushed mint
1½	cups cooked barley
4	cups Chicken Stock (see Index)
2	eggs, lightly beaten
3	cups yogurt

Melt butter over medium heat in a heavy pot and saute onion and garlic until wilted. Add the ground beef, cumin, allspice, and pepper and stir until meat loses its pink color. Stir in the scallions, mint, and cooked barley.

In a large bowl, beat the chicken stock, eggs, and yogurt together with a wire whisk. Add to the pot and heat slowly over low heat, stirring until thickened, for about 10 minutes. Do not boil or it will curdle. Serve hot.

Cock-a-Leekie Soup
Serves 6

1	2½- to 3-pound chicken
12	cups Chicken Stock (see Index)
2	pounds veal bones, cut in small pieces
2	stalks celery with leaves
2	small carrots
6 to 8	thin leeks, split and washed well under cold running water
1	whole bunch parsley
3	whole cloves
2	whole bay leaves
¾	cup medium pearled barley
1	teaspoon curry powder
1	teaspoon ground allspice

Place the chicken, chicken stock, and veal bones in a 5-quart heavy pot. Bring to a boil, then lower heat, and skim the accumulated foam. Simmer for 5 minutes. Tie the celery, carrots, only 1 of the leeks, and the whole bunch of parsley together with string and add to the pot with the cloves and bay leaves. Cover and simmer for 45 minutes.

Lift out chicken to cool. Continue cooking for 30 minutes more and then remove the vegetable bouquet and the bones, and discard. Bring soup to a boil, slowly add the barley, and then lower heat. Cut the tough green parts off the leeks, leaving 1 inch of the green part, and discard. Cut leeks into 1-inch lengths and add to the pot along with curry powder and allspice. Simmer, covered, for 40 to 45 minutes, or until barley is tender.

Meanwhile, remove skin and bones from the cooled chicken and tear the meat into chunks. Add to the soup and heat together for 5 minutes.

Barley, Brown Onion, and Chicken Liver Casserole
Serves 6

1   cup whole hulled barley
4   cups Chicken Stock (see Index)
2   tablespoons melted chicken fat
2   large onions, thinly sliced and separated into rings
8   chicken livers, cut into small pieces
¼   teaspoon black pepper

Garnish:

⅛   teaspoon paprika
3   tablespoons minced parsley

Wash barley in cold water in a small bowl and drain. Boil chicken stock, then add barley, and stir. When it comes to a boil again, stir once again, cover pot, and simmer for 30 minutes, or until the barley is tender and the liquid is absorbed. Remove from heat and let sit for 5 minutes more to allow grains to separate.

While the barley is cooking, heat the chicken fat in a skillet and add the onions.

Cook the onions, stirring occasionally, until they are dark in color. Remove with slotted spoon and add to barley. In the same skillet, cook the chicken livers over medium heat, while stirring, for 3 to 4 minutes, and then add to the barley and onions. Add the pepper and stir. Then transfer to a warmed serving dish and sprinkle with paprika and parsley before serving.

Barley, Mushroom, and Parsley Casserole
Serves 6

3   cups beef stock
1   cup whole hulled barley
3   tablespoons butter
1   large onion, finely chopped
1   pound mushrooms, thickly sliced
1   tablespoon lemon juice
½   teaspoon black pepper
¼   cup finely minced parsley for garnish

Place beef stock in a 4-quart pot and bring to a boil. Slowly add barley. Cover, lower heat, and simmer for 30 to 45 minutes, or until liquid is absorbed and grain is tender.

Meanwhile, heat butter in a skillet and saute the onion until it starts to brown. Then add the mushrooms and cook, while stirring, for 5 minutes. Turn off heat and add lemon juice and black pepper to the onion and mushrooms. Add to barley and mix well.

Before serving, turn into a casserole and sprinkle with parsley.

Barley with Red Beans, Cheese, and Parsley
Serves 6

1 tablespoon soft butter
1 medium-size onion, thinly sliced and separated into rings
1 large clove garlic, finely minced
¼ teaspoon black pepper
⅛ teaspoon dried oregano
1 cup cooked red kidney beans
2 cups cooked whole barley
½ cup finely minced parsley
1 cup grated sharp cheddar cheese
¼ teaspoon ground cumin
2 eggs
1 cup milk

This baked grains-and-beans dish is somewhat like a quiche in texture, with a firm cheese custard.

Generously butter a 9-inch round casserole. (A glazed clay casserole is perfect for this dish.) Preheat oven to 350°F. Place the onion rings on the bottom of the prepared casserole and sprinkle with the minced garlic, pepper, and oregano.

In a bowl, mix the beans, barley, parsley, cheese, and cumin together and spoon over onions. Beat the eggs and milk together and pour mixture over all. Bake for about 45 minutes.

Hamburgers with Barley and Vegetables
Serves 6

1 tablespoon olive oil
½ cup finely minced carrots (about 1 medium carrot)
¼ cup finely minced onions
1 cup finely minced red cabbage (¼ of a small cabbage)
1 pound lean ground beef
½ cup cooked fine pearled barley
2 tablespoons finely minced chives
¼ teaspoon black pepper
1 teaspoon tamari soy sauce
1 egg, lightly beaten

Each one of these 4-ounce hamburgers is a whole meal chock full of vegetables and grain as well as beef.

Heat oil over medium heat in a skillet. Add carrots, onions, and red cabbage. (A food processor minces these vegetables beautifully.) Stir and cook for 1 minute, then lower heat to simmer, cover skillet, and cook vegetables slowly. Let cool slightly.

Meanwhile, in a small bowl, mix ground beef, barley, chives, pepper, and tamari. Then add the cooked vegetables. Add the egg and mix again. Wet hands and form into balls. Flatten into patties and cook in a hot nonstick skillet for 5 minutes on each side.

Lamb Shanks with Barley, Vegetables, and Chick-Peas
Serves 6 to 8

6 lamb shanks, about ¾ pound each, cut into 3 pieces each (total about 4 to 4½ pounds)
½ teaspoon black pepper
1 clove garlic, minced
¼ teaspoon rosemary, crushed
½ cup whole hulled or pearled barley, washed
1 medium-size onion, peeled
2 stalks celery, quartered
1½ cups water
1 medium-size potato, peeled and cut into chunks

2 small turnips, peeled and cut into chunks
4 or 5 small carrots, quartered
2 small yams or sweet potatoes, peeled and cut into chunks
¼ pound string beans
½ pound green peas, shelled, or ½ package frozen green peas
⅔ cup cooked chick-peas
1 tablespoon lemon juice
1 teaspoon grated lemon peel
2 tablespoons finely minced parsley for garnish

Place the pieces of lamb in a large heavy pot. Add the pepper, garlic, rosemary, barley, onion, celery, and water. Bring to a boil, lower heat, and simmer, covered, for 1 hour.

Remove the onion and discard. Add the potato, turnips, carrots, and sweet potatoes and continue to cook for 20 minutes more. Add the string beans, green peas, and chick-peas and stir. Cook for an additional 15 minutes.

Add the lemon juice and the peel. Transfer to a warmed serving dish and sprinkle with parsley before serving.

Flemish Waterzooie *with Whole Barley*

Serves 6

1	5½- to 6-pound chicken, cut into 6 serving pieces (chicken parts can be used)
½	teaspoon white pepper
3	tablespoons butter
3	leeks, washed and sliced ½ inch thick
3	carrots, sliced ½ inch thick
3	stalks celery with leaves, sliced ½ inch thick
1	large onion, thinly sliced
6	sprigs parsley with stems leaves from 2 sprigs thyme, or ½ teaspoon dried thyme
5	whole cloves
¼	teaspoon nutmeg
4½	cups hot Chicken Stock (see Index)
2	cups cooked whole hulled barley
3	egg yolks
2	tablespoons heavy cream
2	tablespoons lemon juice

Garnish:

1	lemon, thinly sliced
2	tablespoons minced parsley

This top-of-stove, delicate, lemony casserole is half-way between a soup and a stew. A complete meal in itself, *Waterzooie* is served in large, deep soup plates.

Sprinkle chicken pieces with pepper and set aside.

In a large, heavy pot, melt butter slowly and then make a bed of the leeks, carrots, celery, and onion in the bottom of the pot. Lay the parsley over the vegetables, and then the chicken pieces in 1 layer over the vegetables and parsley. Sprinkle with the thyme, cloves, and nutmeg. Cover pot and cook over medium-low heat for 10 minutes. Then slowly pour the hot chicken stock over all, cover pot, lower heat, and simmer for 45 minutes, or until chicken is tender.

Remove pot from heat and lift out chicken pieces to cool. Strain the soup into a bowl and pick out and discard the parsley sprigs and the cloves from the vegetables in the strainer, reserving the vegetables. When chicken is cool enough to handle, remove and discard bones and skin and keep the chicken meat in large chunks.

In a large oven-to-table casserole, layer the barley in the bottom. Place the cooked vegetables on top evenly, and the pieces of chicken over all. Cover and keep warm in oven while preparing broth.

Beat the egg yolks and cream with a wire whisk and then add the lemon juice. Return stock to a clean saucepan and heat (do not boil). When hot, add a ladle of hot stock to the egg mixture, beating constantly. Slowly whisk this mixture into the stock and stir constantly over the lowest heat possible. Now switch to a wooden spoon so soup will not be foamy. When slightly thickened (about 5 minutes), pour over chicken and vegetables. Float lemon slices on top and sprinkle with parsley before serving.

Polish Galobki—
Barley and Mushroom
Stuffed Cabbage Leaves with
Sour Cream and Dill Sauce

Makes 24 cabbage rolls

1   large head green cabbage
2   tablespoons butter
1   medium-size onion,
       chopped
¼   pound mushrooms,
       chopped
1½ cups cooked whole hulled
       or pearled barley
1   tablespoon lemon juice
½   teaspoon paprika
¼   teaspoon black pepper
¼   cup minced parsley
2   cups hot beef stock
¾   cup sour cream
1   tablespoon minced dillweed

Cut core from cabbage about 3 inches deep. Boil water in a deep pot (stockpot or pasta pot). Place whole cabbage in boiling water and parboil for 10 to 15 minutes or until leaves are soft and pliable. Lift out cabbage by inserting a 2-pronged fork into the hole left from coring and supporting the other side of the cabbage with a wide spatula. Drain and cool on paper towels. When cooled, separate the leaves carefully. With a sharp knife, carefully cut an inverted V from the tough center part of the rib. The leaf will now lie flat. Do this with each leaf. Line up the leaves on kitchen counter between layers of paper towels, and then prepare the filling.

Melt butter in a skillet, and when hot, saute onion until wilted. Add the mushrooms and barley and stir and cook for 3 minutes. Add the lemon juice, paprika, pepper, and parsley and continue stirring and cooking for 1 minute more. Set aside to cool. There should be about 3 cups of filling.

Depending on the size of the cabbage leaf, spoon 1 tablespoon, more or less, of the filling onto the center of each leaf. Fold sides of cabbage first and roll up from the cut stem end to enclose the filling, but not too tightly or they will expand and burst while cooking. Place rolls seam side down in a large flat-bottom skillet in 1 layer. Slowly pour hot beef stock around rolls. Cover and simmer over very low heat for 1 hour and 15 minutes.

Lift out the rolls and place in 1 layer on a serving dish. Keep warm.

Pour off remaining liquid (about ⅓ cup) and strain. Reserve liquid and wipe out skillet. Return liquid to skillet and stir in sour cream and dillweed. Heat over low heat, stirring, for 2 minutes, and then pour over stuffed cabbage.

Barley-Flake Buttermilk Bread

Makes 1 loaf

2 cups buttermilk
1½ cups barley flour
2 tablespoons barley flakes
1 tablespoon butter
1 teaspoon mild honey
2½ cups gluten flour
1 teaspoon baking powder
¼ teaspoon baking soda
1 egg white, lightly beaten
1 tablespoon toasted barley flakes

This is basically a "quick bread," even though the flour and buttermilk stand overnight to develop a special flavor.

In a small bowl mix buttermilk, barley flour, and barley flakes. Let stand, covered, overnight (or 7 to 8 hours) in a warm place.

Melt the butter and honey in a small skillet. Let cool slightly. Preheat the oven to 425°F. and butter a cookie sheet. Transfer the buttermilk mixture to a large bowl and, with a wooden spoon, stir in the butter and honey mixture.

Mix together the gluten flour, baking powder, and baking soda and beat into the buttermilk mixture. Form into a damp, solid mass with your hands until it forms a large ball. Place on the prepared cookie sheet and flatten slightly. Bake for 50 minutes. After 40 minutes, brush with egg white and sprinkle with the toasted barley flakes. Return to the oven for 10 minutes more.

Note: Barley flour makes a dense bread since it has very little gluten, therefore the addition of gluten flour to lighten it.

Barley-Flake Cracker Bread

Makes 6 crackers

1 cup buttermilk
1 tablespoon butter
2 cups barley flour
½ cup toasted barley flakes

In a saucepan, heat buttermilk and butter slowly over low heat until butter melts. Do not overheat or it will curdle. Remove mixture from heat and let cool for 5 minutes.

Pour into a bowl and add the barley flour and toasted barley flakes. Flour hands and knead a few times until a thick dough is formed. Let rest 5 minutes and then divide into 6 equal pieces. Turn each piece out onto floured waxed paper and roll into a ¼-inch-thick ragged circle.

Heat a griddle. Drape the rolled dough over a rolling pin and unfold over the griddle. Cook slowly over medium heat, pressing down with a wide spatula. Cook about 5 to 8 minutes on one side, then turn and continue cooking. Repeat until 6 are made. To serve, break into pieces and eat warm with butter.

Orange, Carrot, and Barley Grits Pudding with Raisins and Pecans
Serves 6

1 whole seedless orange
4 cups milk
½ cup barley grits
1 cup raisins
1 cup shredded carrots
1 tablespoon butter
1 teaspoon ground cardamom
¼ teaspoon ground cloves
3 tablespoons mild light honey
2 teaspoons orange flower water
10 pecan halves, toasted in butter

Place whole orange in deep saucepan and cover with water. Bring to a boil, lower heat, and simmer for 10 minutes or until soft. (Test with the point of a knife.) Drain water and let cool. When orange is cool enough to handle, cut out stem end with point of knife and cut orange into quarters. Remove any white part from central core of orange. Process orange in a food processor until very fine, and set aside.

Bring milk to the boiling point and slowly add barley grits. Stir in raisins, carrots, and butter. Lower heat, cover pot, and simmer, stirring occasionally, until thick (about 10 minutes). Then stir in cardamom, cloves, honey, and orange flower water.

Rinse a 5-cup mold (preferably a charlotte mold), and spoon dessert into it. Chill for 3 hours.

Before serving, run a knife around side of mold, invert on serving dish, and unmold. Place toasted pecan halves on top like the spokes of a wheel. Cut in wedges to serve.

Vanilla Barley Pudding with Toasted Almonds and Purple Plums
Serves 6

4 cups milk
1 large vanilla bean
1 cup pearled barley
4 tablespoons mild honey
1 teaspoon vanilla extract (optional)
1 tablespoon butter
4 tablespoons slivered almonds
¼ cup heavy cream
6 cooked purple plums, pitted (or cooked peaches, pitted)

Place milk in a large saucepan. Split the vanilla bean, and with the point of a sharp knife, scrape the tiny black seeds into the milk, adding the pod as well. Bring slowly to a boil and then stir in the barley. Cover the pot and lower heat to simmer. Use a flame tamer under the pot to keep the heat as low as possible. Cook for 30 minutes.

When milk is absorbed and barley is tender (bite a kernel to test), stir in the honey. Remove vanilla pod and taste the mixture. If more vanilla is needed, add 1 teaspoon vanilla.

In a small skillet, melt the butter and toast the almonds, and then stir into barley mixture. Serve warm or cold in individual bowls. Pour some cream over each and top with a purple plum or peach.

Born-Again Buckwheat

For those of us who were lucky enough to have a grandmother who could prepare the traditional foods of Central Europe, the images of steaming bowls of Kasha *Varnishkas* still stir up memories of childhood. Others recall stacks of belly-filling pancakes, dark and richly flavored, covered with thick maple syrup, eaten as insulation against the long walk to school on cold mornings. Both of these unforgettable treats were made of buckwheat. There was a time when buckwheat was an important part of America's cuisine. Mark Twain, reporting on a disappointing European trip in 1878, wrote a long list of foods he had missed while on his journey and that he would devour when he returned—among them, buckwheat pancakes.

But somehow, along the way from those days to now, buckwheat lost its prominence. As one writer put it, buckwheat seemed to go the way of the horse and buggy. In China, it has been a staple food for over a thousand years. Russia cultivates 5 times the amount of buckwheat that we do. In fact, here in the United States, we grew *20 times* more buckwheat in 1866 than we do now! But fortunately, it seems to be coming back again. Somehow, the interest in nutritious, tasty ingredients that was a part of the natural foods renaissance of the seventies brought buckwheat out of the closet and onto the shelves of our supermarkets and specialty stores.

Although buckwheat has many of the characteristics and the nutritional structure of grains, it is not truly a grain. Botanically speaking, it is a fruit, related more to rhubarb than it is to wheat or corn. As a result, one of buckwheat's most important attributes is that it is a perfect food for many people who cannot eat wheat products because of allergies.

Like most grains and cereal grasses, buckwheat is on the list of the underutilized foods of the world. Except for its popularity as a food in Russia and Asia—and its starring role in the ubiquitous American pancake—buckwheat is used mostly for fodder, or it is grown to attract bees, who make a distinctively flavored honey from its white blossoms. And yet, with its high-quality protein balance, its rich concentration of iron, B vitamins, and calcium, and its ability to grow almost anywhere on poor soil and to mature in only 60 days, buckwheat is another perfect candidate for new popularity in a world that is looking for reliable food sources.

Basically, there are two kinds of buckwheat on the market: *roasted* and *unroasted*. The process of roasting buckwheat gives it its nutty flavor, dark color, and distinctive aroma. Generally, the roasted buckwheat is called kasha. Since it has a strong flavor, kasha works best with pork, beef, duck, liver, or lamb.

The unroasted white form is called buckwheat, and it can be used with more delicately flavored foods, such as veal or fish. It can be used in soups, souffles, desserts, to stuff vegetables, or as an easily digested cereal for babies or invalids—or for just plain people like us who love the special taste of buckwheat!

The Forms of Buckwheat

Roasted Buckwheat (Kasha)

Fine: Cooks quickly and is less chewy than the other varieties.

Medium: Good for all-around use.

Coarse: Also good for all-around use. The coarse grind is Kasha that is cracked in large particles.

Whole Kasha Groats: Good in pilafs or soups.

Dark Buckwheat Flour: Grayish in color with tiny black specks and contains about 17 percent of the hull. It is stronger in flavor than the light buckwheat flour, and it is usually used alone for pancakes and in combination with wheat flour for baked goods. Since buckwheat is not a true cereal grain, it does not have gluten.

Unroasted Buckwheat

Whole Buckwheat Groats: Pale in color and used for stuffings or pilafs or in dishes where the taste of roasted buckwheat would be too assertive.

Creamy Kernel Buckwheat Grits: An almost white cereal, similar to Cream of Wheat. It is easily digestible and excellent for souffles and desserts, and as cereal in the breakfast bowl.

Light Buckwheat Flour: Can be used in baked goods, sauces, and pancakes. It contains only 7 percent of the dark hull particles.

Buckwheat Seeds: Can be sprouted by using the same procedure as with other sprouts (see page 24), if you can get these seeds fresh from the grower—or if you grow them yourself. However, don't attempt to sprout the unroasted or roasted buckwheat that you buy packaged in a box. Nothing will happen.*

Some Cooking Tips

Just as there are two kinds of buckwheat—roasted and unroasted—there are *two* methods of cooking buckwheat. The instructions on most packages suggest that the kernels be mixed with a beaten egg before adding the boiling liquid. The reason is that the albumin in the egg seals the uncooked buckwheat with a thin binding that helps keep the grains separated while still allowing the cooking liquid to be absorbed.

The second method is the standard method of cooking most cereal grains. Just add the grains slowly to the boiling liquid. However, this method usually results in a more congealed end product, though it can be used when this particular texture is desired. The recipes in the book will specify when this method should be used. Grains cooked by the boiled method keep longer in the refrigerator than those cooked by the egg method.

---

*Birkett Mills is the largest processor and packer in the world, and its buckwheat is sold under the "Wolff's" label in supermarkets and "Pocono" in the natural foods stores. If your local supplier is out of stock, buckwheat can be ordered by mail (see Mail-Order Sources).

Reed Hoffmann/Gannett Rochester Newspapers

Where the Wild Winds Blow

*"Let me wander where my heart may lead me,
Where the wild winds blow on the
        mountainside."*

Each of us, in our dreams of escape and our visions of changing our everyday lives, has some idea of what we'd like to do, a place we'd like to go, far from the tensions and the pressures of urban living. We are fascinated by those who actually pick themselves up and turn those dreams into reality. Many of them do it with great success. Indeed, for some it marks the beginning of prosperous new careers.

Ten years ago, John McMath dropped out of the Madison Avenue advertising rat race and fled to Naples, New York, in the Finger Lakes region. He took a run-down ski cabin and some land that local farmers said would never grow a thing again, and turned them into a complex that comprises over 500 acres. There the gardens, the lush fertile fields, the restaurant, general store, ski trails, and nature walks all make up Wild Winds Farms and Villages.

McMath took the barren land, and without the "help" of pesticides, herbicides, or chemical fertilizer, he turned it into an abundant farm, and gave lie to the presumption that this earth would forever remain barren. Through a soil

enrichment program that included intercropping, crop rotation, compost fertilization, contour plowing, and green manure, the farm now flourishes and thrives.

Over 100,000 people visited Wild Winds last summer, and in winter, the skiers cover the cross-country trails. The restaurant, run by Ellie Clapp, has now been discovered by food magazines and writers from all over the country. It serves home-grown vegetables and wild foods from the land—carrots and onions for the stews; blueberries, blackberries and peaches for the pies; leeks, lettuce, grape leaves, day-lily buds.

There is a special treat in springtime. The farm's buckwheat, harvested the previous autumn and milled into flour, makes the traditional stack of pancakes, while the rich, thick maple syrup that covers them has been gathered from the local trees and boiled down at Wild Winds' own sugaring house. Each weekend during the spring, the guests sit down to Maple Sugaring Pancake Brunch—and the smile on John McMath's face as he watches confirms the decision he made ten years back.

Basic Fluffy Roasted Buckwheat (Kasha)

Yields 4 cups

This is the preferred method of cooking, recommended by the National Buckwheat Institute.

1 egg
1 cup fine buckwheat
2 cups boiling water or stock
1 teaspoon butter

Use a flat-based SilverStone-lined pot with lid. Beat egg and mix with buckwheat. Place in pot and stir constantly over medium heat for 2 to 3 minutes, separating grains and coating them with the egg.

Add boiling liquid and butter and stir. Cover pot tightly, lower heat to simmer, and cook for 5 minutes, or until liquid is absorbed. Place paper towels between lid and pot and let stand for 5 minutes. Fluff with a fork to separate grains.

Variations:

1. Basic Roasted Buckwheat (Kasha), Medium: Use method above and cook for 8 minutes.
2. Basic Roasted Buckwheat (Kasha), Coarse: Use method above and cook for 10 to 15 minutes.
3. Basic Roasted Buckwheat (Kasha), Whole Groats, and Basic Unroasted Buckwheat, Whole Groats: Use method above and cook for 10 to 15 minutes.

Note: Medium, coarse, and whole granulations vary in cooking time— from 10 to 20 minutes, depending upon the depth of the pot. A wide, flat-bottom pot takes less time.

Basic Creamy Kernel Unroasted Buckwheat Grits

Yields 4 cups

5 cups water, or 2½ cups water and 2½ cups milk
1 teaspoon butter
1 cup creamy kernel unroasted buckwheat grits

Boil water rapidly in a SilverStone-lined pot. Add butter and allow it to melt. Then slowly, without disturbing the boil, add the grits, stirring constantly while adding. Cover pot, lower heat, and simmer, stirring occasionally. Cook for 10 minutes, or until liquid is absorbed. Sweeten, if desired, with maple syrup or honey.

Variation: After cooking, spread evenly in an 8-inch-square pan and chill. Cut into 2-inch squares and dredge in buckwheat flour. Brown both sides in butter. The outside has a crunchy texture and the inside is creamy. Serve with maple syrup.

Note: Instead of using water, you may use all milk, if you prefer. We like the half-and-half ratio the best.

Buckwheat Groats, Garlic, and Sorrel Soup with Herbs
Serves 6

Even though a whole head of garlic is used in this soup, gentle cooking insures a mild flavor. The soup is ready to eat within the hour—easy and unusual.

7 cups Chicken Stock (see Index), or half stock, half water
1 whole bulb of garlic, peeled and separated into cloves
½ teaspoon thyme, or ¼ teaspoon dried thyme
½ teaspoon finely minced sage, or ¼ teaspoon dried sage
3 whole cloves
pinch of saffron
1 tablespoon olive oil
½ cup whole buckwheat groats
¼ teaspoon black pepper
2 tablespoons finely minced parsley
3 tablespoons lemon juice
1 cup finely shredded sorrel (about 5 or 6 large leaves)

Heat chicken stock to boiling point in a large, heavy pot. Lower heat and simmer for 5 minutes. Chop garlic coarsely and add to simmering liquid with the thyme, sage, cloves, saffron, and oil. Simmer, covered, for 20 minutes, or until garlic is tender.

Strain soup, pressing garlic against the strainer with a wooden spoon and scraping the puree from the bottom of the strainer back into the liquid. Discard the herbs which remain. Return soup to pot and add the groats and pepper. Simmer for 20 minutes more, or until groats are tender. Stir in parsley, lemon juice, and sorrel and simmer for 1 minute more, or until sorrel changes color from bright green to yellowish green. Serve hot.

Chicken and Fine Kasha Loaf with Mushrooms, Red Peppers, and Herbs
Serves 6 to 8

A nice, light change from the same old meat loaf. This one can be served at room temperature, cold, or hot. Best when made the day before.

2 cups chopped cooked chicken (about 1 pound boned, skinned breasts)
2 cups cooked fine kasha
6 tablespoons butter
½ cup finely chopped scallions
½ cup finely chopped celery
½ cup finely chopped sweet red peppers
1 cup finely chopped mushrooms
2 tablespoons finely minced parsley
½ teaspoon dried thyme
1 teaspoon minced rosemary, or ½ teaspoon dried and crushed rosemary
⅛ teaspoon black pepper
pinch of cayenne pepper
⅓ cup whole wheat flour
1 cup hot milk

In a large bowl, mix chicken with kasha and set aside. Butter an 8½ × 4½ × 2½-inch loaf pan and preheat oven to 325°F. Melt 2 tablespoons of butter in a skillet and saute scallions, celery, and red peppers until wilted. Add the mushrooms and stir and cook for 2 minutes more. Stir mixture into the chicken and kasha along with the parsley, thyme, rosemary, pepper, and cayenne.

In a saucepan, melt 4 tablespoons of butter. Stir in the flour and cook over low heat, stirring constantly, until flour loses raw taste and begins to color slightly. Pour in hot milk and stir with a whisk until very thick. Mix with the chicken mixture and spoon into loaf pan. Smooth surface evenly and bake for 40 minutes, or until top begins to brown. (Cover lightly with foil if surface gets too brown.) Let rest for 5 minutes on a wire rack, loosen, and unmold. Bring to room temperature before slicing, or prepare a day in advance before removing from mold and slicing.

Main Dishes _____

Zrazi — *Kasha and Mushroom Filled Hamburgers with Yogurt-Dill Sauce*
Makes 12 patties

Filling:

2	tablespoons chicken fat
1	small onion, finely chopped
1	cup mushrooms, coarsely chopped
1½	cups cooked coarse kasha
⅛	teaspoon black pepper

Melt the chicken fat in a medium-size skillet and add the onion. Stir until wilted and then add the mushrooms. Cook, while stirring, for 2 minutes. Add the kasha and pepper and cook, while stirring, until blended. Set aside to cool.

Meat:

1½	pounds lean ground beef
1	small onion, grated
2	slices whole grain bread
1	tablespoon finely minced parsley
½	cup tomato juice
⅛	teaspoon black pepper

In a large bowl, mix the beef and onion together. Tear bread into pieces and soak in water for a few minutes in another bowl. Then squeeze out water and crumble into the meat. Add all remaining ingredients and mix well. Wet hands and form into 24 balls, each the size of a golf ball. Place on a sheet of waxed paper and flatten each ball into a ½-inch-thick patty. Using 2 tablespoons of filling for each, place filling in center of 12 patties. Top with the remaining 12, enclosing the filling by pressing the edges of meat together with the fingers.

Heat a nonstick-surface skillet over medium heat, add the *zrazi,* and cook for about 5 minutes on each side, turning carefully. (Do not overcook or meat will be dry.) Transfer to a heated platter and keep warm. While meat is cooking, prepare the sauce.

Yogurt-Dill Sauce:

2	cups plain yogurt
1	tablespoon grated onions
4	tablespoons shredded cucumbers (optional)
1	tablespoon finely minced dillweed
⅛	teaspoon paprika

In a small saucepan, mix all ingredients together, except paprika. Heat over low heat so sauce will not curdle. Spoon some sauce over each *zrazi* and sprinkle with paprika.

Kasha Varnishkas — *Whole Kasha Groats and Pasta*
Serves 6

2 tablespoons chicken fat
1 large onion, coarsely chopped
1 egg, lightly beaten
1 cup whole kasha groats
2 cups boiling water
1 tablespoon butter
¼ teaspoon black pepper
1½ cups cooked pasta (½ cup uncooked pasta: small shells or bows)

Heat chicken fat in a heavy black iron skillet. Saute onion until brown, stirring occasionally. Transfer to a SilverStone-lined pot and wipe out iron skillet.

In a bowl, mix beaten egg and kasha together. Heat dry skillet again and when hot, add kasha-egg mixture, stirring constantly, until grains are sealed and separated.

Heat pot with cooked onion, add kasha, stir until blended, and then add boiling water. Lower heat, cover pot, and cook over very low heat for 25 minutes. Then add butter, pepper, and pasta. Cook 5 minutes more and remove from heat. Let stand 5 minutes before turning out onto a warmed serving platter.

Note: Can be prepared ahead and rewarmed in oven for 15 minutes, covered.

Whole Buckwheat Groats with Lemon, Dill, and Red Pepper
Serves 6

4 cups cooked whole buck-wheat groats
3 tablespoons butter
1 clove garlic, finely minced
1 cup thinly sliced scallions (2 large scallions)
1 cup finely chopped celery with leaves (2 large stalks celery)
½ medium sweet red pepper, finely diced (about ⅔ cup)
¼ teaspoon black pepper
3 tablespoons minced dillweed
1 tablespoon finely minced parsley
1 teaspoon grated lemon rind
1 whole lemon

This pilaf, made with unroasted buckwheat, is meant to be served as a side dish or as a stuffing for the more delicate chicken, veal, or fish.

Place the cooked buckwheat in a large bowl and set aside. In a large skillet, melt butter and add the garlic, scallions, celery, and red pepper. Cook, while stirring, for 5 to 8 minutes, or until soft but not brown.

Empty contents of skillet into the bowl with the buck-wheat. Then add the pepper, dillweed, and parsley and mix. After the lemon rind is grated and added to the buckwheat, peel the skin and white heavy membrane from the lemon, remove any pits with the tip of a knife, cut the lemon sections into very small pieces, and toss with the pilaf. Use as stuffing, or cover with foil and heat in a 350°F. oven for 10 minutes.

Whole Kasha with Mixed Dried Fruit, Walnuts, and Herbs
Serves 6

This pilaf can be used for stuffing duck, goose, or pork. It may also be served mixed with cooked poultry or alone.

1 tablespoon chicken fat, or other poultry fat

1 cup finely chopped onions

1½ cups finely chopped celery with leaves

2 tablespoons finely minced sage

2 tablespoons thyme leaves

¼ teaspoon black pepper

1 teaspoon grated lemon rind

4 cups whole cooked kasha groats (cooked in chicken stock for extra flavor)

1 cup diced mixed dried fruit (steam fruit for 5 minutes to soften in vegetable steamer if being used for pilaf)

½ cup coarsely chopped walnuts

Heat chicken fat in a large skillet and cook onions, stirring occasionally, until wilted. Add the celery, sage, thyme, and pepper and cook, while stirring, for 5 minutes more. Stir in the lemon rind and then combine with the cooked kasha. Add the fruit and walnuts and toss again. Serve hot as an accompaniment or as a stuffing. Reheat any extra pilaf, wrapped in foil, for 15 minutes along with stuffed meat or poultry.

Blinis *with Melted Butter, Chives, and Sour Cream*
Makes about 36 6-inch *blinis*

In Russia, the *blini* binge usually starts a week before Lent. These delicate crepelike pancakes, not at all like our American buckwheat griddle cakes, herald the return of the spring sun. Traditionally served with black caviar, our version is less costly, and, we feel, equally elegant.

 1 package dry yeast (¼ ounce)
 4 tablespoons lukewarm
      water
 ½ teaspoon mild honey
1½ cups milk
 ½ cup dark buckwheat flour
 ½ cup unbleached white flour
 2 eggs, separated
 4 tablespoons butter, melted
 2 tablespoons sour cream
      clarified butter for greasing
      crepe pan

Garnish:

      melted butter
 2 tablespoons finely minced
      chives
      sour cream

In a medium-size bowl, sprinkle yeast over warm water. Add honey and stir to dissolve. Let stand for 10 minutes until frothy. Then stir in the milk, sift both flours over the bowl, and beat well with a wooden spoon. Cover with a tea towel and let stand for 1 hour in a warm place until doubled in bulk.

Beat the egg yolks only until yellow and add to the yeast mixture along with the melted butter and sour cream. Beat well again, cover once more, and let rise for another hour.

Then whip the egg whites with an eggbeater until soft peaks form. Beat down batter and fold in beaten egg whites.

Heat a 6-inch crepe pan with a nonstick surface and brush lightly with clarified butter. (Plain melted butter may burn.) Pour about 3 tablespoonfuls of batter at a time into pan. Remove pan from heat and rotate to cover bottom evenly with batter. Cook over medium heat until edges start to look dry. Remove from heat and cool for a few seconds for easier lifting. Lift with a round spatula, turn, and cook for about 30 seconds. Turn out onto a tea towel and keep warm until all the batter is used up. Serve with extra melted butter mixed with chives, and a bowl of sour cream to be passed at the table.

Creamy Buckwheat Grits, Prunes, and Orange Souffle

Serves 6

Squirrel away scooped orange halves in your freezer, and bake this souffle in orange cups, or in a conventional tall-sided ceramic dish.

8 pitted prunes, cut in small pieces; reserve a few pieces for garnish
2 large navel oranges
⅓ cup mild honey
2 eggs, separated
1 tablespoon grated orange rind
1 cup cooked creamy kernel buckwheat grits
3 tablespoons butter
4 tablespoons light buckwheat flour
¼ teaspoon ground cloves

Preheat oven to 350°F. and butter a 1½-quart souffle dish. Place prunes on the bottom and set dish aside. Cut oranges in half, and, working over a bowl to catch any juice, scoop out insides with a curved grapefruit knife and peel membranes away from orange sections. Discard any seeds and membrane and scrape any remaining pulp and juice with the tip of a teaspoon into the bowl. There should be about 1¼ cups of pulp and juice. Then add the honey. Beat the egg yolks only, and add to the orange pulp along with the orange rind and creamy grits. Beat well and set aside.

In a saucepan, melt the butter and stir in the buckwheat flour with a wire whisk. Add the orange-egg yolk mixture and whisk over low heat until thick. Remove from heat and stir in cloves. Let mixture cool slightly.

Beat egg whites until stiff. Then add 1 cup of mixture to the egg whites. Stir and then fold egg whites gently into the orange mixture. Pour at once into prepared souffle dish (or reserved orange halves) and bake for 30 to 45 minutes. Sprinkle with a few chopped prunes and serve at once.

Though it has become the staple grain of Eastern Europe, Asia Minor, and almost every Middle Eastern country, no one has ever taken the time to standardize the spelling of what should be a simple culinary word. *Bulgur.* Depending upon whose grandmother wrote the recipe, the country in which it originated, or the ingenuity of the cook, the name has come to us in an endless variety of spellings: *bulghur, bulghar, bulgor, boulgur, boulghour, borghul, burghul,* and *burghoul!*

By whatever name, however, it is basically whole wheat that has been cracked, parched, and processed by steaming. It is then dried, left whole, or cracked into various grinds. And, because it is only minimally processed, it retains nearly all the nutrients of whole wheat.

During the years of writing and researching this book, we kept finding a classic example of misinformation being repeated, since obviously each writer researches by using every other author's book! Put simply, as it was by a columnist for a major newspaper, "Bulgur is simply cracked wheat," and she went on to say that the two were interchangeable.

Well, bulgur is *not* simply cracked wheat, since it is already cooked (steamed) and needs only soaking to prepare it for any recipe. Cracked wheat, on the other hand, is *uncooked* and requires at least 15 minutes of simmering time before it can be used. At the very least, using cracked wheat where we call for bulgur might make an unchewable dish, at worst, it could result in a chipped tooth (were it not cooked first.)

Most of the bulgur used in this country comes from either Kansas or California. The Kansas variety is a darker grain, and it has a stronger flavor and less delicate color than the California bulgur. Also, it cannot be purchased in the various grinds. California bulgur, on the other hand, is the kind that is usually sold in natural foods stores or in the Middle Eastern markets that can be found in most of our major cities. It generally comes in four forms, it can be

Bulgur: A Grain by Any Other Name . . .

purchased in bulk, and our recipes were developed by using the California grain. If you can't find it in your area, use the Mail-Order Sources where we shop for our own whole grain needs.

The Forms of Bulgur

#1 Fine Grind: Usually used for making various *kibbi* recipes. It has the most delicate taste of all the grinds. It can also be used unsoaked and then baked or fried.

#2 Medium Grind: A good all-purpose coarse grind usually used for cold salads such as *tabbouleh* and for stuffings.

#3 Coarse Grind: Usually used alternately with the whole grain (according to preference) for pilafs and salads. This grind has a chewier texture than the others. It can also be toasted while dry and the liquid poured over it afterward.

Whole Grain Bulgur: Used mostly for soups and pilafs, since it retains its shape better than the ground bulgur. Even after soaking, whole bulgur is still rather toothy. Add about one hour extra soaking time if you use the whole grain, in order to cut down on your cooking time. It can also be dry toasted and hot liquid poured over it.

In the recipes that follow, we indicate which grind of bulgur should be used and whether to use it presoaked or dry.

Basic Bulgur #2 Medium Grind
Presoak Method
Yields 1½ cups

½ cup #2 medium bulgur
1½ cups boiling water

Pour boiling water over bulgur in a medium-size bowl. Cover bowl and let soak for a minimum of 1 hour. The grain will absorb most of the liquid. Line a strainer with a piece of cheesecloth and drain the bulgur. Take up the ends of the cheesecloth and squeeze out all remaining liquid.

It is now ready to use in various recipes that follow, unless otherwise directed. It can also be heated with milk and fruit and a sweetener added for breakfast.

Note: Between 1 and 2 cups of presoaked and drained bulgur are usually used in recipes for 6 people. The amounts vary, depending on additional ingredients.

The presoak method can also be used with any of the other grinds.

The Glorious Oriental Pastry and Grocery Company

On Atlantic Avenue in Brooklyn, not far from the Brooklyn Bridge, there is an enclave of Arabic delights—tiny restaurants, bakeries redolent with the smell of newly made pita breads, and specialty grocery and pastry shops. Baklava, Syrian and Turkish sweets, spinach and cheese pies fill the small shops. The restaurants offer a world of Middle Eastern specialties—Lebanese, Syrian, Moroccan, and even an occasional French establishment influenced by the cooking of Algeria.

For the past 20 years, we have been buying our dried fruits, nuts, spices, and freshly milled grains at a shop run by the Moustapha family:

The Oriental Pastry and Grocery Company. It is one of the few places in New York, for example, where we can be certain to get the correct grinds of bulgur, all neatly displayed in sacks and sold in bulk.

Over the years, of course, we've gotten to know the brothers in the family, and no visit is complete without a taste test of dried apricots, a small piece of *baklava* freshly baked in the ovens in the rear, a few olives of different varieties, and a crumble of *halvah* to whet the palate before dinner. Everything in the shop is also sold by mail order, and we've included their address with the Mail-Order Sources.

Bulgur, Cashew, and Alfalfa Sprout Pate

Serves 6 to 8

2	tablespoons grated onions
½	cup toasted and finely chopped cashews
1	cup presoaked #1 fine bulgur
1	cup alfalfa sprouts
2	cups creamed cottage cheese
4	tablespoons finely minced parsley
2	tablespoons lemon juice
1	tablespoon tamari soy sauce
½	clove garlic, finely minced
¼	teaspoon whole celery seeds
½	teaspoon paprika
⅛	teaspoon cayenne pepper

Garnish:

1	cup alfalfa sprouts
6	slivers sweet red pepper

Combine onions, cashews, bulgur, alfalfa sprouts, and cottage cheese in a bowl and mix well with a wooden spoon. Add half the parsley, reserving the rest for part of the garnish.

In a small cup, mix the remaining ingredients together and add to the large bowl. Stir again and pack in an 8½ × 4½ × 2½-inch loaf pan. Cover and chill for at least 1 hour. Unmold and decorate edge of platter with alfalfa sprouts. Sprinkle with remaining parsley and make X's with slivers of red pepper on top. Slice and serve with crisp bread or crackers.

Bulgur, Spinach, Egg, and Water Chestnut Dip

Serves 6 to 8

10	cups fresh spinach leaves, stems removed (about 10 ounces)
3 or 4	scallions
1	cup presoaked #2 medium bulgur
2	hard-cooked eggs
1	8-ounce can drained water chestnuts
1½	cups sour cream
1	tablespoon Barth's instant chicken broth
¼	teaspoon black pepper several radishes, thinly sliced, for garnish

Chop the spinach in a food processor in several batches. Then process the scallions. Transfer to a large mixing bowl and toss with the bulgur. Process the hard-cooked eggs until finely chopped and then the water chestnuts, and add to the bowl. Mix the sour cream, instant chicken broth and pepper together and toss with the spinach mixture. Mound smoothly in a bowl and press the radish slices around the edge of the mound. Serve with whole grain crackers or pieces of whole wheat pita bread.

Bulgur and Lamb
Covered Indian Eggs
with Cucumber-Yogurt Sauce
Makes 6 Indian eggs

An unusual first course, or double the recipe and serve as a main course.

½ pound lean ground lamb
1 small onion, grated
1 clove garlic, finely minced
½ cup presoaked #1 fine
      bulgur
2 tablespoons finely minced
      parsley
1 teaspoon finely minced leaf
      coriander
3 drops hot pepper sauce
1 teaspoon lemon juice
¼ teaspoon each: ground
      cumin, ginger, turmeric,
      and ground coriander
1 small egg, lightly beaten
3 hard-cooked eggs
1 teaspoon butter

Mix all ingredients together except the hard-cooked eggs and butter.

Preheat the oven to 400°F. Butter an oven-to-table baking pan with half the butter. Divide the meat mixture into 3 parts, wet hands in cold water, and form the meat over each egg to enclose completely. Place in pan and dot with remaining butter. Bake for 20 to 25 minutes, cool slightly, and slice in half. Serve at room temperature and spoon some of the following sauce over each egg.

Cucumber-Yogurt Sauce:
Yields ¾ cup

½ cup plain yogurt
2 tablespoons finely minced
      green scallion tops
2 tablespoons shredded
      cucumber
    pinch of white pepper

Blend all ingredients and allow flavors to develop for at least 1 hour.

Bulgur and Lentil Soup with Mustard Greens
Serves 6

1   cup green lentils
½   cup dry whole grain bulgur
10   cups water
1   tablespoon Barth's instant beef broth or beef stock
1   whole clove garlic
¼   teaspoon cayenne pepper
5   parsley stems, finely minced
3   tablespoons Oriental sesame oil
1½   cups finely minced onions (2 large onions)
1   cup grated carrots
2   cups shredded mustard greens (or spinach or sorrel)
2   tablespoons apple cider vinegar
2   tablespoons tamari soy sauce

Pick over and wash lentils and bulgur. Drain and add to a large, heavy pot with the water. Bring to boil and add instant beef broth or beef stock, garlic, cayenne, and parsley stems. Lower heat. Cover pot but leave ajar. Cook for 1 hour and 15 minutes. Remove garlic clove and discard. Meanwhile heat oil in a skillet and saute the onions over low heat for 10 minutes, stirring occasionally, until they begin to brown. Add to soup with carrots and greens. Cook for 5 minutes more. Add vinegar and tamari before serving.

Kibbi

The spirit of hospitality . . . a Middle Eastern tradition.

The rule is that "no guest may leave hungry"—and "the food equals the affection." The host or hostess shows regard for a guest by the quantity and variety of food that is served. The guest, in turn, shows regard by the amount of food that is eaten. There are numerous dishes served, but no meal ever excludes some form of lamb and bulgur mixture.

Once you master the basic raw lamb and bulgur mixture, the other variations are a snap.

It is called *koubbeh, kibbey, kibbeh, kibbi, kufte, kofte, or kuftee,* depending on what part of the Middle East it comes from. This dish with bulgur and ground lamb is prepared in even more ways than it is spelled. However, no matter how you spell it, or prepare it, we think it's delicious.

The basic recipe follows, along with several variations. This raw mixture by itself is treated in several forms. It is also served uncooked, similar to steak tartare. The basic recipe can also be cooked as well in several ways that follow.

Basic Raw Lamb and Bulgur

Serves 6

3½ to 4   pounds boned leg of lamb, trimmed of all fat and cut into chunks
1   large onion
1½   cups presoaked #1 fine bulgur
½   teaspoon paprika
¼   teaspoon cayenne pepper
¼   teaspoon black pepper
1   tablespoon lemon juice
3 to 4   tablespoons ice water

Grind lamb very fine in a food processor. There will be about 1½ pounds of ground lamb. Transfer to a bowl; remove ½ pound of ground lamb and set aside for another dish. Place onion in the food processor and chop very fine. Remove and add to the bowl. Mix the bulgur into the meat and onion mixture and then the paprika, cayenne, pepper, and lemon juice. Divide mixture in half and return half to the food processor, adding 1½ tablespoons of ice water until a smooth, pasty mixture is formed. Process the remaining mixture in the same manner and then mix both halves together. This mixture is served in the following ways:

- Spread in a mound and flatten the top with a wide spatula dipped in cold water to smooth the surface, until a 1½-inch flat, round cake is formed. Score a cross on top, sprinkle with finely minced parsley, and dribble 2 tablespoons of melted butter over the top. To eat, scoop up with pieces of pita bread.
- Wet hands and scoop up about 1 tablespoon of the mixture at a time and roll into finger shapes. Dip in a mixture of finely minced parsley and scallions and roll a small leaf of romaine lettuce to enclose it.
- Wet hands and form a patty, 2 inches in diameter. Press thumb into center and pour melted butter into the well that is formed.
- Pinch off olive-size pieces of this raw mixture, poach them in chicken broth, and serve as miniature meat dumplings with soup.
- Wet hands and form mixture into sausage shapes (about 3 to 4 inches long and 1½ inches thick) around an oiled metal skewer. Brush with melted butter and broil, turning frequently, until brown. When serving, slip off skewer with a piece of pita bread as a holder.

Main Dishes _____

Deep Fried or Poached Stuffed Lamb and Bulgur Patties
Serves 6

Filling:

3 tablespoons butter
¼ cup pine nuts
2 large onions, finely minced
¼ green pepper, finely minced
¼ sweet red pepper, finely minced
½ pound lean ground lamb (reserved from recipe of Basic Raw Lamb and Bulgur)
¼ cup finely minced parsley
¼ teaspoon Syrian Mixed Spices (see Index)
2 teaspoons dried currants

Heat butter in a skillet and toast pine nuts until they are tan, then remove and set aside. Add the onions and green and red peppers to the same skillet and cook slowly until vegetables are soft. Add the meat and stir until it loses its color. Stir in the parsley, Syrian Mixed Spices, currants, and toasted pine nuts. Let cool slightly before using.

Outer Cover:

1 recipe Basic Raw Lamb and Bulgur (see recipe in this section)

Have a bowl of ice water handy to dip hands into frequently. Dip hands in water and scoop up an amount of the mixture about the size of a small egg. Form into a hollow using the thumb and forefinger of the right hand, rotating the bulgur and lamb mixture in the palm of the left hand. Press sides to form an even cavity, making the walls about ½ inch thick. Place about 1 tablespoon of the filling in each hole and with wet hands bring top edges around and seal to enclose filling. Taper both ends slightly like a football and place on a waxed-paper-lined plate. Chill for 30 minutes, uncovered, before cooking.

To Fry: Heat enough peanut or corn oil at 375°F. on a fat thermometer and fry, a few at a time, until golden. Drain on paper towels and serve with wedges of lemon.

To Poach: Prepare a broth of lamb bones and water (or use homemade beef stock or instant beef stock) mixed with an 8-ounce can of tomato sauce. Place stuffed patties in liquid and simmer, turning carefully, for 15 to 20 minutes.

Irish Steel-Cut Oat Brown Bread   For this recipe, see page 121

Pasta with Broccoli, Tomatoes, Cheese, and Green Peppercorns   For this recipe, see page 248

Falafel — *Chick-Pea and Bulgur Patties with Yogurt-Tahini Sauce*
Makes 18 patties

Falafel is served from street carts all through the Middle East. It reminds us of a healthier version of a hamburger when served in a whole wheat pita bread.

1 cup cooked chick-peas
2 teaspoons finely minced garlic
1 cup whole wheat bread, soaked in water and squeezed dry
⅓ cup dry #1 fine bulgur
2 tablespoons lemon juice
1 egg, lightly beaten
1 tablespoon finely minced leaf coriander
2 tablespoons finely minced parsley
1 teaspoon cumin
½ teaspoon paprika
⅛ teaspoon cayenne pepper
⅛ teaspoon black pepper
1 teaspoon baking powder
peanut or corn oil for frying

Chop chick-peas in a food processor until fine. Add all remaining ingredients and mix until well blended. Then wet hands and form mixture into walnut-size balls. Flatten slightly and place on a plate lined with waxed paper, uncovered. Chill for at least 1 hour. Then fry in very hot oil in a large skillet, in 1 layer. Turn to brown both sides. Drain on paper towels and serve hot or at room temperature with Yogurt-Tahini Sauce.

Yogurt-Tahini Sauce:
Yields ¾ cup

1 small clove garlic
¼ cup tahini (sesame seed paste)
¼ cup plain yogurt
1 tablespoon lemon juice
3 tablespoons cold water
1 teaspoon tamari soy sauce
¼ teaspoon ground cumin

Chop garlic very fine in a food processor. Then add all remaining ingredients and blend. Chill for at least 1 hour to blend flavors.

Note: This sauce can also be used for salads and is especially good with fresh spinach.

Filled Baked Lamb and Bulgur

Serves 6 to 8

Don't pass this recipe by just because you are in the market for something less substantial than a main course. As you will see in the directions, this recipe also works well as an hors d'oeuvre.

1 recipe Basic Raw Lamb and Bulgur (see recipe in this section)
1 recipe Filling for Deep Fried or Poached Stuffed Lamb and Bulgur Patties (see recipe in this section)
¼ pound clarified butter

Preheat oven to 350°F. and brush a 9 × 13 × 2-inch pan with some melted butter. Divide half the raw lamb and bulgur mixture and, with wet hands, spread and smooth the surface evenly for a bottom layer. Spoon the filling over this layer evenly. For the top layer, wet hands and scoop up about 2 tablespoons of the mixture at a time. Flatten with hands until about ½ inch thick and place over filling, overlapping each flat piece slightly. Wet finger tips and smooth surface evenly.

Score surface into diamond shapes any size you wish, pour clarified butter on top and bake 20 to 25 minutes, basting with the liquid that accumulates. (If there is too much liquid, drain with baster for last 5 minutes.) Slip under broiler for 2 to 3 minutes to brown top. Cut into previously scored diamond shapes to serve either as hors d'oeuvres, if small, or a main course, if cut into larger portions.

Note: This recipe can also be prepared in a different form—similar to a pie without the top crust. Butter a 10-inch oval or round oven-to-table baking dish and press 1 recipe raw lamb and bulgur on bottom, pushing up a 1½-inch rim all around the sides of the baking dish. Spoon the filling in the center and spread evenly. Bake for 25 to 30 minutes and serve cut into wedges like a pie.

Rolled Chicken Breasts Stuffed with Bulgur, Fruit, and Nuts

Makes 6 rolled chicken breasts

Bulgur Stuffing:

2 tablespoons butter

2 stalks celery with leaves, finely chopped

2 large scallions, finely chopped

2 cups presoaked #2 medium bulgur

1 cup Chicken Stock (see Index)

12 pitted dates, quartered

2 tablespoons currants

2 tablespoons toasted pine nuts

1 teaspoon Syrian Mixed Spices (see Index)

Melt butter in a large skillet and saute celery and scallions over medium heat until soft. Add the bulgur and stir for a few minutes, and then add all the remaining ingredients. Mix and transfer to an oven-to-table baking dish. Remove 6 generous tablespoons of the stuffing and reserve. Place the remaining stuffing in a low oven to keep warm while preparing the chicken rolls.

Chicken:

6 large chicken breasts, skinned and boned

¼ teaspoon black pepper

2 tablespoons butter

2 tablespoons corn oil

2 tablespoons grated orange rind

juice of 2 oranges

1 tablespoon grated lemon rind

juice of 1 lemon

2 tablespoons mild honey

6 coriander leaves for garnish

Place the chicken breasts between 2 pieces of waxed paper and gently pound with side of a cleaver to ¼-inch thickness. Sprinkle with pepper and place 1 tablespoon of bulgur stuffing on each chicken cutlet. Roll up to enclose the stuffing and skewer with a toothpick. Heat the butter and oil over medium heat and saute the chicken, turning carefully to brown on all sides. Remove from skillet with a slotted spoon and arrange over stuffing in oven to keep warm. In the same skillet, add the orange rind and juice, lemon rind and juice, and honey. Bring to a boil, lower heat, and simmer for a few minutes. Spoon sauce over chicken rolls and some over bulgur stuffing. Garnish with 1 coriander leaf on each chicken roll.

Bulgur, Chick-Pea, and Tomato Salad with Yogurt-Mint Dressing
Serves 6

A light dish for hot weather when appetites drag.

1½ cups presoaked #2 medium bulgur
1 cup cooked chick-peas
½ cup finely chopped scallions
2 medium-size tomatoes, diced
½ cup finely minced parsley
¼ teaspoon black pepper
   romaine lettuce leaves

Mix all ingredients together in a bowl except the lettuce. Add the Yogurt-Mint Dressing and mix lightly with 2 forks. Serve on lettuce leaves.

Yogurt-Mint Dressing:
Yields 1⅓ cups

1 scallion, minced
1 cup yogurt
¼ cup olive oil or safflower oil
1 tablespoon finely minced mint, or ½ tablespoon dried mint
2 tablespoons lemon juice
¼ tablespoon black pepper

Blend all ingredients in a blender. Chill for 1 hour to meld flavors.

Bulgur, Lentil, and Mushroom Pilaf with Yogurt and Chives
Serves 6

¾ cup green lentils (picked over and washed)
2 cups Vegetable Stock (see Index)
3 tablespoons olive oil
1 medium-size onion, finely chopped
½ pound fresh mushrooms, sliced (about 1½ cups)
¾ cup dry whole or #3 coarse bulgur
¼ teaspoon black pepper
1 cup plain yogurt
2 tablespoons finely minced chives

Combine lentils and vegetable stock in a medium-size saucepan and cook over low heat for about 20 minutes, or until tender but still slightly firm. Remove from heat and set aside. Preheat oven to 350°F. and butter a 1½-quart casserole. Heat oil in a large skillet and saute onion, mushrooms, and bulgur. Add pepper, stir, and cook for about 5 minutes. Add the lentils and liquid and pour into prepared casserole. Cover and bake for 25 to 30 minutes. Mix the yogurt with chives and spoon on top of hot pilaf—or serve cold, blending the yogurt and chives into pilaf.

Butter Pecan, Carrot, and Bulgur Pilaf
Serves 6

3 tablespoons butter
½ cup broken pecans
1 medium-size carrot, shredded
2 cups presoaked whole or #3 coarse bulgur
½ cup Chicken Stock (see Index)
¼ teaspoon black pepper
1 teaspoon tamari soy sauce
1 tablespoon finely minced tarragon, or 1 teaspoon dried tarragon

This pilaf goes well with poultry or pork.

Melt butter in a medium-size skillet and add pecans. Toss and toast for 2 to 3 minutes. Remove with a slotted spoon and reserve. In same skillet, add carrot and toss for 1 minute. Then add bulgur, chicken stock, pepper, and tamari. Cook, stirring, for 5 minutes until heated through. Add tarragon and sprinkle with buttered pecans.

Tabbouleh — *Bulgur, Parsley, and Mint Salad*

Serves 6

2 cups presoaked #2 medium bulgur

3 cups finely minced parsley (about 2 large bunches)

¼ cup finely chopped mint, or 4 teaspoons dried mint

3 scallions, finely minced

¼ teaspoon black pepper

¼ teaspoon ground cumin

2 tomatoes, cut into ½-inch cubes

3 tablespoons lemon juice

3 tablespoons oil (2 tablespoons safflower oil and 1 tablespoon olive oil)

Garnish:

romaine lettuce leaves

thinly sliced cucumber

In a large bowl, gently mix together all the ingredients, except lemon juice and oil, with a wooden spoon. Add the lemon juice, toss, and chill for 1 hour to blend the flavors. Before serving, toss again with oil. Serve in a mound with romaine lettuce leaves arranged like the spokes of a wheel. Scatter cucumber slices over lettuce.

Europeans look with suspicion upon corn as a staple. To them, it is essentially a food for animals (with a few exceptions like *mamaliga* and *polenta*). Perhaps that is because corn seems peculiarly American. In fact, while wheat was being domesticated in the Middle East and oats were being cultivated in Northern Europe and rice in Asia, Indian corn (maize) was being grown and eaten in the Western Hemisphere, and had been an important crop for close to 5,000 years among developing Andean civilizations. The American Indians—the Shawnees and the Navajos, the Mohawks and the Cherokees—worshipped corn. To this day, the Pueblo Indians in New Mexico perform the Summer Corn Dance every August, for if they were to miss even a single year, they say, the earth would not grow crops, the rain would not fall from the sky, children would not be born, and the stars would not turn. The tribe, indeed the universe, would disintegrate.

For the Mexicans, for the Indian tribes of the Plains, the Woodlands, and the Great Lakes, for the colonists who first landed in New England, corn was a critical crop for survival, and it turned up everywhere in a hundred different forms. The pioneers who opened the West survived on "hawg and hominy"—salt pork and corn. Cornmeals and flours were the basis for the dishes that now rank as classics in American cuisine: hasty pudding, Indian pudding, Johnnycakes, anadama bread, hoe cakes, corn chowder, and that good old Southern standby, grits. The myths, the legends, and the recipes that originate with corn, could fill a book of their own. What follows is a mouth-watering sampling of the versatility of this remarkable, native American grain.

An Amazing Maze of Maize

The Forms of Corn

Whole Corn—Dried: White, yellow, or blue. Used for home grinding into meal, for parching, or for preparing whole hominy. It can be soaked and cooked whole and used for various dishes when fresh corn is not available. "Blue corn" is a Southwestern Indian corn, usually obtainable only in that area of the country.

Cornmeal—Yellow or White: Labeled either "stone ground" or "water ground" (though the latter term actually refers only to the power source). Cornmeal is of medium-fine consistency and the corn germ is retained. The various brands differ considerably in performance and in the quality of the final product. We tested several brands (including Indian Head, Erewhon, and Quaker) and found the most consistently good results with Indian Head, a readily available brand. A good, whole ground cornmeal (unlike some) does not require the addition of other flours to prevent crumbling. Cornmeal is used in breads, griddle cakes, various loaves such as scrapple or *tamale* pies, and in soups. The yellow cornmeal contains more carotene than the white.

Corn Germ: The central core of the kernel, the part where the new plant sprouts or germinates. Ten pounds of corn will provide one pound of germ, and it's used in the same way wheat germ is used. It can serve as an extender for meat, be sprinkled on cereal or yogurt, and be used in baked goods and salads. So far as we know, only Fearn's distributes the product. It has a popcornlike taste and lots of nourishment. It's highly perishable, so it must be refrigerated after opening.

Whole Hominy: Known by various names: *mote, pozole, samp* and *nixtamal.* It is available in yellow and white, but more commonly in the latter. It is also sold dried or canned (processed and packed in water). It is whole corn that is processed by using one or more procedures, with slaked (hydrated) lime or a combination of unslaked lime, calcium carbonate, lye, or wood ash. (Tom Ney at the Rodale Test Kitchens recommends the unslaked lime process as pref-

erable to the others.) The lime combined with water acts to loosen the hulls and partially cook and puff up the kernels. The corn is then washed to remove the hulls, dried, and used for dishes such as soups and stews, or toasted as a snack (called corn nuts). When it's dried and ground, it becomes the only cornmeal that can be used to make *tortillas.*

Hominy Grits: Made from undegerminated, coarsely ground (preferably stone-ground) white corn. They're used to prepare souffles and breads, or eaten plain in many parts of the country, as part of any meal, just like potatoes.

Masa Harina: Finely ground flour made from whole hominy. It's used for *tortillas* and many other Mexican and South American-influenced recipes. For those of us who don't have the time or inclination to prepare our own *masa harina* from *nixtamal,* Quaker distributes the product.

Corn Flour—Yellow or White: Corn ground to a finer consistency than cornmeal and without the grainy texture of the meal. It can be used for breading foods as well as in waffles, pancakes, wheat-free pastas and breads, and for mixing with other flours.

Puffed Corn: Round, airy, and light puffs of corn and, so far as we know, manufactured only by El Molino. They can be used as a breakfast cereal with fruit and milk, or they can be made into sweet candy snacks.

Cornstarch: A finely milled powder that is made from a high-starch variety of corn called indentata. It's usually used as a thickening agent for sauces, soups, or puddings, and it also has a history as a folk medicine, applied on the skin during those hot summer days to ward off prickly heat.

Popcorn: A type of whole, dried corn, pearl-yellow, and similar to flint corn, very much like the crop that was found in America in 1607.

A Casual Glossary of Corn Breads

Like Ruth, we sometimes stand amidst (among) the alien corn. Traditionally, the South is known to use white cornmeal, while the North uses yellow. However, the dividing line is crossed when we discover that the old-time Rhode Island specialty, Johnnycake, uses *white* for the traditional recipe. When we look still further, we find that both the North *and* the South have many similar recipes, all called by different names, and many corn breads are exactly alike, but carry several dissimilar aliases.

Actually, *all* corn breads are variations and combinations of the following ingredients, no matter what their names:

- *Liquid:* Some use sweet milk, some boiling water, others use buttermilk.
- *Shortening:* Fat, butter, bacon fat, lard, or oil.
- *Flavoring:* Sometimes a bit of sweetening, but usually something salty.
- *Leavening:* Sometimes baking powder, or baking soda, or even yeast on occasion, plus the addition of eggs.
- *Cornmeal:* Yellow or white cornmeal. (Although, in the South they would never use that "Northern yellow stuff!" nor any sweetening.)

In an attempt to clarify the debate, we've come up with a general and very casual dictionary of corn breads. If, in your own particular section of the country, you have still other names for these breads, contact us at Rodale Press.

Batter Bread or Skillet Corn Bread: Usually contains baking powder and is somewhat firmer in texture than spoon bread. It is baked in a cast-iron skillet.

Corn Dodgers: Similar to the Johnnycake batter, but a bit thicker, they shout, "Dodge!" if they come in your direction. The thick batter is shaped into tiny, pinched-off cakes, and then dropped into a heavy, heated cast-iron skillet with bacon fat glazing them while they cook. They're served very crisp and hot. If we take corn dodgers, add an onion, and fry them in the same pan where we've just cooked our fish, voila! We have hush puppies.

Corn Sticks: Corn bread baked in the shape of ears of corn, using a special, molded pan.

Hush Puppies: The hush puppy got its name, of course, from being a dog pacifier in the South. Pieces of corn-bread batter, legend tells us, were pinched off to fry quickly, and thrown to the howling dogs to keep them quiet while the evening corn bread was baking. Obviously, someone tasted one before throwing it out to the dogs and decided that an error in judgment had been made. Why waste it on the dogs! It's been a Southern specialty for *people* ever since!

Johnnycake, Journey Cake, Jonnycake, or Shawnee Cake: Supposedly originated with the Shawnee Indians to be used on long journeys because of its good keeping quality. The Rhode Islanders, on the other hand, claim it as their own. In a sense, these cakes are the forerunners of our modern pancakes, since they are baked on a griddle. They're small and crisp, and they contain no eggs.

Pones: Smaller versions of the same bread, but just slightly softer. The mark of the pone is the indentation made by the fingers of the cook who shapes them, sort of a personal imprint. Our dear friend Kaye, in Memphis, refers to the excess weight on her thighs as "my pones."

Shingle Bread, Hoe Cake, or Ash Cake: A stiffer form of batter bread that has a rich history in America. In parts of the South, it was baked in the field on a scoured and greased hoe blade, hence the "hoe cake." In other parts of the country, it was baked on a new house shingle, in front of an open fire, hence the name "shingle bread." When this same batter was baked in the ashes of the fire in a heavy skillet, it became "ash cake."

Spoon Bread: More like a pudding or souffle than a bread. However, it is aptly named, since it is eaten with a spoon. It contains several eggs to give it a custardy texture, and you can add two cups of cheddar cheese to make it a "cheese spoon bread."

Basic No-Lumps Cornmeal

Serves 6

1 cup stone-ground cornmeal
(white or yellow)
1 cup cold water
3 cups boiling water

Combine cornmeal and cold water in a measuring cup or small bowl. Gradually pour mixture into boiling water in a nonstick-surface saucepan, stirring constantly with a whisk. Return water to boiling, stirring constantly. Then lower heat, cover pot, and continue to cook for 5 to 10 minutes over very low heat, stirring frequently.

Note: There are some people who prefer pouring boiling water over dry cornmeal, stirring with a whisk, then pouring mixture into the saucepan and cooking for the required time. Both methods work if you stir constantly until smooth. Whole dried corn can be freshly ground into cornmeal in a blender. One cup corn kernels will make 1⅛ cups cornmeal.

Confetti Corn Germ Balls

Makes 18 balls

¾ pound lean ground beef
¾ cup corn germ
1 egg, beaten
2 tablespoons finely minced
sweet red pepper
2 tablespoons finely minced
scallions (green part)
⅛ teaspoon black pepper
¼ teaspoon ground cumin
2 tablespoons melted
chicken fat

Mix all ingredients together, reserving ½ cup of the corn germ. Let stand for 5 minutes and then shape into walnut-size balls. Roll each one in the reserved corn germ. Chill for 10 minutes on waxed paper in the refrigerator.

In a heavy iron skillet, heat chicken fat until very hot. Cook balls until browned, turning frequently (about 4 to 5 minutes). The centers should be slightly pink.

Masa Harina *and* Shrimp Fritters
Makes 24 fritters

6 large shrimp (about ½ pound), peeled and deveined

2 scallions, finely minced

1 tablespoon finely minced cilantro or parsley

3 drops hot pepper sauce

¼ teaspoon cumin

¾ cup *masa harina*

1 teaspoon baking powder

1 egg, separated, plus 1 extra egg white

¼ cup milk

corn or peanut oil for frying

Chop shrimp very fine (a food processor does it quickly), add the scallions, cilantro or parsley, hot pepper sauce, and cumin, mix, and set aside.

Mix the *masa harina* and baking powder together and set aside.

Mix the egg yolk with the milk and add it to the shrimp mixture. Then stir the milk-egg-shrimp mixture into the *masa harina.*

Beat the 2 egg whites until stiff and fold in. Heat oil in a heavy skillet and drop batter by the teaspoonful into hot oil. Brown on one side for 2 to 3 minutes and then turn with tongs to brown the other side. Drain on paper towels and serve at once.

A Glossary of *Tortilla* Terms

Chimichanga: A Mexican version of a Jewish *blintza*—a cheese-filled and wrapped *trigo* or wheat flour *tortilla*—topped with sour cream.

Enchiladas: Stuffed and rolled *tortillas* baked in a sauce. The fillings vary—meat, cheese, or a combination of both. The sauce is either red, made with tomatoes and hot chilis, or is a smooth green chili-based puree. (The hotness can be varied with the variety of chili pepper used.) *Enchiladas* are often baked in layers like Italian lasagna, and then cooled with sour cream.

Nachos: Stacks of *tortillas,* cut into wedge-shaped pieces, sprinkled with hot chili peppers and cheddar and Jack cheeses and slipped under a broiler or baked in the oven until the cheeses melt. This peppery mouthful is usually eaten as an hors d'oeuvre.

Taco: A crisply fried and folded *tortilla.* It is usually filled with ground meat and a spicy sauce, and then covered with shredded lettuce, avocado, and cheese—a Mexican version of a cheeseburger.

Tortilla: A Mexican version of a pita bread without the pocket. It is a flat, round bread prepared from ground, lime-soaked corn and water, or *masa. Tortillas* are also made with wheat flour, called *trigo.* The flavor and aroma are tantalizing with the smell and taste of smokey corn.

Tostada: *Chalupa* or little boat. It is fried flat and then topped with an assortment of goodies—an open-faced taco or Mexican version of the *Smorrebrod,* Scandinavian open-face sandwiches served at smorgasbord tables.

Tostaditas: Tiny versions of the *tortilla* cut out with a 2-inch cookie cutter and fried. They are similar to the *totopos* and Doritos, which are *tortillas* cut into wedges from a larger *tortilla,* fried, and used as scoops.

Tortillas

Makes 12 tortillas

2 cups *masa harina*
1¼ cups warm water

Place *masa harina* in a mixing bowl and gradually add the warm water, blending with a wooden spoon. Use hands to knead dough until smooth (about 3 to 4 minutes). Divide dough into 12 walnut-size balls, place in a bowl, and cover with a towel or aluminum foil. Let stand for about 5 minutes. When making each *tortilla,* keep remainder of dough covered so that it doesn't dry out.

Heat a heavy iron skillet, griddle, or *comal* (a Mexican version) over medium-high heat. Flatten each ball by patting it 2 or 3 times between the palms of your hands and place the dough on a *tortilla* press with a piece of plastic or a small plastic food storage bag (6¾ × 8¼-inch) placed on the bottom plate. Cover dough with a second plastic bag. Close the lid and press just hard enough to flatten the dough. (Dough should be placed closer to the top of the press to make a perfect circle when pressure is applied.) Open press and peel top plastic off slowly, being careful not to break the thin circle. Then, lift the entire bottom piece of plastic along with the *tortilla* off the press and turn it upside down on the first piece of plastic. Then peel the second piece off slowly. Lift *tortilla* with plastic and turn it off the plastic gently and onto the ungreased hot skillet. Cook for about 30 seconds. The edges should look dry and the underside will be speckled with brown. Turn with a spatula and bake for 1 minute, then turn back to first side and bake another 30 seconds. The *tortilla* will puff up. Wrap in foil, or a towel or napkin to keep warm and soft. After you make each *tortilla,* add it to the pile in the towel and cover.

Note: The plastic should peel off easily once you get the knack. If it seems too dry, add more water to the dough. If the plastic sticks, add more *masa harina.*

You can freeze *tortillas* for several weeks. When you're ready to use them, just reheat them in a slow oven.

To use leftover or stale *tortillas,* make *tostadas, tostaditas,* or *nachos* (see Glossary of *Tortilla* Terms).

Tortillas, of course, can be made in advance, then reheated by using any of the methods we've listed below.

Steaming: Stack *tortillas* on a rack over boiling water. Cover tightly and steam for a few minutes. Wrap in a towel or large napkin to keep warm. A Chinese wok with a perforated rack or Chinese bamboo steamer is excellent.

Oven Method: Using a plant mister, spray water over *tortillas.* Wrap in aluminum foil and warm in a 250°F. oven for a few minutes until hot and soft.

Sauteing: Heat oil or butter in a skillet and fry *tortillas* on both sides. Fold in half, as you turn with tongs, to make a semicrisp *taco,* or leave flat and whole as a *tostada* should be.

Frying: Heat oil in a deep fat fryer to 400°F. Hold *tortilla* with tongs and fry one at a time for *tostadas* or fry each, gently folded in half, for *tacos.*

Grilling: Sprinkle *tortillas* with water using a plant mister and heat both sides on an ungreased heavy iron griddle for a few seconds.

Leftover *Tortillas*

Cut *tortillas* in eighths, in wedge-shaped pieces, and fry crisply in oil. Then try these snacks:

- Spread with leftover mashed beans, a tiny piece of hot pepper, and a sprinkling of Jack cheese. Toast in oven until cheese melts.
- Use with an avocado dip made with mashed avocado, lime juice, grated onion, minced hot pepper, and chopped tomato.
- Top with grated cheddar cheese and chili powder. Bake in oven until cheese melts.
- Shake pieces in a bag with chili powder and make a homemade and inexpensive version of the commercially made Doritos.

Basic Stone-Ground Hominy Grits

Yields 3 cups

4 cups cold water
1 cup stone-ground hominy grits

Use a nonstick pot with a cover. Bring water to a boil and very slowly add grits, stirring constantly with a wooden spoon. When mixture starts to boil again, lower heat to simmer, cover pot, and cook, stirring occasionally, for 25 to 30 minutes. Let stand for 5 minutes.

Cornmeal, Pork Sausage, and Sage Loaf
Serves 6

This loaf is excellent as a breakfast, luncheon, or supper dish accompanied by scrambled eggs.

6 cups water
1 medium-size onion, peeled and cut in half
1 carrot, cut into 3 pieces
1 clove garlic, peeled
1 stalk celery with leaves, cut in half
5 whole peppercorns
3 sprigs parsley
1 thin slice ginger root
1 pound Italian-style sausage (about 6 sausages)
1 tablespoon finely minced sage, or 1 teaspoon dried sage
2 tablespoons grated onions
1 tablespoons tamari soy sauce
¾ cup yellow cornmeal
½ cup cold water

Combine the 6 cups of water, the onion, carrot, garlic, celery, peppercorns, parsley, and ginger root in a large, heavy pot and bring to a boil. Lower heat and simmer for 25 minutes. Add the sausage and continue to simmer for 30 minutes. Remove sausage and cool. When cool, peel off the casing, cut sausage into small pieces, and put in a bowl. Strain the stock and discard the vegetables. (There should be 3 cups of liquid.)

Add the sage, grated onions, and tamari to the chopped sausage. Bring stock to a boil in a nonstick pot. Mix the cornmeal with the cold water and stir into the boiling stock with a wire whisk. Stir and cook over medium heat for 10 minutes, or until quite thick. Add the reserved sausage mixture and stir.

Rinse an 8½ × 4½ × 2½-inch loaf pan with cold water (do not dry the pan) and spoon mixture into pan. Cover with aluminum foil and refrigerate for several hours or overnight.

When ready to serve, unmold loaf, blot dry on paper towels, cut into ¾-inch slices, and dip into corn flour. Saute in a bit of corn oil or butter until heated and browned. Serve with scrambled eggs, or alone.

Cornmeal and Sage Pie
with Chicken Liver Pate
Serves 6

Crust:

¾ cup yellow stone-ground
  cornmeal
¼ cup whole wheat flour
1½ teaspoon baking powder
1 egg
½ cup milk
2 tablespoons grated onions
⅛ teaspoon black pepper
2 tablespoons finely minced
  sage, or 1 teaspoon dried
  sage
¼ cup soft butter, cut into very
  small pieces

Preheat oven to 400°F. and butter a 10-inch pie plate. Mix together the cornmeal, flour, and baking powder in a small bowl. In another, larger bowl, beat egg and milk together and then stir in remaining ingredients. Pour into pie plate and bake about 15 to 18 minutes. Remove and frost top with a layer of Chicken Liver Pate and return to oven for 5 minutes. Decorate top with fresh sage leaves. Serve warm, cut into wedges.

Chicken Liver Pate:

2 tablespoons chicken fat
2 medium-size onions, thinly
  sliced
½ pound chicken livers
  (about 3 or 4)
1 hard-cooked egg
¼ teaspoon black pepper

Melt chicken fat in a heavy skillet. Add onions and saute over medium heat, stirring occasionally, until very brown. Push onions aside, increase heat, and add the livers. Saute quickly for 2 minutes, turn, and saute the other side until the livers lose their pink color. Turn off heat and let cool for 10 minutes. When cool, chop finely with hard-cooked egg (a food processor takes about 5 or 6 strokes) and add pepper.

Hominy Grits Souffle with Garlic and Cheddar Cheese

Serves 6

2	cups milk
2	cups water
¾	cup stone-ground hominy grits (*not instant* grits)
4	tablespoons butter, melted
¼	teaspoon black pepper
⅛	teaspoon grated nutmeg
½	teaspoon hot pepper sauce
2	cups (about ½ pound) grated sharp cheddar cheese
1½	teaspoons finely chopped garlic
6	large eggs, separated

Boil milk and water together and slowly, without disturbing the boiling liquid, add the grits. Lower heat, stir with a wooden spoon, and cook in a double boiler over boiling water with pot covered. Stir occasionally until grits are tender (about 30 minutes).

Preheat oven to 425°F. Combine cooked grits with butter, pepper, nutmeg, hot pepper sauce, half the grated cheese, and the garlic. Let cool.

Beat egg yolks, add to the hominy-cheese mixture, and stir until blended. Beat the egg whites until stiff. Add half, fold them in, and then fold in the other half. Spoon into a well-buttered, 2½-quart souffle dish with deep sides, sprinkle with the rest of the cheese, and bake for about 25 to 30 minutes. Serve immediately.

Mamaliga with Goats'-Milk Cheese and Garlic Butter

Serves 6

6	cups boiling water or Chicken Stock (see Index)
2	cups yellow cornmeal
6	tablespoons butter
1	large clove garlic, finely minced
½	pound crumbled goats'-milk cheese such as feta, Brinza, or Katzkaval
1	tablespoon finely minced parsley
	few gratings of fresh black pepper
1	cup sour cream or yogurt

Gradually add liquid to cornmeal, beating constantly with a wooden spoon or whisk. Cook over low heat in a nonstick pot, stirring often, for 25 to 30 minutes, or until the cornmeal pulls away from the pan and forms a very thick, smooth mass. Then invert the pot and let this mass fall out into a round platter.

Meanwhile, heat the butter with the garlic and keep warm. When ready to serve, use a piece of fine string (fishing line or guitar string is suitable) and cut the cornmeal in half horizontally. Carefully remove top half with a wide spatula and pour half the garlic butter and cheese on bottom half. Replace the top half and pour remaining garlic butter and cheese on top. Sprinkle with parsley and pepper, and pass the sour cream or yogurt separately to spoon on top.

Corn-Bread Ring
with Sausage and Red Peppers
Serves 6

This elegant, fine-textured corn-bread ring made with
corn flour has the colorful surprise of pimientos and
whole sausages in its center.

Filling:

1   pound Italian-style sausage
      (about 6 sausages)
1   clove garlic, finely minced
2   tablespoons minced onions
1   tablespoon finely minced
      parsley
1   teaspoon finely minced
      sage, or ½ teaspoon
      dried sage
      pinch of red pepper flakes
4   whole pimientos, rinsed,
      dried on paper towels,
      and cut in half
½   cup shredded mozzarella
      cheese

Prick sausages with the point of a knife and cook
slowly in a heavy skillet on all sides until lightly browned,
turning frequently. Remove sausages and drain all but
1 tablespoon of accumulated fat. In the same skillet, saute
garlic and onions until wilted, stirring frequently. Let cool
for a few minutes and then add the parsley, sage, and red
pepper flakes. Set aside.

Ring:

2   cups yellow corn flour (its
       finer texture prevents ring
       from crumbling)
1   cup gluten flour
1½   tablespoon baking powder
1   egg, beaten
2   cups milk
4   tablespoons butter, melted

Prepare corn bread by first sifting and then mixing all
dry ingredients with all the liquid ones and beating to
combine well. Lavishly butter a ring mold (9½ inches in
diameter and 2½ inches deep) and preheat oven to 425°F.
Spoon half the corn-bread batter on bottom of ring
mold. Spoon some of the onion mixture over, then arrange
the pimientos in a circle over that. Sprinkle with the
mozzarella cheese and lay the whole sausages on top. Spoon
the remaining corn-bread batter over all and bake for 20 to
25 minutes. Run a knife carefully around the mold and let
stand for 10 minutes before inverting and unmolding onto a
warmed serving platter.

Pozole—*Basic Whole Hominy*

Serves 6

1 pound whole dried white
    hominy
5 cups water

Soak dried hominy overnight in enough water to cover by 3 inches. When ready to cook, drain, rinse, and place in pot with 5 cups of fresh water. Bring to a boil. Lower heat, cover pot, and simmer for 2½ to 3 hours, or until kernels are tender. Keep in refrigerator or freezer and use as needed.

Main Dishes

Whole Hominy
with Sausage and Apple Patties

Makes 6 patties

In this recipe, the tart-sweet taste of sliced apple is sandwiched between 2 thin pork patties.

2 tablespoons corn oil
1 clove garlic, finely minced
1 medium-size onion, finely
    chopped
3½ cups cooked whole hominy
⅓ cup light cream
1 cup shredded sharp cheddar
    cheese
1 pound Homemade Pork
    Sausage (see Index)
1 egg, beaten
2 tablespoons milk
1 cup soft whole grain bread
    crumbs
2 medium-size apples
2 teaspoons lemon juice
1 tablespoon finely minced
    leaf coriander or parsley
    for garnish

Preheat oven to 400°F. and butter a large oven-to-table casserole. Heat oil in a large skillet and saute the garlic and onion for 2 to 3 minutes, or until wilted. Stir occasionally. Stir in the hominy and cream and spoon into the prepared casserole. Sprinkle with the cheddar cheese, reserving 6 teaspoons.

In a bowl, mix the sausage meat with the egg, milk, and bread crumbs. Wet hands and form mixture into 12 balls. Flatten each ball between 2 pieces of waxed paper into thin patties about 3½ inches in diameter. Set aside.

Core apples and remove ends. Then slice each apple into 4 slices. Remove two slices and save for another use. Sprinkle the remaining 6 slices of apple with lemon juice. Place each slice of apple between 2 patties, and with wet hands enclose the apple slice. (There will be 6 stuffed patties.)

Using a nonstick skillet, quickly brown patties on each side and then lay them over the hominy mixture. Sprinkle each one with 1 teaspoon of reserved cheese. Cover casserole with foil and bake for 30 minutes. Sprinkle with minced coriander or parsley before serving.

Pozole
Serves 6

This stew, made with dried whole hominy, is a traditional New Mexican and Pueblo Indian feast-day favorite.

10 ounces dried whole white hominy
5 cups water
2 pounds center cut pork chops, bone in, or
   3 pounds pork shoulder
3 tablespoons corn oil
2 cloves garlic, finely chopped
2 large onions, finely chopped
¼ teaspoon paprika
¼ teaspoon black pepper
2 cups Chicken Stock (see Index)
1 or 2 dried, long red mild chili peppers, seeded and torn into small pieces
1 tablespoon thyme leaves, or 1 teaspoon dried thyme
1 tablespoon oregano leaves, or 1 teaspoon dried oregano
2 medium-size tomatoes, coarsely chopped
1 or 2 green jalapeno peppers, roasted, peeled, and minced
1 tablespoon minced cilantro or parsley for garnish

Soak hominy overnight in enough water to cover by 3 inches. Drain, rinse in cold water, and place in a heavy soup pot. Add 5 cups fresh water and bring to a boil. Meanwhile, remove bones from meat and add bones to pot. Lower heat and simmer, covered, for 2 hours.

Cut the meat into 1-inch cubes and set aside. In a large skillet, heat 2 tablespoons of the corn oil and add the garlic and onions. Cook over medium heat until nicely browned (about 8 to 10 minutes). Remove onion mixture and, in the same skillet, add the remaining tablespoon of oil. When hot, add the cubes of pork and sprinkle with paprika and black pepper. Stir and cook for 15 minutes over high heat until meat is browned. Add the onions to the skillet, stir, and then add mixture to the hominy.

Add the chicken stock, dried red pepper, thyme, and oregano (more stock or water may be needed while cooking). Simmer for 1 hour more.

Add tomatoes and jalapeno peppers and cook for 30 minutes more. Before serving, remove bones, add meat scraps (picked from bones), and sprinkle with cilantro or parsley.

Note: Dried hominy—sometimes called *mote* or *pozole*—can be found in Hispanic markets (see Mail-Order Sources).

Mexican Tamale *Pie*

Serves 6

3	cups Chicken Stock (see Index)
1½	cups yellow cornmeal
2	tablespoons corn oil
1	clove garlic, finely minced
1	medium-size onion, coarsely chopped
⅓	cup finely minced green peppers
1	pound lean ground beef
2 or 3	large ripe tomatoes, cut in small cubes
1	cup cooked corn kernels
1	tablespoon chili powder
¼	teaspoon black pepper
¼	teaspoon ground cumin
1	teaspoon oregano leaves, or ¼ teaspoon dried oregano
½	pound Monterey Jack cheese, shredded
1	tablespoon leaf coriander, finely minced for garnish

Heat chicken stock and slowly add cornmeal, stirring with a wooden spoon to prevent lumps. Cook, stirring constantly, over medium heat until thick and smooth (about 10 minutes). Let cool slightly.

Butter a 9-inch round, deep quiche dish or casserole. Wet hands and spread cornmeal on bottom of pan and against the sides. Preheat the oven to 350°F. while preparing the filling.

In a large skillet, heat the oil. Add the garlic, onion, and green peppers and saute, while stirring, over medium heat until wilted. Then add the ground beef, breaking up the pieces with the spoon, and cook until the meat begins to lose its pink color. Add all the remaining ingredients, except the cheese and coriander, stir, and simmer the beef mixture, uncovered, for 10 minutes. Stir occasionally. Pour into the cornmeal-lined pan, sprinkle with shredded cheese, and bake in preheated oven for 30 minutes. Remove from the oven and sprinkle with minced coriander.

The *Polenta* Tradition

In Northern Italy, where *polenta* is a specialty, a U-shaped copper pot is used especially for this dish. (We use SilverStone nonstick for all grains, including *polenta*.) The reason for the pot's shape and composition is that it heats evenly and allows the cornmeal to come away from its sides when stirred.

Stirring is a considerable task, done slowly with a wooden spoon for 45 minutes, and usually over a wood fire. The shape of the pot acts as a mold so that the cooked *polenta* forms a lovely mound when it is turned out onto a wooden board. It is then cut in half, horizontally, with a piece of strong thread.

Polenta — *Cornmeal Italian Style* —
with Wild Mushroom and Tomato Sauce
Serves 6

The Northern Italians from the Bergamo district eat *polenta* with "little birds." Our recipe is served with Wild Mushroom and Tomato Sauce. It can also be eaten plain with butter and Parmesan cheese.

6 cups boiling Chicken Stock
   (see Index), or water
2 cups yellow cornmeal
½ cup butter, melted
¾ cup freshly grated
   Parmesan cheese
1 tablespoon finely minced
   parsley

Pour hot chicken stock or water into a large bowl and slowly stir in cornmeal with a wooden spoon or whisk until there are no lumps. Then place in a nonstick pot and cook over low heat, stirring frequently, for 30 to 35 minutes, or until a very thick mass forms and pulls away from the sides of the pot.

Oil all sides of a 9 × 5 × 3-inch loaf pan and spoon the *polenta* into the pan, smoothing the surface with a spatula. Cool and then chill in refrigerator for several hours. When firm, invert onto a wooden board and cut slices with a strong, fine string. (Fishing line or a guitar string is good.) Cut each slice about ¼ inch thick and then in half crosswise forming rectangular pieces.

Preheat oven to 400°F. and butter a shallow 1½-quart oven-to-table baking dish. Make layers of the rectangles, placing first layer lengthwise and the next crosswise. Spoon some of the melted butter and Parmesan cheese over each layer and bake until hot and bubbly (about 20 minutes). Set under broiler for a few seconds to brown top slightly. Sprinkle with parsley. Serve as is, or with the Wild Mushroom and Tomato Sauce.

Wild Mushroom and Tomato Sauce:

1 cup boiling water
1 ounce dried Italian
   mushrooms *(porcini)*
2 tablespoons olive oil
2 cloves garlic, finely minced
1 medium-size onion, finely
   chopped
1½ cups chopped tomatoes
1 tablespoon tomato paste
1 tablespoon finely minced
   parsley with stems
½ teaspoon mild honey
¼ teaspoon black pepper

Pour water over mushrooms and soak for 15 minutes. Strain liquid through a fine-mesh strainer and reserve. Rinse mushrooms under cold water to get rid of any gritty matter, cut into small pieces, and set aside.

In a medium-size skillet, heat olive oil, then add garlic and saute until soft but not brown. Add the remaining ingredients and the liquid from the mushrooms. Simmer for 15 minutes, uncovered. Add the mushrooms last and simmer for 10 minutes more. Serve sauce with *polenta*.

Note: This sauce can also be used for pasta or rice.

Popcorn Panorama

Even though we have no record of the Incas attending their local movie theaters, they were eating popcorn in great quantities about 5,000 years ago. They also strung popcorn for decoration in their religious ceremonies, much as we do today when we adorn our Christmas trees in puffy white garlands. The ancients, however, couldn't begin to match American consumption of popcorn, currently at about 400 million pounds a year! In fact, there are movie theater owners around the country who claim that the popcorn sold at their concession stands, not Hollywood's output, saved the film industry. Their profit, they say, comes from *popcorn,* not from admissions.

We remember the home-baked cookies sent to the GIs during World War II, comfortably wrapped in popcorn to absorb the shock of travel, and even today, about 10 percent of the popcorn crop is used for cushioning material in packing and shipping, and about 60 percent of it is consumed in the home. When we add the amounts sold at the theaters, it is truly a vast, and very American, phenomenon!

If we eliminate the salt and any other chemical preservatives, popcorn has only 55 calories per cup, and is rich in magnesium, with 12 percent protein, 77 percent carbohydrates, and much-needed cellulose for roughage. It's fun to make, and you don't have to go to the movies to enjoy your own unsalted, no-chemical version. Corn poppers are readily available—modest or fancy—or you can pop the corn very simply in a large pot with a tight lid, or over an open fire using a long-handled popcorn basket. Because we're gadget freaks, we bought a popcorn maker.

Before you start, here are a few rules for popping corn successfully:

- Use a container that is heavy enough to hold the heat. The lid must allow moisture to escape as the corn pops.
- If you use a wire basket over an open fire, don't keep the corn too close to the flame or it will scorch before popping. Shake and agitate the basket or heavy skillet to facilitate popping.
- Corn will pop when the temperature reaches about 420°F.
- To test, put oil in bottom of popper and drop in a kernel of corn. When it pops, you know the temperature is correct for adding the rest of the corn.

Popcorn may be popped a few hours ahead and warmed before serving. Spread in a large roasting pan and heat in a slow oven (250°F.) for 20 minutes. Then "drizzle" or "sprinkle" any of the following toppings over *hot* popcorn, and serve—

Herbed Popcorn:

4 tablespoons butter, melted
6 cups popped corn
½ teaspoon dried oregano
¼ teaspoon crushed rosemary
½ teaspoon dried basil
1 teaspoon thyme
¼ teaspoon black pepper

Drizzle melted butter over popcorn. Whirl herbs in blender, sprinkle over popcorn, and toss.

Garlic Butter and Parsley Popcorn:

4 tablespoons butter
1 clove garlic, finely minced
6 cups popped corn
1 tablespoon finely minced
    parsley

Melt butter and add garlic, cook over low heat for 1 minute, and then drizzle over popped corn. Toss well, sprinkle with parsley, and toss again.

Cheese Popcorn:

4 tablespoons butter, melted
6 cups popped corn
½ cup grated Parmesan,
    cheddar, or Swiss cheese,
    or crumbled blue cheese

Drizzle melted butter over corn, sprinkle with cheese, and toss again.

Peanut, Honey, and Wheat Germ Popcorn:

3 tablespoons butter
4 tablespoons mild honey
6 cups popped corn
¾ cup peanuts
¼ cup wheat germ

Preheat oven 350°F. Line a jelly-roll pan with aluminum foil and then butter the foil. In a small saucepan, melt butter, then add honey, and heat together. Drizzle butter-honey mixture over popcorn and toss. Spread on pan in a thin layer. Bake for 15 to 20 minutes, or until crisp. When cooled slightly, sprinkle with wheat germ and toss again.

Maple Walnut Popcorn:

4 tablespoons butter
¾ cup coarsely chopped
    walnuts
6 cups popped corn
3 tablespoons maple sugar

Melt butter, add walnuts and toast, while stirring, for a few minutes. Drizzle over popcorn and toss. Sprinkle with maple sugar and toss again.

Or . . .

Just drizzle butter, or use no butter. If the popcorn is freshly made, you may not need any. Sprinkle with any of the following and enjoy your own custom-made popcorn: garlic powder, onion powder, kelp powder, cayenne powder, any dried herb or combination of dried herbs, curry.

Try floating some plain or seasoned popcorn in your soup instead of croutons.

Double Corn Pudding with Jalapeno Peppers and Cheddar Cheese

Serves 6 to 9

1¾ cups cooked corn kernels, crushed
¼ cup milk
1 cup stone-ground yellow cornmeal
¼ pound butter, melted and cooled
¾ cup buttermilk
2 medium-size onions, finely chopped
2 eggs, beaten
½ teaspoon baking soda
2 cups grated sharp cheddar cheese
2 or 3 jalapeno peppers, seeded and minced

Preheat oven to 350°F. and butter a 9-inch-square baking pan. In a large bowl, stir together corn kernels and milk. Add all the remaining ingredients, except the cheese and jalapeno peppers. Beat well and then turn half of this mixture into the prepared pan. Cover evenly with half the cheese and sprinkle with the peppers. Sprinkle the remaining cheese over the peppers and then pour the remaining batter evenly over the cheese-pepper layer. Bake for 1 hour. Cool 15 minutes and then loosen sides by running a knife around the edges before cutting into serving portions.

Breads

Apple, Carrot, and Raisin Corn Muffins

Makes 12 muffins

1 cup yellow cornmeal
1 cup whole wheat flour
4 teaspoons baking powder
   pinch of baking soda
½ cup raisins
2 eggs, beaten
1 cup milk plus ½ teaspoon vinegar or soured milk
3 tablespoons mild honey
4 tablespoons butter, melted
1 green apple, peeled and grated
1 carrot, grated
1 tablespoon grated orange rind

Preheat oven to 400°F. and butter a 12-cup, 2½-inch-deep muffin pan. Mix together cornmeal, flour, baking powder, baking soda, and raisins in a bowl and set aside.

In another bowl, combine eggs, milk, honey, and melted butter. Then add the grated apple, carrot, and orange rind to the liquid ingredients. Mix the dry and liquid mixtures together and spoon equal amounts into the prepared muffin cups. Bake about 20 to 25 minutes, or until golden. Let cool slightly on a rack before removing from pan.

Chili-Corn Spoon Bread with Sweet Red Peppers
Serves 6

1 cup dried whole corn,
   cracked in blender or
   food processor (not too
   fine)
3 cups milk
2 tablespoons grated onions
3 eggs, separated
3 tablespoons butter
1 small sweet red pepper,
   seeded and finely minced
½ teaspoon chili powder
⅛ teaspoon white pepper
1 teaspoon mild honey
1 tablespoon corn germ

Preheat oven to 375°F. and butter a 2-quart souffle dish. Place cracked corn in a large bowl and set aside.

Place half of the milk, the grated onions, and egg yolks into a food processor and mix well. Keep mixture in food processor bowl.

Melt butter in a skillet and add sweet red pepper, chili powder, and white pepper. Stir and cook for 1 minute. Let cool slightly and then add to the milk and egg yolk mixture. Add honey and blend.

Add the remaining 1½ cups milk to the dry corn, and then combine with the egg-milk mixture. Beat the egg whites until stiff and fold in. Spoon into prepared souffle dish and bake for 40 minutes. Remove from oven and sprinkle with corn germ. Return to oven and bake for 10 to 15 minutes more.

Corn Flour and Corn Germ Waffles
Makes 3 waffles

1 cup yellow corn flour
½ cup corn germ
½ teaspoon baking soda
1 teaspoon baking powder
2 tablespoons butter or corn
   oil
2 tablespoons mild honey
1½ cups buttermilk
1 egg, beaten

Mix dry ingredients together in a bowl. Melt butter and heat honey in a small saucepan and let cool.

In another bowl, mix buttermilk and egg together and add the cooled honey-butter mixture. Combine with the dry ingredients. Using 1¼ cups of batter for each waffle, bake according to directions given for your own waffle iron. Serve hot with any kind of fruit, ice cream, or syrup.

Breads

Dried Herb
and Fresh Onion Corn Sticks
Makes 14 sticks

These corn sticks are baked in a heavy iron corn-stick mold.

1   cup white cornmeal
1   cup whole wheat flour,
      sifted
2   tablespoons baking powder
2   teaspoons dried herbs: a
      combination of thyme,
      savory, sage, oregano,
      and rosemary
¼   teaspoon black pepper
1   egg, beaten
1   cup milk
1   tablespoon mild honey
4   tablespoons butter, melted
      and cooled
1   medium-size onion, grated
½   clove garlic, grated

Preheat oven to 425°F., butter 2 heavy iron corn-stick pans, and preheat pans for 5 minutes. Mix together the cornmeal, flour, baking powder, herbs, and pepper in a bowl.

In another bowl, beat together the egg, milk, honey, and melted butter. Add the grated onion and garlic to the liquid ingredients. Add the dry ingredients and combine swiftly, mixing for a few strokes only.

Remove the preheated pans from oven and spoon 2 tablespoons of batter into each form. Bake 10 to 15 minutes, or until golden brown. Cool on a rack for a few minutes before unmolding. Serve warm.

Green Peppercorn Pones
Serves 6

1   cup plus 2 tablespoons
      white cornmeal
½   cup boiling water
¼   teaspoon baking soda
⅓   cup sour cream
3   tablespoons butter, melted
2   tablespoons grated onions
1   teaspoon water-packed
      green peppercorns,
      drained
1   tablespoon finely minced
      parsley

Place the cornmeal in a small bowl, add the boiling water, and mix. (Mixture should be crumbly.) Cover and refrigerate for 1 hour.

Preheat oven to 450°F. and heat a large, heavy, preferably iron, pan. While oven and pan are heating, add the sour cream, 1 tablespoon of the melted butter, and the remaining ingredients to the cornmeal mixture and mix well.

Pour remaining butter into hot pan to coat bottom. Then drop batter by the tablespoonful into the hot pan, leaving space between each pone. Press surface lightly with fingers to form a slightly thin oval. Bake for 20 to 25 minutes and serve warm.

Lace-Edge Cornmeal Batter Cakes
Serves 6

1 cup white cornmeal
½ teaspoon baking soda
1 egg
1¼ cups buttermilk
  butter and corn oil for
    frying
  warm honey or maple syrup

Place cornmeal in a mixing bowl. Add baking soda and egg and beat with a whisk. Slowly add the buttermilk, beating constantly.

In a 12-inch skillet, heat butter and corn oil until very hot. Drop batter by the tablespoonful from about 6 to 8 inches above the pan, allowing the edges to spatter, forming crisp lace edges. Allow 2 inches between cakes, since they spread while cooking. When brown, turn and brown the reverse side. Repeat until all the batter is used, stirring batter well each time a new batch of cakes is made. It is not necessary to use more butter and oil for each batch, but if the cakes seem to stick, heat additional butter-oil mixture before continuing. Serve hot with warm honey or maple syrup.

New England Johnnycakes
Makes 14 cakes

No one has ever settled the great Johnnycake controversy: Is it Johnnycake, Jonnycake, Journey Cake, or Shawnee Cake? Did it originate on Rhode Island's Eastern or Western Shore? In fact, did it originate in Rhode Island at all? Should it be made with flint corn or dent corn? Our recipe is an attempt to be neutral, and we attended the October Johnnycake Festival in Usquepaugh, Rhode Island, to sample them firsthand (all in the interest of scientific research!).

1 cup stone-ground white
    cornmeal
¾ cup boiling water
1 tablespoon soft butter, cut
    into small pieces
1 teaspoon mild honey
3 tablespoons cold milk
  butter for griddle

Place the cornmeal in a bowl and gradually add the boiling water, stirring with a wooden spoon. Add the remaining ingredients and mix well. The batter will be thick.

Heat a griddle and melt butter. Drop batter by tablespoonful, lower heat to medium, and cook slowly, about 5 minutes on each side, until crisp and golden on the outside and soft on the inside. Additional butter may be needed while baking to form a crisp crust.

Skillet Corn Bread
with Zucchini and Jack Cheese
Makes 1 skillet corn bread

1   pound shredded zucchini
1   cup yellow cornmeal
1   teaspoon baking powder
⅛   teaspoon black pepper
¼   teaspoon baking soda
1   cup buttermilk
4   tablespoons butter, melted
2   scallions, finely minced
1   tablespoon finely minced
     oregano, or ½ teaspoon
     dried oregano
½   cup shredded Monterey
     Jack cheese (about
     4 ounces)
     paprika

Place shredded zucchini in a strainer and let stand for 15 minutes. Then squeeze out remaining liquid from the zucchini between palms of hands and set the zucchini aside. Preheat oven to 425°F.

In a medium-size bowl, mix together all the dry ingredients. Add the buttermilk and 2 tablespoons of the melted butter. Pour the rest of the melted butter in a heavy 8-inch cast-iron skillet and preheat the skillet for 5 minutes in the oven.

Add all the remaining ingredients to the batter, except the paprika. Stir in the zucchini and pour batter evenly in the skillet. Sprinkle with paprika and bake for 20 to 25 minutes, or until edges are brown. Before serving, let bread cool to room temperature and then cut into pie-shaped wedges. Bread will have a creamy texture rather than a breadlike texture.

Yellow Corn Muffins
with Tomato and Basil
Makes 12 muffins

A muffin that envelops a fresh cherry tomato and a basil leaf.

1½   cups yellow cornmeal
¼   teaspoon baking soda
     pinch of cayenne pepper
1   cup sour cream
2   eggs, beaten
1   teaspoon mild honey
1   tablespoon butter, melted
1   cup minced scallions
6   basil leaves, cut in half
6   cherry tomatoes, cut in half
½   cup cooked corn

Preheat oven to 400°F. and butter cups of muffin pan. In a bowl, mix cornmeal, baking soda, and cayenne. Set aside. In another bowl, combine the sour cream, eggs, honey, and melted butter.

Combine the dry ingredients and the liquid with a few strokes and then stir in the scallions. Put 1 heaping teaspoonful of this batter into each muffin cup. Then add a piece of basil, half a cherry tomato, and a teaspoon of corn. Spoon another heaping teaspoon of the batter into each cup and bake for 25 to 30 minutes, or until golden. Cool on a wire rack for a few minutes before removing from muffin cups.

During the writing of any cookbook, there is a nonstop hum of activity in the kitchen as recipes are tested, revised, and finally committed to paper for posterity. Since each recipe is tested to serve six people, there is no way on earth that two thin cooks can consume even a small portion of the daily output. As a result, great quantities of breakfast, lunch, and dinner are presented to friends; sometimes "test parties" are held in order to gather comments and criticism, as well as to avoid the awful waste of food that might otherwise occur.

As this book developed, friends in the village began to wait for certain test phases. Herb, passing us on his bicycle, waved and shouted, "Don't forget to call me when you get to buckwheat!" Tina wanted to test the rice dishes. *Everyone* waited for pasta invitations. Our friend Rochelle was asked to sample the millet tests after she commented during a walk this summer, "Oh, I know all about millet! I feed it to my parakeet!"

Millet is another (yet another!) "stepchild" of the human food chain, at least here in the United States. However, knowing its remarkable nutritional value, it's hard to understand why millet has become known as "the poor man's cereal." (Brown rice carries a similar designation!) Millet has served as an alternative to rice for centuries in Korea, Japan, and the north of China. In fact, one-third of the people living in the Orient use millet as a daily food source.

The taller, healthier natives of northern China might owe their height and strength, at least in part, to eating millet instead of rice; the long-lived Hunzas in the Himalayas also use the grain as a major food source. It is found in Africa, from the north, where it is made into a porridge called *tuo zaafi,* to the Sahara Desert, where it is used in a small flat bread called *taguella,* and down into Ethiopia where millet makes the national bread of the country, *injera.* In Western Europe and the United States, of course, we use it mostly for hay, pasture—and for the birds.

Millet: The Unsung Grain

Millet is one of the most nutritious of the grain family, easy to digest, rich in essential amino acids, phosphorus, and B vitamins, with an iron content higher than any grain except amaranth. It is also one of the most outstanding antacid foods in the world, a perfect addition to the diets of ulcer and colitis patients.

The cook can use it for any course, in any meal, either by itself or in combination with other grains. We use it as a stuffing for baked vegetables, poultry, and fish, and in our soups and stews; it makes a marvelous base for casseroles, and serves as a superb whole grain substitute for *couscous*. And, because it does not have an imposing flavor, it's delicious in custards and desserts.

We strongly recommend it. It has become one of our very favorite grains. And whether you eat it just because it has so many good things in it, or because you love the taste of it, as we do, we think you'll agree that this is one grain that is *not* strictly for the birds!

Basic Whole Millet I

Yields 4 cups

1 cup whole millet
2 teaspoons butter, melted, or safflower oil
2 cups boiling water

If you wish the grains to remain separated, follow this method. For a stickier texture, use the Basic Whole Millet II recipe.

Toast millet in a heavy skillet over medium heat in 1 teaspoon of melted butter or oil, stirring and shaking the pan until the grains are light tan and you begin to smell a nutty aroma.

In a separate nonstick saucepan, bring water to a boil. Add the remaining teaspoon of butter or oil and the grains, stir, cover pan, and simmer over very low heat for 25 to 30 minutes, or until all the water is absorbed. Slip a double sheet of paper toweling between pot and lid. Cover pot again and let stand to absorb moisture for 10 minutes. Remove cover and discard paper towels. Fluff with a fork before serving. Cooked millet grains can be kept in a covered container and refrigerated for 1 week to 10 days, and frozen for 3 to 4 months. If frozen, defrost before using.

Note: If cooked millet is used in dishes other than desserts, substitute chicken, vegetable, or beef stock in place of the water for added flavor.

Basic Whole Millet II

Yields 4 cups

2½ cups water
1 cup millet

In a SilverStone-lined pot, bring water to a boil. Add millet, stir, lower heat, cover, and simmer, stirring occasionally, for 25 to 30 minutes, or until liquid is absorbed. Let rest, covered, for 5 minutes. Millet should be sticky and fairly thick.

The Forms of Millet

Millet—Whole or Groats: Always hulled, since the outer layer is indigestible. The resultant grain is tiny and golden.

Puffed Millet: The whole grain puffed under pressure. It is an excellent food for those on diets, who want to restrict the amount that they eat and still get sufficient nourishment. Puffed millet can also be used in puddings and bread to give added lightness.

Millet Flour: A still finer grind than the meal. As far as we can determine, millet flour is not commercially available at this time. Millet can be ground into flour, as we do it, in a small electric mill.

Millet Meal: A fine ground meal used for baked goods. It can be purchased already prepared, or you can grind it yourself from whole millet by using a home mill or a small electric spice grinder.

————————————————————————————— **Cereal**

Millet with Nuts, Seeds, and Shredded Pears
Serves 6

2 cups cooked millet
¼ cup sunflower seeds
½ cup chopped walnuts
2 firm pears, shredded
4 tablespoons maple syrup
2 tablespoons raisins
  milk

Toss all ingredients together in a bowl. Serve with a pitcher of milk to be poured over cereal at the table.

————————————————————————————— **Soup**

Cold Cucumber, Buttermilk, and Millet Soup
Serves 4 to 6

2 medium-size cucumbers, shredded
2½ cups hot Chicken Stock (see Index)
2 cups buttermilk
½ cup sour cream
1 cup cooked millet
¼ cup finely minced scallions plus 2 tablespoons for garnish
  few drops of hot pepper sauce
  paprika for garnish

Place cucumbers in a bowl and add hot chicken stock, buttermilk, sour cream, and millet. Process this mixture in a blender, a few batches at a time, until very fine. Add all but 2 tablespoons of the scallions. Stir in hot pepper sauce. Chill for 1 hour before serving. When ready to serve, sprinkle with reserved scallions and a dusting of paprika.

Broccoli and Millet Souffle
Serves 6

Millet insures that the souffle won't fall. Cheddar cheese gives it flavor. Broccoli and mushrooms give it added snap. Vegetarians love it—and so does everyone else.

$\frac{1}{4}$ c dry = 1 c cooked

3 cups cooked millet

1½ cups lightly steamed broccoli florets, finely chopped

2 tablespoons butter

1 small onion, grated

½ pound mushrooms, coarsely chopped

1 tablespoon finely grated lemon rind

1 cup grated sharp cheddar cheese

¼ teaspoon arrowroot

1 cup milk

6 eggs, separated

few drops of hot pepper sauce

pinch of cream of tartar

Preheat oven to 350°F. and butter a 6-cup souffle dish. In a large bowl, mix the millet and chopped broccoli. Set aside.

Melt the butter and add the onion and mushrooms. Stir and cook for 5 minutes. Then add to millet and broccoli mixture. Stir in the lemon rind and cheese. Dissolve arrowroot in milk and then add to mixture.

Beat the egg yolks until foamy and add to the mixture, along with the hot pepper sauce. Beat the egg whites with a pinch of cream of tartar until stiff and then fold into the millet mixture. Spoon into prepared souffle dish and bake for about 50 minutes to 1 hour, or until center is firm.

Broccoli and Millet Souffle   For this recipe, see page 104

Whole Wheat Pinwheel Roulade Stuffed with Spinach and Pine Nuts   For this recipe, see page 189

Carrot, Alfalfa Sprout, and Millet Croquettes
Serves 8

These meatless croquettes are as tasty and satisfying as a hamburger. They may be served in whole wheat pita bread with dollops of yogurt.

- 2 tablespoons peanut oil
- 1 large clove garlic, finely minced
- 1 large onion, finely chopped
- 1 cup finely chopped celery with leaves
- 1½ cups cooked Basic Whole Millet II (see recipe in this section)
- 1 cup alfalfa sprouts
- 1 cup shredded carrots
- 2 eggs, beaten
- ½ cup millet flour
- 1 teaspoon baking powder
- ¼ teaspoon black pepper
- ¼ teaspoon ground cumin
- ½ cup finely minced parsley
  - peanut oil for frying
  - lemon wedges or yogurt for dressing

In a large skillet, heat oil and saute garlic, onion, and celery over medium heat for 5 to 8 minutes, stirring occasionally. Let cool slightly and then mix with all remaining ingredients.

Form mixture into flat patties with wet hands. (If mixture is too wet, add more flour; it should be moist, but still hold its shape when patties are formed.) Wipe out skillet and heat oil until very hot. Place patties in the hot oil and brown both sides. Lift out carefully with slotted spoon and drain on paper towels. Serve at room temperature with lemon wedges or yogurt.

Chicken Couscous *Moroccan* with *Hot* Harissa *Sauce*

Serves 6 to 8

2 tablespoons butter
1 tablespoon olive oil
1 3½-pound chicken, cut into
    10 small pieces (or
    combine ½ pound beef,
    cut into cubes plus
    ½ chicken, cut into pieces
    and ½ pound lamb, cut
    into pieces)
1 teaspoon grated ginger
1 clove garlic, finely minced
¼ teaspoon crushed saffron
¼ teaspoon black pepper
¼ teaspoon ground cinnamon
¼ teaspoon ground cloves
¼ teaspoon grated nutmeg
3 cups Chicken Stock (see
    Index)
1 recipe Basic Whole Millet I
    (see recipe in this section)
¾ pound onions, cut into
    ½-inch-thick slices
    (about 2 large onions)
5 small turnips, peeled and
    cut in half
4 carrots, cut into 3 to
    4 pieces each
3 small zucchini, washed,
    trimmed, and cut into
    1½-inch pieces
1 cup cooked chick-peas
⅓ cup raisins
1 lemon, cut into eighths
¼ cup blanched whole
    almonds, toasted in butter
2 tablespoons minced parsley

Melt butter and heat oil together in the bottom of a large, deep, heavy pot. Add the chicken pieces, skin side down, and cook over medium-high heat until brown. Sprinkle with ginger, garlic, saffron, pepper, cinnamon, cloves, and nutmeg and turn to brown other side, stirring occasionally. Then add chicken stock, bring to a boil, cover, lower heat to simmer, and cook for 30 minutes. At this point, the millet grains can be cooked and kept warm and Hot *Harissa* Sauce prepared.

After 30 minutes, tuck onions, turnips, and carrots around the chicken. Baste vegetables once, using a turkey baster. Do not stir at any time. Cover pot and continue to cook for 20 minutes more. Then add the zucchini, chick-peas, raisins, and lemon wedges. Cover pot and continue to cook until zucchini is tender. To serve, mound the millet grain in the center of a large warm platter and sprinkle with the toasted almonds. With tongs or a slotted spoon, lift out vegetables and chicken pieces and arrange attractively around the mound of millet. Sprinkle with parsley. Bring remaining sauce in pot to a boil and serve in a separate bowl to be spooned over all at the table. The incendiary classic *Harissa* sauce should be passed along with the broth and used sparingly.

Hot *Harissa* Sauce:

8 small dried hot red peppers
1 clove garlic
¼ teaspoon caraway seed
⅛ teaspoon ground cumin
⅛ teaspoon ground coriander
1 tablespoon olive oil
2 tablespoons liquid from
   stew

Bring peppers to a boil in enough water to cover. Let cool and drain, reserving the liquid. Wearing rubber gloves, split peppers and discard the seeds. Then mash with the remaining ingredients with a mortar and pestle until pureed. (A blender will not mix so small an amount.) Add 1 or more tablespoons of reserved water to thin the sauce a bit. Pass separately with a warning.

Note: *Couscous* is a classic Islamic Sabbath dish. It is to North Africa what pasta is to Italy and rice is to China. It is not a whole grain, however, but a semolina-flour-based pasta which is forced through a sieve and then dried to give it a grainlike shape. It resembles whole millet almost to a T.

Classic *couscous* requires many time-consuming steps in its preparation to steam the dough pellets and keep them separate. The *couscous* must be washed and drained, dried, kneaded, and raked with the fingers to separate the pellets. The *couscous* is then steamed, uncovered, for 25 minutes over meat and vegetables vigorously boiling in stock. It is our view that the vegetables get overcooked and mushy—not to mention the vitamin loss—and the meat usually falls apart. Then the drying and finger-raking is repeated, and so is the steaming.

We find it easier to pour some toasted millet into boiling stock and simmer for 25 minutes. Who wouldn't? The meat and vegetable contents of this dish vary from country to country, with what is on hand and what is in season, and with the imagination of the cook. The Algerians, for example, may use beef, goat, lamb, or chicken, or a combination of several meats. Sometimes they add pumpkin and fava beans as vegetables. It is fun to try our version and then make up your own.

Layered Vegetables and Millet Mold

Serves 6 to 8

2 tablespoons soft butter

½ cup fine dry whole grain bread crumbs

1½ cups cooked millet

2 cups coarsely chopped, cooked green string beans (about ½ pound)

2 cups coarsely chopped, cooked cauliflower

2 cups coarsely chopped, cooked asparagus

1 cup thinly sliced leeks, white part only, or white part of scallions

1 cup grated Parmesan cheese

2 tablespoons finely minced parsley

1 tablespoon finely minced oregano, or 1 teaspoon dried oregano

5 eggs

1 tablespoon tamari soy sauce

¼ teaspoon white pepper

1 cup light cream or half-and-half

Preheat oven to 350°F. Line the bottom of a 2½-quart springform pan with foil going up part of the sides (about 1 inch) to prevent custard from leaking out. Butter foil evenly and sprinkle with bread crumbs, rotating pan so crumbs adhere to side of pan. Shake out excess. Place millet evenly on bottom of pan. Then layer each vegetable over the millet in the order given (string beans, then cauliflower, and so on). Sprinkle ⅓ cup of the cheese and part of the parsley and oregano over each layer, leaving the last layer plain.

Beat the eggs with the remaining ingredients and then slowly pour over layered vegetables, allowing liquid to seep down. Place in another, larger pan and pour 1 inch of boiling water into the bottom of second pan. Bake for about 1 hour, or until center is firm. Remove from oven and let stand for 10 minutes. Place on a serving plate and remove the sides of the springform, leaving the base. Carefully turn down edge of foil and cut away with scissors, or cover the edge with a ring of parsley to hide it. If any liquid forms on serving plate, blot it up with paper towels.

Note: If these are not your favorite vegetables or they are out of season, substitute Brussels sprouts or broccoli for cauliflower, and carrots for asparagus, or use a layer of red peppers and chopped Swiss chard or spinach. But don't forget to squeeze excess liquid out before layering.

For variation, include leftover, cooked, finely minced chicken. It makes the custard base firm and adds to the flavor.

Herbed Millet, Tomato, and Vegetable Salad
Serves 6

2½ cups cooked millet
1 cup tomatoes, skinned and diced
½ cup finely diced green pepper (about ½ large pepper)
¾ cup finely diced zucchini (about ½ pound)
½ cup finely minced scallions
2 tablespoons finely minced basil
2 tablespoons finely minced parsley
¼ cup mayonnaise
1 teaspoon Dijon-type mustard
¼ teaspoon black pepper
2 tablespoons white wine vinegar
leaf lettuce

Place all ingredients except mustard, pepper, vinegar, and lettuce in a medium-size bowl and toss with a fork. Combine mayonnaise, mustard, and pepper in a small bowl, add vinegar, and beat with a wire whisk until smooth. Toss with vegetable-millet mixture and serve cold on lettuce leaves.

Millet, Onion, and Black Pepper Diamonds
Makes approximately 2 dozen crackers

½ cup millet flour
½ cup unbleached white flour
1 teaspoon baking powder
¼ teaspoon black pepper
2 tablespoons tahini
2 teaspoons honey
1 teaspoon onion powder
¼ cup cold water

These crackers have a nice bite of pepper. However, if you prefer, you can use more onion and less black pepper.

Preheat oven to 350°F. and butter 2 cookie sheets. Combine the flours, baking powder, and black pepper in a bowl. In a small cup, mix the tahini and honey together and then add to the dry ingredients. In the same cup, mix the onion powder with the water and add to the mixture. Mix with hands until a ball of dough forms.

Divide dough in half for easier handling and roll each half between 2 sheets of lightly floured plastic wrap or waxed paper to ¼-inch thickness. Cut into diamond shapes and lift carefully onto cookie sheets. Bake until edges start to brown (about 15 to 20 minutes). Rotate pans after 10 minutes to prevent burning. Remove with a spatula to a wire rack to cool. Store in airtight containers.

Breads _____

Puffed Millet Banana Walnut Bread
Makes 1 loaf

2   eggs, separated
1   cup sour cream
¼   cup butter, melted, or safflower oil
⅓   cup maple syrup
1   teaspoon vanilla extract
2   ripe bananas, sliced
1   cup millet meal
1½ cups unbleached white flour
½   cup puffed millet
2   teaspoons baking powder
    pinch of baking soda
1   cup chopped walnuts
1   teaspoon cinnamon
¼   teaspoon mace
⅛   teaspoon ground cloves

This bread is delicious spread with ricotta or cottage cheese.

Preheat oven to 350°F. and butter a 9¾ × 5¾ × 2¾-inch loaf pan. In a food processor, process egg yolks with sour cream, butter or oil, maple syrup, vanilla, and bananas. In a large bowl, mix all the remaining dry ingredients. Beat egg whites until stiff and set aside.

Combine the liquid ingredients with the dry, stirring with as few strokes as possible. Then fold in the beaten egg whites. Pour into loaf pan and bake for 1 hour, or until center tests done. Cool on a rack in the pan for 10 minutes, then remove from pan and cool on rack again.

Desserts _____

Millet Cheese Cake
Makes 1 8-inch cake

2   cups creamed low-fat cottage cheese (1 pound)
1   cup plain yogurt
½   cup mild honey
1   tablespoon cornstarch
2   teaspoons vanilla extract
1   teaspoon grated lemon rind
1   tablespoon lemon juice
4   eggs, separated
1½ cups cooked millet
    pinch of cream of tartar

A luscious, low-calorie cheese cake with millet in the filling and a base of millet for the crust.

Preheat oven to 325°F. and butter an 8-inch round pan. In a food processor or blender, blend cottage cheese, yogurt, honey, cornstarch, vanilla, lemon rind, and lemon juice. Blend in several batches, emptying each into a large mixing bowl. In the last batch, add the egg yolks only. Blend and then stir into the rest of the mixture. Stir in ¾ cup of the cooked millet. Press the remaining millet into the bottom of the pan evenly. Beat the egg whites with the cream of tartar, fold into the cheese mixture, then pour over millet base. Bake 40 to 45 minutes, or until center of mixture is firm. Let cool completely before loosening sides and cutting into wedges. Serve from pan.

Millet, Dried Fruit, and Nut Logs
Makes 2 12-inch logs

¼ pound shelled walnuts
¼ pound whole blanched almonds
1 teaspoon grated orange rind
1 cup cooked millet
¼ pound currants
¼ pound pitted dates
¼ pound raisins
¼ pound dried apricots
1 tablespoon frozen orange juice concentrate

In a food processor, chop walnuts and almonds together until fine. Remove to a large bowl and mix with orange rind and millet. Oil the blades of the food processor with safflower oil and add all the remaining ingredients except the orange juice concentrate. Process until the fruits are very fine. Then add the orange juice concentrate and the nuts mixture. Process again until well mixed and the mass starts to form a ball.

Oil hands well and divide mixture into 2 pieces. Lay 1 piece on waxed paper on a counter and with oiled hands, roll and press into a log shape, 12 inches long by 1 inch in diameter. Repeat with other piece. Wrap individually in plastic wrap and let ripen at room temperature for 3 days. Slice the log into ½-inch slices with an oiled knife. The logs will keep several weeks in the refrigerator, covered with plastic wrap.

Millet and Maple-Walnut Custards
Serves 6

3 eggs
½ cup maple syrup
2 cups low-fat milk
1 teaspoon vanilla extract
1 teaspoon arrowroot
¼ cup cooked millet
¼ teaspoon allspice
¼ cup chopped walnuts

Preheat oven to 350°F. In a mixing bowl, beat eggs. Then add maple syrup, milk, vanilla, and arrowroot and beat again. Distribute the cooked millet evenly between 6 6-ounce custard cups and pour custard over the millet. Place cups in a large baking pan (9 × 13 × 2 inches) and add 1 inch of boiling water to the pan. Sprinkle the custards with allspice and bake for 40 minutes, or until the center of custard is firm. Remove from hot water and cool on a wire rack to room temperature. Chill and top with chopped walnuts before serving.

Millet with Nuts
and Steamed Dates
Serves 6

A light, delicate way to end a meal. Any leftovers
can be served with hot milk for breakfast.

24 whole dates
3 cups cooked hot Basic
    Whole Millet I (see
    recipe in this section)
½ teaspoon almond extract
2 tablespoons soft butter, cut
    into small pieces
1½ cups finely ground mixed
    walnuts and almonds
4 tablespoons date sugar
1 teaspoon cinnamon

Steam dates in a vegetable steamer for 5 minutes and
set aside. In a large bowl, mix the hot millet lightly with
the almond extract and butter. In another bowl, combine
the nuts, date sugar, and cinnamon. Toss this nut mixture
with the millet and lightly mound on a platter. Ring the
platter with the steamed dates. Serve warm with cream,
if desired.

Note: A Mouli hand grater grates the nuts in a light,
airy fashion. An electric grater or blender produces a pastier
blend. If you don't have a Mouli grater, crumble the nut
mixture between the palms of your hands in order to
distribute it evenly when adding it to the millet.

About a year ago, just before our trip to Akron, Ohio, a well-traveled friend who knew about this book, laughed and suggested that we stay the night at the "Oatmeal Hilton" in Quaker Square. At first, we thought he was teasing, but we checked with our travel agent and found that there is, indeed, a Quaker Square Hilton in Akron, lovingly dubbed the "Oatmeal Hilton" because of its unusual construction.

When the Quaker Oats Company left Akron in 1970 for Chicago, they deserted 36 huge, 120-foot-high silos in the downtown area. By ingenious planning, the silos were cut and used as the basic design for the hotel complex, not a small job by any means, since the walls are seven-inch-thick reinforced concrete. We can only report that we dreamt of oats all night long and that you can, of course, get that dish for breakfast in the downstairs dining room.

Considering that every man, woman, and child in this country is aware of oats, mostly in the form of breakfast cereal, it is amazing how little oats they eat—*over 90 percent* of the crop goes to feed animals! In terms of nutrition, it is a grain that is easily digested, has excellent-quality protein and B vitamins, and contains calcium as well as cholesterol-trapping fiber and polyunsaturated fats. Still, it is uphill for oats. Possibly, as Waverly Root has said, oats have

"Oat Cuisine"

gotten a bad press for centuries. Pliny, writing of the German penchant for oats, asked, "How can one eat the same food as animals?"

Perhaps the oat began as a poor relation to the grain family because it started out as an unloved, unwanted weed that found its way into the fields of wheat and barley, to be pulled up by the farmers and burned. But, slowly, the people who lived under less-than-favorable agricultural conditions found that oats could survive beautifully in the colder climates where other grains were decimated by the weather. Thus in ancient days, oats proliferated in Northern Germany and Denmark, as well as in Switzerland and Scotland.

For the Scots, no celebration would be complete without the appearance of oats—whether in haggis or in the drink called *atholi brose*, an incredibly potent beverage made by straining the liquid that results from raw oats soaked in water. We include special recipes dedicated to our Scottish friends as a tribute to their—and our—love of oats. They could not have chosen a better source of energy to get them through the brutal, damp winters of their homeland.

The Forms of Oats

Oat Groats: Untreated, natural, hulled oats. Only the outermost inedible "chaff" or "hull" is removed, with very little change in the basic nutritional value of the grain. Groats can be cooked whole or they can be ground. They're excellent when mixed with wheat berries. Oats in this form take the longest cooking time.

Steel-Cut Oats (sometimes called Scotch Oats): Natural, unrefined oat groats that are cut into two or three small pieces for tasty, chewy cereals. They're processed with a small amount of heat, and therefore they retain most of their B vitamins. They require a fairly long cooking time, but they have good crunch, and they're generally used for "Scottish-style" recipes like oat cakes, griddle cakes, cookies, scones, and porridge. Steel-cut oats can also be blended with various flours for baking.

Rolled Oats: Large, separate flakes that are first steamed and then flattened ("old-fashioned" rolled oats). For added flavor, they can be toasted slightly in the oven, then crumbled between the palms of the hands, or whirled in a food processor or blender to make the flakes smaller in size. Rolled oats are usually used in cereals, cookies, cakes, and breads. They cook in about five minutes, so there's no need to buy the packaged, "quick" or "instant" oats—both of which have been preprocessed (heat treated) for fast cooking and thus have less nutritive value.

Oat Flour: Finely ground from whole oat groats, with much of the bran remaining. It is, therefore, almost as nutritive as the whole groats themselves. The flour can be blended with other flours in the baking of bread, but it has no gluten, so that it will not rise unless it is mixed with a gluten-rich flour. Oat flour can also be used as a thickening agent in sauces, soups, and stews. It's a good substitute flour for people on wheat-restricted diets, and it's excellent for infants. The addition of oat flour to your baked goods will help them to remain fresher for a longer period of time, since the grain has a strong, natural antioxidant. As a matter of fact, oats and derivatives of the grain were used for just that purpose long before the discovery of chemical preservatives.

Basic Old-Fashioned Rolled Oats Porridge
Serves 6

This is what mother fed us when we were kids, only we called it "oatmeal." "Porridge" was something British kids ate. We found out one day (another childish fantasy shot down) that "oatmeal" is really oat *flour* and what we called "oatmeal" was, indeed, porridge.

3 cups boiling water
2 cups rolled oats

2 people:
1 c
2/3

2/3 c dry rolled oats   54 calories approx.

Add oats slowly to the boiling water. Stir once to moisten, cover tightly, and remove from heat. Allow to sit for 8 to 10 minutes. Serve with butter, milk, or honey.

Note: Our directions are quite different from the ones on the commercial box of old-fashioned rolled oats. Their directions suggest that you *cook* the oats for 10 minutes. By using the directions we've given, however, you can save time and energy in the morning. Once the pot of water is brought to a boil, remove it and set a timer—Mel generally shaves and I put on my mascara, the alarm goes off, and *voila,* breakfast is ready!

Cereals

Creamy Oats Porridge
Serves 6

This is a creamier version of the Basic Old-Fashioned Rolled Oats Porridge (above). If you thin this porridge by adding more milk or water, it becomes gruel.

2 cups rolled oats
2 cups water
2 cups milk

Cover the oats with the water and milk and bring to a boil. Cook for 10 minutes over low heat and serve hot with butter or honey.

Cereals

Toasted Steel-Cut Oats Porridge
Serves 6

Untoasted steel-cut oats will take from 30 to 40 minutes of cooking time. We find that toasting the steel-cut oats cuts down on cooking time, and adds an extra nutty taste as a breakfast bonus.

1   cup toasted steel-cut oats
4   cups boiling water

To toast steel-cut oats, whirl the oats in a food processor or blender a few times to break down the grain a bit. Spread the oats in a large roasting pan and toast them for 20 minutes in a 350°F. oven, stirring occasionally.

Slowly sprinkle the toasted oats into boiling water without disturbing the boil. Lower the heat and simmer for 15 minutes, uncovered, stirring once during the cooking time. Cover pot and let rest for 5 minutes before serving.

Note: You can toast a whole pound at one time, then use what you need and store the rest in an airtight jar.

Soup

Quick Oat and Tomato Soup
Serves 6

1   cup rolled oats
4   tablespoons butter
1   large onion, chopped
2   medium-size cloves garlic, chopped
4   large, ripe tomatoes, peeled and chopped
5   cups Chicken Stock (see Index)
1   2-inch strip of orange peel
2   basil leaves, or ½ teaspoon dried basil
3   tablespoons finely minced parsley for garnish

In a heavy skillet, add the oats and toast over medium heat, stirring until they turn golden (about 5 to 10 minutes.) Be careful not to let them burn.

In a large saucepan, heat the butter and add the onion and garlic. Cook for 5 minutes, stirring until the onion is wilted. Add the tomatoes and stir for 2 minutes more. Then add the chicken stock, orange peel, and basil and bring to a boil. Lower heat to medium and cook for 8 minutes. Serve hot, sprinkled with parsley.

Whole Oat Groats with Celery and Herbs
Serves 6

This tasty side dish can also be used as a stuffing for poultry or pork.

6 tablespoons butter
3 cups cooked whole oat groats (see Grains Cooking Chart)
1 medium-size onion, finely chopped
1 green pepper, diced
1 cup finely chopped celery and leaves
½ teaspoon powdered sage
¼ teaspoon dried thyme
1 teaspoon tamari soy sauce
¼ teaspoon black pepper
2 tablespoons finely minced parsley for garnish

In a skillet, melt 3 tablespoons of the butter. Add the cooked groats, stir, and saute until toasted (about 5 minutes). Remove to a bowl and set aside.

In same skillet, heat the remaining 3 tablespoons of butter and then add the onion and green pepper. Cook, stirring, for 3 minutes, and then add the celery and all the other ingredients except the parsley. Cook over medium heat for 2 minutes more. Add the groats to the vegetable mixture and heat, stirring a few times. Serve hot, sprinkled with parsley.

_____ **Breads**

Applesauce, Oat, and Nut Bread
Makes 1 loaf

1½ cups whole wheat pastry flour
2 teaspoons cinnamon
1 teaspoon baking soda
1 teaspoon baking powder
½ teaspoon nutmeg
⅓ cup soft butter
⅓ cup mild honey
1¼ cups thick applesauce
2 eggs, beaten well
1 cup rolled oats
1 cup chopped walnuts
½ cup raisins

Preheat oven to 350°F. and butter a 9 × 5 × 3-inch loaf pan. Sift the flour, cinnamon, baking soda, baking powder, and nutmeg together and set aside.

Beat butter with a wire whisk or a food processor until it is creamy. Add the honey, beat again, and then add the applesauce and eggs. Add the dry ingredients and blend well. Stir in the oats, nuts, and raisins and pour into the pan. Bake for about 55 minutes to 1 hour. Test center of the bread with a cake tester. Cool in pan for 10 minutes, then remove and cool completely on a wire rack. Serve warm with softened cream cheese or cottage cheese.

Basic Rolled Oat and Wheat Germ Breakfast Mix
Yields 6 cups

1½ cups rolled oats
 2 cups whole wheat flour
 ½ cup wheat germ
 ½ cup nonfat dry milk
 2 tablespoons baking powder
 ¼ teaspoon cream of tartar
 1 cup butter, cut into small
    pieces

This time-saving mix is custom-tailored to suit your own nutritional or dietary needs, unlike commercial mixes that usually contain salt and/or white flour.

Combine all dry ingredients in the bowl of a food processor. (If you don't own a food processor, use a pastry blender or 2 knives to cut the butter into the dry ingredients.) Add the pieces of butter and process until the mixture is crumbly. Store in a tightly covered jar in the refrigerator.

Note: Once you've made this convenient and versatile basic mix, it can be used in making the following recipes: Oat Waffles, Oat-Banana Nut Muffins, Oat and Buttermilk Biscuits, Oat-Blueberry Pancakes, and Scottish Oat Bannocks.

Buttermilk Oat Scones
Makes 12 scones

 1 cup steel-cut oats
 ¾ cup buttermilk, warmed
1¼ cups whole wheat flour
 ½ cup oat flour
 1 teaspoon baking soda
 ¼ cup soft butter

Upon tasting the tests for this recipe, two of our island neighbors were plunged into a fit of nostalgia for the afternoons in Scotland when scones were served with tea before a roaring fire.

Preheat oven to 350°F. Place the oats in a pie pan, and toast in oven for 20 minutes, stirring often to prevent burning. When oats are slightly golden, remove and let them cool. Reset the oven for 400°F. Butter a cookie sheet. In a small bowl, combine the oats and the buttermilk and let stand for 10 minutes. In a large bowl, mix both flours with the baking soda. Using a food processor or a pastry blender, cut the butter into the flour mixture and blend until crumbly. Then add buttermilk and oats mixture. Using your hands, knead the mixture 4 or 5 times until it forms a dough. Flour your hands and divide the dough into 2 parts, pressing each part into a circle ½ inch thick. This can be done directly on the cookie sheet, using half the sheet for each circle. Score each circle with a fork to make 6 triangular wedges. Bake for 12 to 15 minutes, or until the scones are golden brown. Cut along scored markings and serve hot.

Note: Actually, there are many types of scones, and you'll find them at breakfast, lunch, or dinner in Scotland. Traditionally, you eat them covered with melted butter, marmalade, or honey.

Irish Steel-Cut Oat Brown Bread
Makes 1 large loaf

²⁄₃ cup toasted steel-cut oats,
     whirled in a food
     processor
3 cups buttermilk, warmed
2 teaspoons tamari soy sauce
5 cups whole wheat flour
1 tablespoon baking soda

This is another of those easy, no-yeast, no-knead breads that can be whipped up in little over an hour, from mixing to taking it steaming hot and crusty from the oven. Not only is it simple to prepare, but toasted for breakfast, it becomes a special treat.

Preheat oven to 400°F. and butter and lightly flour a cookie sheet. In a bowl, combine the toasted oats and the buttermilk and then add the tamari. Let stand for 15 minutes.

In a large bowl, mix the flour with the baking soda. Gradually add the oat and buttermilk mixture to the flour. The dough should be workable and slightly damp.

Turn the mixture out onto a floured board. Knead with floured hands just until it forms a ball (about 5 or 6 times). Place the dough on the cookie sheet and cut a deep cross into it. Bake 45 to 50 minutes, or until it sounds hollow when thumped on the bottom. Cool on a wire rack.

Oat-Banana Nut Muffins
Makes 6 muffins

1 large banana
1 egg, beaten
⅓ cup yogurt
2 tablespoons mild honey
1 cup Basic Rolled Oat and
     Wheat Germ Breakfast
     Mix (see recipe in this
     section)
⅛ teaspoon baking soda
¼ cup broken walnuts
¼ cup raisins
½ teaspoon cinnamon

Preheat oven to 400°F. and generously butter 6 cups of a muffin tin (2½-inch-size cups). In a mixing bowl, mash the banana with a fork. Add the egg, yogurt, and honey and mix well.

In another bowl, add all the remaining ingredients and mix thoroughly with a wooden spoon. Add the yogurt mixture to the dry ingredients and mix. Fill each muffin cup to the top and bake for 20 to 25 minutes, or until golden brown. Let cool in the pan for 5 minutes and then turn out onto a wire rack. Serve warm.

Oat-Blueberry Pancakes
Makes 30 small pancakes

1½ cups Basic Rolled Oat and
Wheat Germ Breakfast
Mix (see recipe in this
section)
1 cup milk
2 tablespoons butter, melted
1 egg, beaten
1 tablespoon mild honey
pinch of baking soda
¼ teaspoon cinnamon
¾ cup blueberries (if berries
are frozen, thaw enough
to soften slightly)

Place basic breakfast mix in a mixing bowl. In another bowl, combine the milk, melted butter, egg, honey, baking soda, and cinnamon. Add the liquid to the basic breakfast mix and stir. Then stir in the blueberries. Drop the batter from a large tablespoon onto a hot, lightly buttered griddle. Cook over medium heat until bubbles form on the surface of the pancakes. Turn with a spatula and cook on the other side. Serve at once with maple syrup.

Note: To freeze blueberries, wash the berries and lay them out on paper toweling to dry thoroughly. Place them in a single layer on a large cookie sheet and put the entire sheet in your freezer compartment. In a few hours, the berries will be totally frozen and will feel like small pellets. Pour them into heavy plastic bags and put the bags back in the freezer. Each time you need berries, just pour out the amount called for and put the bag back in the freezer. You'll appreciate your foresight in January and February!

Oat and Buttermilk Biscuits
Makes 12 biscuits

These tiny biscuits are a delicious mouthful. Since they're easily made with the basic breakfast mix, they can be whipped up for the family in less than half an hour.

1 cup Basic Rolled Oat and
Wheat Germ Breakfast
Mix (see recipe in this
section)
¼ cup buttermilk
1 tablespoon butter, melted

Preheat oven to 450°F. Place the basic breakfast mix in a large bowl. Then add the buttermilk gradually, mixing lightly with a fork and using just enough to make a soft, nonsticky dough. Turn out on a lightly floured board and knead about 6 to 8 times. Pat or roll out ½ inch thick and cut with a floured 1½-inch biscuit cutter or the edge of a glass. Roll each biscuit in melted butter and place close together on a baking pan. Bake for 12 to 15 minutes and serve warm with butter.

Oat, Fruit, and Nut Muffins

Makes 18 muffins

1¼ cups whole wheat flour
1½ cups rolled oats (whirled in a blender)
2 tablespoons wheat germ
1 tablespoon finely minced orange rind
½ cup coarsely chopped dates
½ cup chopped walnuts
2 unpeeled Delicious apples, shredded
1 teaspoon cinnamon
1¼ teaspoons baking soda
½ cup boiling water
¼ cup butter, melted
⅓ cup mild honey
1 egg, lightly beaten
1½ cups buttermilk
2 tablespoons orange juice

Preheat oven to 375°F. and butter 18 2½-inch muffin cups.

In a large bowl, combine the whole wheat flour, rolled oats, wheat germ, orange rind, dates, walnuts, apples, and the cinnamon. Mix well with a wooden spoon.

In a cup, mix the baking soda with the boiling water. Let it cool slightly. In another bowl, mix melted butter with the honey. Add the egg, buttermilk, and orange juice, and then the baking soda liquid. Slowly add the liquid ingredients to the dry ingredients, mixing well. Spoon the mixture into the muffin cups, filling them about three-quarters full. Bake for 35 minutes. When cool enough to touch, remove to a rack and cool completely.

Oat Waffles

Makes 6 waffles

2 eggs, separated
1¼ cups milk
3 tablespoons butter, melted
3 cups Basic Rolled Oat and Wheat Germ Breakfast Mix (see recipe in this section)

Preheat waffle iron. Beat egg yolks with milk and melted butter. Add the basic breakfast mix and stir only until the ingredients are moistened. Beat egg whites until stiff and fold into batter.

Lightly oil the waffle iron and spoon about 1 cup of batter onto the grids, or follow the manufacturer's directions accompanying your waffle iron. Bake until lightly browned. Serve with honey, fruit, or maple syrup.

Scottish Oat Bannocks
Makes 14 bannocks

1½ cups Basic Rolled Oat and Wheat Germ Breakfast Mix (see recipe in this section)
¼ teaspoon baking soda
1 egg, beaten
¾ cup milk
1 teaspoon mild honey

These are feather-light, yet hearty. You can prepare them the night before and, in the morning, cook them in just a few minutes.

Place basic breakfast mix in a bowl and add baking soda. Mix together. In another bowl, beat egg, milk, and honey together. Make a well in the center of the dry ingredients and add the liquid mixture. Beat until smooth. Let stand in the refrigerator overnight. The batter will thicken.

In the morning, heat a griddle over medium heat. Butter lightly and drop the batter by the tablespoonful without crowding, since the bannocks spread. Cook over low to medium heat until bubbles form on the surface. Then turn with a spatula and bake on the other side for 2 to 3 minutes. Serve warm with butter and honey or maple syrup.

Yorkshire Potato Oaties
Makes about 24 oaties

2 large Idaho baking potatoes, peeled and boiled
8 to 10 tablespoons oat flour (or rolled oats whirled in a blender until fine)
2 tablespoons milk
½ small onion, grated
4 tablespoons butter, melted
⅛ teaspoon nutmeg
¼ teaspoon cayenne pepper
additional melted butter for garnish

Mash potatoes and add all remaining ingredients to make a stiff dough. (Begin with 8 tablespoons of oat flour and if dough seems too damp, add the remaining 2 tablespoons.) Divide dough into 4 parts for easier handling. Press down with hands on a floured board until dough is ¼ inch thick. Cut parallel lines 3 inches apart and within those lines, cut triangles.

Repeat until all the dough is used. Lift carefully with a wide spatula, place on a lightly buttered griddle, and cook over medium heat. When the underside is dappled brown and somewhat dry, turn and brown the other side. Serve with melted butter trickled over each oatie.

Apple-Oat Spice Dessert
Serves 6

1 cup whole wheat pastry flour
1 cup rolled oats
6 tablespoons date sugar
⅛ teaspoon baking soda
6 tablespoons butter, cut into small pieces
3 or 4 red Delicious apples, peeled and very thinly sliced
1 teaspoon lemon juice
½ teaspoon finely minced lemon rind
½ teaspoon cinnamon
¼ teaspoon nutmeg
2 tablespoons butter, melted

Preheat oven to 350°F. Butter an 8-inch-square baking pan. In a large bowl, mix flour, oats, date sugar, and baking soda. Add the pieces of butter and mix until crumbly with a food processor or a pastry blender. Set aside.

In another bowl, combine apple slices with lemon juice, lemon rind, cinnamon, nutmeg, and half the melted butter. Divide the oat mixture in half and press it onto the bottom of the buttered baking pan with your fingertips. Add the apple mixture as a next layer and then add the remaining oat mixture, pressing down again. Drizzle the remaining melted butter over the top and bake for 35 to 40 minutes, or until top is golden and the apples seem tender.

When slightly cooled, cut into 6 large portions and serve topped with Scottish *Cranachan* (see recipe in this section), heavy cream, or sour cream.

Oat and Nut Orange Florentines
Makes 5 to 6 dozen cookies

1 cup rolled oats
4 tablespoons whole wheat pastry flour
pinch of baking soda
2 tablespoons finely minced orange rind
½ cup finely chopped walnuts
1 egg
¼ cup maple syrup
½ cup mild honey
1 teaspoon vanilla extract
½ cup butter, melted and cooled

Preheat the oven to 350°F. Generously butter 2 cookie sheets. Whirl the oats in a food processor or blender a few times and place them in a bowl. Add the flour, baking soda, orange rind, and nuts. Stir and set aside.

In another bowl, beat the egg. Add the maple syrup, honey, vanilla, and melted butter. Beat well and then add to the dry ingredients. Mix again. Drop by ½ teaspoonfuls onto the buttered cookie sheets, leaving about 2½ inches of space between each cookie. They will spread out while baking. Bake 5 to 8 minutes, or until edges of the florentines are golden brown. *Loosen all cookies at once with a spatula while they are still soft.* Then remove them carefully to a wire rack to cool completely.

Oat and Orange Cake with Orange-Nut Glaze

Serves 9

Cake:

- ⅔ cup boiling water
- ¾ cup rolled oats
- ¼ cup soft butter
- ½ cup date sugar
- 2 tablespoons mild honey
- 1 egg
- ¼ cup frozen orange juice concentrate, thawed but not diluted
- ½ teaspoon vanilla extract
- 1 cup whole wheat pastry flour
- ¼ cup oat flour
- ½ teaspoon baking powder
- ½ teaspoon baking soda
- ½ teaspoon cinnamon

Preheat oven to 350°F. and butter an 8-inch-square baking pan. In a small bowl, pour the boiling water over the rolled oats. Stir and set aside to cool.

Cream the butter and date sugar until fluffy. Add honey and egg and beat well. Add orange juice concentrate and vanilla and beat again. In another bowl, mix all the dry ingredients together.

Combine a third of the dry ingredients with half of the oats and beat well. Add the remaining dry ingredients and the rest of the oats and beat again. Turn the batter into the buttered pan and bake 35 to 40 minutes, or until cake tester comes out clean when inserted in the center of the cake. Cool in pan on rack.

Orange-Nut Glaze:

- 2 tablespoons butter
- ¼ cup maple syrup
- 1 tablespoon orange juice concentrate
- ½ cup flaked coconut
- ½ cup chopped walnuts

In a small saucepan, warm butter and maple syrup. Add the rest of the ingredients and cook, stirring, for 1 minute. Spread over top of cake and slip under broiler for about 2 minutes, watching carefully so glaze doesn't burn. When cake is cool, cut into 9 squares.

Scottish Cranachan (an Orange Oat Cream)

Yields 1½ cups

This toasted oat cream is usually served over fresh berries. It can also be used as a sauce for cakes and desserts. The original version calls for 2 tablespoons of Drambuie liqueur, but this adaptation is a delicious compromise.

¼ cup steel-cut oats, whirled in blender
1 cup heavy cream
1 tablespoon sour cream
2 tablespoons mild honey
2 tablespoons frozen orange juice concentrate, thawed but not diluted
1 teaspoon finely minced orange rind

Preheat oven to 350°F. Place the oats in a pie pan and toast in oven for 20 minutes, stirring often to prevent burning. When oats are slightly golden, remove them from the oven and set aside to cool.

Whip cream until it stands in soft peaks. Stir in all the remaining ingredients. Add the cooled, toasted oats to the cream.

Note: This is a country of rolled oats, and steel-cut oats may be more difficult to find. Look for Erewhon Brand or for McCann's Irish Steel-Cut Oats, which may be on your supermarket shelf.

Cashew-Apricot Granola

Yields about 6 cups

3 cups uncooked rolled oats
1 cup wheat flakes (rolled wheat)
½ cup wheat germ
½ cup bran
¾ cup chopped raw cashews
½ cup sunflower seeds
6 tablespoons flaked coconut
½ cup safflower oil or butter, melted
½ cup mild honey
1 cup coarsely diced apricots
½ cup raisins

Preheat oven to 300°F. In a large bowl, mix all the ingredients except the oil or melted butter, honey, apricots, and raisins. Gradually add the oil or butter and mix again. Then add the honey slowly and mix until evenly distributed. Spoon the granola mixture into a large, flat roasting pan and toast for 30 minutes. Stir occasionally. When the grains are toasted, crisp, and somewhat dry, remove the pan and let cool slightly. Before serving, add the diced apricots and raisins. (We find that heating the apricots and raisins along with the grains tends to dry them out, thus the addition after the baking process.)

When the granola is completely cool, store in a tightly covered container in the refrigerator.

Note: The basic granola mix without the fruit can be used in other recipes in this section.

Granolas _____

Maple Walnut Granola
Yields about 4½ cups

2 cups rolled oats
1 cup chopped walnuts
⅓ cup safflower oil
¼ cup maple syrup
½ teaspoon vanilla extract
1 cup chopped mixed dried
    fruits

Preheat oven to 300°F. Mix all ingredients except the dried fruits and spread them out in a roasting pan. Bake for 40 minutes, stirring several times to toast evenly. When cool, add the chopped mixed dried fruits. Serve with milk.

Note: For those with wheat allergies, use this granola as a base (without fruit) for other recipes in this section.

Applesauce Raisin Granola Cookies
Makes about 48 cookies, depending upon size

½ cup butter, melted
⅔ cup mild honey
1 cup applesauce
2 eggs, beaten
1 teaspoon vanilla extract
2¼ cups whole wheat pastry
    flour
1 teaspoon cinnamon
2 teaspoons baking powder
½ cup flaked coconut
    (optional)
½ cup raisins
2 cups Cashew-Apricot
    Granola, without fruit
    (see recipe in this section)

Preheat oven to 350°F. and butter several cookie sheets. In a medium-size bowl, mix butter, honey, applesauce, eggs, and vanilla until smooth. In another bowl, mix flour, cinnamon, and baking powder. Add the coconut (if desired), raisins, and granola to the dry ingredients, stir, and then add to the liquid ingredients. Beat well.

Drop batter by the tablespoonful onto the prepared cookie sheets and flatten each cookie with the back of the spoon. (They do not spread.) Bake for 15 to 20 minutes. Remove at once with a spatula to wire racks for cooling.

Apple-Prune Granola Betty
Serves 6

4 or 5 red Delicious apples
¼ teaspoon lemon juice
1 teaspoon grated lemon rind
1½ teaspoons cinnamon
3 tablespoons mild honey
8 pitted prunes, cut in pieces
1 cup Cashew-Apricot
Granola, without fruit
(see recipe in this section)
4 tablespoons butter, melted

Preheat oven to 350°F. and butter an oven-to-table flat casserole. Peel and slice the apples thinly to the core and place them in a medium-size bowl. Sprinkle with lemon juice and toss. Add lemon rind, cinnamon, honey, and prunes. Mix well and spread evenly in prepared casserole. Sprinkle granola over apples and drizzle melted butter over the top. Bake for 40 minutes, or until apples are soft (test with the point of a sharp knife). Serve warm with cream, or if you're dieting, top with yogurt.

Apricot-Granola Miniature Muffins
Makes 12 muffins

Kids seem to love these tiny bite-size muffins with an apricot surprise on the bottom.

12 apricot halves, soaked in
water for 10 minutes
½ cup Cashew-Apricot
Granola, without fruit
(see recipe in this section)
¼ cup boiling water
1 tablespoon butter
2 tablespoons mild honey
1 egg
2 tablespoons milk
1 teaspoon vanilla extract
1 teaspoon grated orange rind
¾ cup whole wheat pastry
flour
1½ teaspoons baking powder

Preheat oven to 350°F. and butter a miniature 1¾-inch muffin tin (or line it with paper cups). Place 1 apricot half in the bottom of each cup. Place granola in a small bowl, add boiling water, and let stand.

Heat butter and honey together until butter is melted and set aside to cool slightly.

In another bowl, beat egg, milk, and vanilla together and then beat in the honey-butter mixture. Add the orange rind.

Mix the flour and baking powder together. Add the moistened granola to the liquid ingredients, then add the flour. Do not overbeat. Fill each cup to the brim and bake for 10 to 15 minutes. Let cool for 10 minutes in the pan on a wire rack before removing.

Frozen Granola Bananas
Serves 6

½ cup plain yogurt
2 tablespoons mild honey
3 firm bananas
½ cup Cashew-Apricot Granola, with fruit (see recipe in this section)

Mix the yogurt and honey in a small bowl. Peel and cut each banana in half lengthwise and then in half crosswise. Line a cookie sheet with waxed paper. Dip each piece of banana in the yogurt mixture and coat evenly. Lay the coated bananas on the waxed-papered cookie sheet and place in freezer for 1 hour.

When the yogurt coating is firm, remove the tray of bananas and dip each one in the yogurt mixture once again. Place the granola on waxed paper and roll the bananas in the mixture to coat them evenly. Return them to cookie sheet (still covered with waxed paper) and return to freezer. Freeze again for 15 to 20 minutes. Defrost about 5 minutes before serving.

Granola, Cheese, and Carrot Balls
Makes 20 balls

Try this healthful hors d'oeuvre or snack.

½ cup shredded sharp cheddar cheese
1 3-ounce package soft cream cheese
1 medium-size carrot, finely shredded (about 1 cup)
½ cup Cashew-Apricot Granola, without fruit (see recipe in this section), whirled fine in a blender
3 tablespoons finely minced parsley

In a food processor, beat both cheeses together until well blended. Add the shredded carrot and mix to blend. Cover and chill mixture in refrigerator for 30 minutes.

Then, using a teaspoon to scoop the cheese, form into tiny balls about 1 inch in diameter. (The mixture will be fairly soft.) Roll each ball first in granola and then in parsley. Press coating with fingers so it will adhere. Chill before serving.

Granola Pie Shell
Makes 1 pie shell

1½ cups Cashew-Apricot
    Granola, without fruit
    (see recipe in this section)
¼ cup soft butter, cut into
    pieces

Whirl granola in a food processor. Add butter and mix again. Press into a 9-inch pie pan. Bake in a 350°F. oven for 5 to 10 minutes. Cool and fill with puddings, cheese, fruits, or other fillings. Use in place of graham cracker crusts for more nutrition and better flavor.

Pineapple Granola Stuffed Acorn Squash
Serves 6

3 acorn squash, split and
    seeded
½ cup Cashew-Apricot
    Granola, with fruit (see
    recipe in this section)
1½ cups crushed pineapple
1 tablespoon minced orange
    rind
½ teaspoon mace
2 tablespoons mild honey
2 tablespoons butter

Place squash in a baking pan with 1 inch of hot water on bottom. Preheat oven to 350°F. Mix granola, pineapple, orange rind, and mace together and distribute evenly in cavity of squash. Trickle honey over top and dot with butter. Bake for 1 hour, or until tender.

Variations:
1. Stuff large apples with granola before baking.
2. Top rice pudding or fresh stewed apple with granola and bake for 10 minutes before serving.

Homemade Swiss Oat Muesli

Yields 4½ cups

Swiss *muesli* is soaked or "wet" oat-based cereal with apples, nuts, and other grains. It originated in Switzerland and is, perhaps, the forerunner to the more recent "granola revolution."

Prepare this recipe the night before (or at least 3 hours ahead) so that the flavors will blend sufficiently. The mixture should be thick.

1½ cups rolled oats

2 cups low-fat milk plus
   2 tablespoons nonfat
   dry milk

1 cup dried apples, cut into
   small pieces, or 4 whole,
   fresh red apples, grated

1 tablespoon lemon juice

2 teaspoons vanilla extract

½ teaspoon cinnamon

⅛ teaspoon nutmeg

⅓ cup frozen apple juice
   concentrate

½ cup coarsely chopped
   pitted prunes (about 8 or
   9), or ½ cup raisins

¼ cup toasted slivered
   almonds

¼ cup wheat germ

½ cup sunflower seeds
   (optional)

2 tablespoons mild honey
   (optional)

Mix all ingredients together except the nuts, wheat germ, and sunflower seeds. Soak overnight in the refrigerator. In the morning, add the remaining ingredients and mix. Eat as is or with extra milk and honey.

Note: *Muesli* can be kept in the refrigerator for several days. We usually double the recipe and use the basic mix for a pudding or cookies.

Muesli *Cookies*

Makes 36 cookies

2 cups leftover Homemade Swiss Oat *Muesli,* including almonds and wheat germ (see recipe in this section)
1 egg, beaten
2 tablespoons shredded orange rind
¼ cup date sugar (only if honey is not used in basic mix)
¾ cup whole wheat pastry flour

Mix all ingredients together. Preheat oven to 350°F. and butter several cookie sheets. Drop heaping teaspoonfuls of the mixture 2 inches apart. Flatten with fork and bake for 10 to 15 minutes.

Muesli *Pudding*

Serves 6

2 cups leftover Homemade Swiss Oat *Muesli* (see recipe in this section)
2 eggs, separated
½ cup date sugar (optional)
1 cup milk
1 tablespoon shredded orange rind
1 teaspoon vanilla extract
1 tablespoon butter

Garnish:

wheat germ
almonds

Preheat oven to 350°F. Mix *muesli* with beaten egg yolks, date sugar, milk, and orange rind. Add vanilla. Beat whites of eggs and fold into pudding. Spoon mixture into buttered 8-inch-square heat-proof dish. Dot with butter and sprinkle with the wheat germ and almonds. Bake for 35 to 40 minutes or until firm. Serve warm with or without whipped cream.

Rice: "The Bread of Asia"

If we think back on the trips we've taken, the films we've shot all over the world, there is a universal memory that stays with us when we think of rice. Calf-deep in the flooded fields, row upon row of people bend to plant rice seedlings, the rhythm of their movements timed to the beat of a drum or the cadence of a repetitive chant. Always in a warm, wet climate, the rows of plants are deftly plunged into the earth below the water—and we can imagine them vividly. We see the women of the Po Valley in Italy, skirts pulled up around their waists as they move; the terraced fields in the Philippines, and the paddies of Thailand, dotted with the planters wearing wide-brimmed, braided hats to keep the sun from their heads. At least, that was the prevalent image until we produced a film that took us to the rice fields of Central California!

The paddies are very much the same, the flooded fields making a wet bed for the seeds that will soon be sown. On a nearby field, a biplane stands, its engine running as two sturdy young men lift a tube to the nose of the plane, and rice seed is pumped quickly into the chutes and down into the body of the aircraft. It takes but a few seconds, and then the plane roars off the dirt strip and wobbles into the air, heading for the rice fields a few miles away. At the end of the field to be seeded stands a young woman, waving a flag to guide the pilot. He starts the run down the flooded field, seeds flowing from the belly of the plane in a cloud of tiny brown spots that will float into their beds, soon to grow and to be harvested by machine.

We stood on the embankment with the farmer, Mr. Sopwith, in awe at the speed with which it was all done. On the third pass of the biplane, Mr. Sopwith turned to us and commented, "I understand that in Asia they do all this by hand!" Indeed they do, and modern technology has cut 400 man-days per acre down to less than 2 man-days to plant, fertilize, and harvest the fields of rice. And though we grow less than 1 percent of the world crop, we export nearly 10 billion pounds a year—75 percent of the entire rice crop that we grow!

However, though most of the world exists on rice as a staple (thus, "the bread of Asia"), the *form* (milled and polished) in which it is eaten makes it less than adequate as a prime source of nutrition. It is a cultural thing, very much like the idea fostered by the Roman patricians that refined wheat flour was superior to the coarse whole grain used by the slaves and peasants for making bread. In Japan and China, the unmilled form of rice (brown rice) is considered "the poor people's rice." During World War II, when the starving Japanese were given rations of nutrition-rich brown rice, they immediately went home and put the grain through their own homemade milling machines in order to remove the bran and the embryo buds to turn the rice into their beloved polished variety.

We presumed that the Asians' love for rice meant that at least the educated part of the population understood what happens when you mill the nutrition out of it. No wonder we were both amused and horrified to read that the government of China is now trying to convince the working population to use *instant* rice and other convenience foods. Less time in the kitchen would mean more time on the factory assembly line. America, unfortunately, is not much better. With 7,000 varieties from which to choose, we eat only two: 99 percent of our consumption of rice is white or long grain, milled and polished; only 1 percent of our consumption is unmilled (brown) rice!

Brown Rice or White Rice?

The twentieth-century milling machines only duplicate what has long been taking place all over the world in transforming brown rice to white. We just do it more efficiently. The rice kernel is stripped of the husk, the bran, and the germ, leaving only the endosperm and practically no nutrition. Though the ancient methods of pounding rice managed to keep most of the nutrients intact, our methods remove most of the iron, almost all of the fiber, the B vitamins, half the vitamin E, 10 percent of the protein,

70 percent of the other minerals, and more! Yet Americans prefer to buy and to eat "enriched" rice, "instant" rice, polished rice.

Some people object to brown rice because they find that it is chewier, has a nuttier flavor, and is stickier than white rice. We, on the other hand, find its flavor and consistency a plus. Just as we think it unfair to compare "tissue-paper" packaged white bread with homemade whole grain loaves, so do we think it unwarranted to judge white rice against the unmilled brown rice. American consumers have sided with the food processors and packagers (again).

Our advice is "do not compare." Become more aware (if you have not already switched to whole grains), and follow our method and our recipes. We think you'll discover with us a new taste sensation with brown rice, and you'll probably never go back to the nutritionally inferior white rice again. We speak from experience, for both of us are converts, and we have even begun to use brown rice in our Chinese cooking, something that not even our Asian friends do. You might even begin to throw brown rice at weddings!

The Forms and Varieties of Rice

Long Grain Brown Rice: Light and fluffy texture. Good in pilafs, salads, and poultry stuffings.

Short Grain and Medium Grain Brown Rice: Tender and moist. These shorter grains have a better cohesive quality, and therefore they work best for croquettes, rice balls, pancakes, and puddings.

Sweet Glutenous Brown Rice: Good in puddings and desserts. The grains are plumper and paler than the other varieties. If sweet rice is not available where you live, short grain rice may be substituted.

Brown Rice Flour: A fine-milled flour from which part of the bran and hull have been removed. Brown rice flour can be used for breads, cakes, muffins, noodles, pancakes, and biscuits. When used alone, without the addition of whole wheat flour, it is excellent for people who need gluten-free diets. However, baked goods will be somewhat more moist and more dense when rice flour is used alone. It can also be used as a thickening agent for sauces.

Brown Rice Cream: A coarsely ground rice. It can be prepared at home in a blender or a spice grinder. It is also available premilled and prepackaged. It can be used for breakfast cereals and puddings.

Brown Rice Flakes: Heated and pressed flat under pressure. The manufacturing process is similar to that of rolled oats. It's fine for quick-cooked, hot, morning breakfast cereal in place

of oatmeal, and it can be used for textural interest in breads and other baked goods.

Puffed Brown Rice: Puffed under pressure and then expanded by filling the grains with air. It is an excellent cold breakfast cereal when served with milk and fresh fruit. If you need to eat less, if you're overweight, puffed brown rice automatically reduces your intake while allowing you to get excellent nutrition. Puffed rice can also be used to make candy and other snacks.

Rice Bran: The outside layer of the rice kernel. It contains the hull, the bran, and a small part of

Basic Nonsticky Long Grain Brown Rice

Yields 8 cups

How to cook a perfect batch of basic brown rice every time.

2   cups long grain brown rice
5   cups water
1   tablespoon butter

Pick over rice, removing any foreign matter. In a 5-quart, wide-bottom, SilverStone-lined pot with a tight-fitting lid, bring water to a boil. Add butter and allow it to melt. Slowly add rice. Bring to a boil again, lower heat, cover pot tightly, and simmer, covered, for 45 minutes. Then turn off heat. Fluff rice with a fork and cover pot again. Let stand, covered, for 10 minutes more.

Note: Cooked rice can be refrigerated for 1 week and used as needed. It can also be frozen for up to 6 months. Frozen rice should be thawed completely before reheating. To reheat refrigerated and thawed rice, add 2 tablespoons liquid for each 1 cup of rice and simmer in a SilverStone-lined, covered pot for 5 minutes.

Short grain brown rice, prepared exactly the same way, yields 7 cups cooked rice.

There is little difference between short and medium grain brown rice. We find them interchangeable. However, there are so many strains and varieties of rice that they may cook up differently. Learn to adjust cooking techniques to the brand or kind of rice you generally buy.

the germ. It's also high in dietary fiber, and it can be used as an excellent extender with ground meat.

Rice Polish: The flour taken off the rice during the process of making white rice. It retains a part of the germ and the bran, and it also has a high content of vitamins, iron, and fiber. It can be used in all your baked goods in the same manner as wheat germ.

Converted Rice: Sometimes called "parboiled" rice. It is steamed and pressurized before being milled into white rice, moving some of the nutrients into the kernel of the grain. After the milling process, converted rice contains more of the original nutrient values than white rice. So in a pinch, if you must buy white rice, or if you can't readily find brown rice, look for the indication that the rice is "converted."

Precooked White Rice: Partially cooked after milling. It is then dehydrated so that with a small amount of water and very little cooking it will be reconstituted quickly.

Wild Pecan Rice: Gently milled to retain most of its bran. The taste is evocative of roasted pecans, adding an interesting dimension to curries and stuffings for game and poultry. This unique grain was developed by Louisiana State University and is produced by the oldest rice mill in the United States, down in New Iberia, Louisiana. It is available in limited quantities at selected stores across the country and by mail order (see Mail-Order Sources).

Wild Rice: Not really a variety of rice, but a rare aquatic grass. It is, indeed, wild, and it grows and is harvested in the Great Lakes region. We devote a separate chapter to wild rice and its preparation.

Basic Brown Rice Cream

Serves 6

A delicious and easily digested hot cereal for infants, invalids, and people with wheat allergies.

1 cup brown rice cream
4 cups cold water or milk

Place rice cream in a SilverStone-lined pot over medium heat. Stir and toast for 1 to 2 minutes. Slowly add cold water, stirring constantly with a wire whisk to prevent lumping, bring to a boil, lower heat, cover pot, and simmer, stirring occasionally for 4 to 5 minutes, or until cereal is thick and creamy.

Variations:
1. Serve with milk or cream, a dab of butter, and a sprinkling of cinnamon.
2. Mix with ½ cup plumped raisins and ½ teaspoon cinnamon and spoon into an 8-inch-square pan. Chill, cut into squares, and cook in butter until brown on each side. Serve with maple syrup.

Note: If you cannot find prepackaged rice cream, it can be made by toasting 1 cup of the whole grain at 350°F. for 10 to 15 minutes in the oven and then grinding in an electric spice mill or coffee grinder.

Steamed Rice Rolls Stuffed with Shrimp and Scallions
Makes 6 rolls

2 cups water

1 cup sweet glutenous brown rice

½ pound shrimp, shelled and deveined

2 tablespoons tamari soy sauce

2 scallions, green part only

½ teaspoon grated ginger root
few grains of cayenne pepper

⅛ teaspoon Chinese 5 Spices, optional (available in Oriental food supply stores)

Bring water to a boil in a SilverStone-lined pot. Slowly add rice and stir. Bring to a boil again, cover, lower heat, and simmer for 30 minutes. Remove from heat and let stand, covered, for 10 minutes. Then remove cover and cool enough so that you can handle the rice without burning your hands.

Meanwhile, tear off 6 12-inch squares of aluminum foil and set aside. While rice is cooking, place shelled, cleaned raw shrimp in tamari to marinate, turning once after 15 minutes. Then discard tamari.

Using a blender or food processor, chop the scallions and shrimp together until they form a pasty consistency. Add remaining spices to shrimp mixture. Then wet hands and scoop up equal amounts of rice to distribute into 6 portions, placing the rice to one side of each piece of foil. Wet a teaspoon and press the back of the spoon on each mound of rice, making an indentation. With wet hands, enclose rice (which should be sticky) to cover filling, pressing with fingers to make a sausage shape, about 4 inches long and 1½ inches thick. Then roll up the foil. Twist ends of foil tightly to seal. Place in a large pot of boiling water to cover and cook for 40 minutes. Water should cover rolls at all times, so add more if necessary.

Then lift packets out with tongs to drain on paper towels. Cool for 30 minutes, then open and slice with a wet knife into ¾-inch-thick slices. You may use tamari as a dipping sauce if you like. You can also prepare in advance, refrigerate, and reheat in foil in boiling water for 10 minutes.

Note: Sweet glutenous brown rice is used here since it is a sticky rice and holds its shape well.

Saffron Rice Mold with Chicken, Dried Fruit, Walnuts, and Yogurt   For this recipe, see page 145

Baked Orange Rice Custard with Dates and Honey   For this recipe, see page 157

Suppli al Telefono—*Rice and Cheese Croquettes*
Makes 12 croquettes

This recipe originates in Rome. When the croquettes are pulled apart, the cheese forms strings which resemble telephone wires—hence the name.

3 cups cooked short grain brown rice
2 eggs, beaten
½ small onion, grated
⅛ teaspoon black pepper
12 slices mozzarella cheese, cut into 2-inch-long strips about ½ inch thick
¾ cup whole grain dry bread crumbs
6 tablespoons olive oil
6 tablespoons peanut oil

Mix rice, eggs, onion, and pepper together in a bowl. Take 1 tablespoon of the rice mixture and flatten it in the palm of your hand. Lay a strip of cheese in center and place another tablespoon of rice on top. Roll into a log shape between the palms of your hands, enclosing the cheese. Then roll in bread crumbs. Chill for 30 minutes on waxed paper.

Heat both oils together until hot and fry 2 or 3 rolls at a time until brown on all sides. Drain on paper towels and serve at once.

Priest's Soup—*A Rice and Red Lentil Soup*
Serves 6 to 8

This thick soup dates back to Biblical times and is sometimes called Esau's Potage. The Armenians call it *Vartabed Abour* or Priest's Soup, since the legend of Esau was told so often by the priests.

6 cups Chicken Stock (see Index)
1 cup small red lentils, picked over of foreign matter
¼ cup long grain brown rice
3 medium-size onions, sliced and separated into rings
2 tablespoons finely minced parsley with stems
¼ teaspoon Allepo pepper, or a combination of sweet paprika and cayenne pepper
¼ cup olive oil or butter extra paprika for garnish

Heat 4 cups of chicken stock and add lentils and rice. Bring to a boil, then lower heat, cover pot, and simmer for 10 minutes. Add only 2 of the onions, stir, and cook over low heat for 20 minutes more. Stir in the remaining chicken stock, parsley, and pepper and continue cooking 10 minutes more.

While soup is cooking, heat oil or butter in a heavy skillet and add the remaining onion. Saute until brown and crisp. Lift out with slotted spoon and drain on paper towels. Sprinkle over soup before serving and add a few grains of additional sweet paprika for color, if desired.

Main Dishes

Chicken and Rice Salad
with Marinated Mushrooms
Serves 6

Mushrooms and Dressing:

¼ cup lemon juice
½ teaspoon grated lemon rind
½ cup olive oil
¼ teaspoon black pepper
¼ cup finely minced scallions
2 tablespoons finely minced tarragon
¼ pound mushrooms, thinly sliced

Mix together lemon juice, lemon rind, olive oil, pepper, scallions, and tarragon and pour over mushrooms. Let stand at room temperature for 1 hour while preparing the salad.

Salad:

3 cups cooked long grain brown rice
2 cups diced cooked chicken
3 medium-size tomatoes, cubed
½ cup cooked green peas
2 tablespoons finely diced green peppers
¼ cup finely minced parsley for garnish

Toss all salad ingredients together, except the parsley. Pour mushrooms and dressing over all and toss again. Sprinkle with parsley before serving.

Chinese Chicken Fried Rice with Scallion Pancakes
Serves 6

Scallion Pancakes (prepare first):

- 1 tablespoon peanut oil
- 2 eggs, well beaten
- 1 tablespoon tamari soy sauce
- 2 tablespoons finely sliced scallions
- 2 drops Oriental sesame oil

Chicken Fried Rice:

- 4 tablespoons peanut oil
- 1 cup finely sliced scallions
- 1 cup frozen green peas, or lightly steamed green beans
- 1 cup coarsely chopped water chestnuts, rinsed and dried
- 1 cup mung bean sprouts
- 1 cup diced cooked chicken (cooked pork, cooked beef, or uncooked shrimp may be used)
- 3 tablespoons tamari soy sauce
- 1 tablespoon Chinese rice wine
- 2 or 3 drops hot pepper sauce
- 4 cups cold, cooked long grain brown rice
- 2 cups sliced almonds, toasted
- 1 tablespoon finely minced cilantro (Chinese parsley), or parsley

The rice must be prepared one day in advance and chilled overnight so that the grains do not stick together. Chilling on a cookie sheet in one layer does the trick.

Heat half the peanut oil in a 12-inch skillet. Combine eggs, tamari, scallions, and sesame oil, mix well, and pour half the mixture into the heated skillet. Quickly rotate the pan until a paper-thin layer is formed covering the bottom and part of the sides of the pan. Cook until edges are slightly brown and surface is slightly dry. Grasp edge of pancake gently and flip to other side. Cook for a few seconds, then invert on waxed paper, and repeat with remaining batter. Then roll each pancake and cut into ½-inch shreds. Set aside and prepare rice.

In a wok or large, heavy skillet, heat 2 tablespoons of the peanut oil until very hot. Add scallions, peas or beans, water chestnuts, and sprouts and stir and cook for 30 seconds. Add the chicken and toss for 1 minute. Mix the tamari, rice wine, and hot pepper sauce together and stir into the chicken mixture. Then spoon into a bowl and set aside.

Wipe out wok and heat remaining 2 tablespoons peanut oil until very hot. Add rice and stir fry until rice is hot (about 2 to 3 minutes). Stir in the chicken and vegetables and stir-fry for a few seconds more until heated through. Turn out onto a warmed serving platter. Sprinkle with toasted almonds, reserved scallion-pancake shreds, and cilantro or parsley.

Main Dishes_____

Ground Beef, Rice, and Yellow Split Pea Balls with Lemon and Mint

Makes 12 balls

¼ cup short grain brown rice
4 tablespoons dried yellow split peas
2 cups water
1½ pounds ground beef
6 scallions, finely minced (about ¾ cup)
2 tablespoons grated onions
2 tablespoons finely minced parsley
2 tablespoons finely minced dillweed
¼ teaspoon black pepper
¼ teaspoon turmeric
1 teaspoon Syrian Mixed Spices (see Index), or 1 teaspoon allspice
1 egg, beaten
2 tablespoons butter
1 large onion, thinly sliced
1 cup Chicken Stock (see Index)
2 tablespoons tomato paste
juice of ½ lemon
2 sprigs mint

Garnish:

lemon slices
sprigs of mint

Bring rice, split peas, and water to a boil, lower heat, cover pot, and simmer for 35 minutes, or until rice is partially cooked. Set aside and let cool slightly.

In a large mixing bowl, mix ground beef with scallions, onions, parsley, dillweed, pepper, turmeric, Syrian Mixed Spices or allspice, and egg and set aside. In a large skillet, melt butter and saute onion until golden. Add the chicken stock. Mix together tomato paste and lemon juice and then add to skillet. Bring to a boil, add sprigs of mint, lower heat, and simmer, covered, for 5 minutes. To the beef mixture, add the rice and split peas. Wet hands and form this mixture into 12 large apple-size balls. Carefully place into skillet. Cover and simmer for 10 minutes. Remove cover and baste balls with pan juices. Continue to cook for 20 minutes, basting occasionally, and then remove balls with a slotted spoon to a serving dish. Remove mint and bring sauce to a boil. Cook for 1 minute, stirring constantly. Pour over meatballs, garnish with slices of lemon and mint, and serve.

Saffron Rice Mold
with Chicken, Dried Fruit,
Walnuts, and Yogurt

Serves 6

This Persian rice mold, perfumed with saffron and studded with fruit and nuts, is the perfect choice for a party buffet.

¼ cup currants
6 pitted prunes
12 pitted dates
6 dried apricots
6 dried peaches
1 cup boiling water
¼ cup coarsely chopped walnuts, toasted
3 cups cooked short grain brown rice
8 tablespoons butter, melted
¼ teaspoon saffron steeped in 1 tablespoon hot water
½ cup plain yogurt
1 teaspoon grated lemon rind
1½ teaspoons Syrian Mixed Spices (see Index) or 1 teaspoon allspice
2 cups diced cooked chicken breasts (about 1½ breasts)

Preheat oven to 400°F. Put the dried fruits in a bowl and pour boiling water over all. Let steep for 10 minutes. Then pour off water and reserve. Cut all the fruit into small pieces and set aside.

In a separate bowl, mix the walnuts with only 2 cups of the cooked rice and set aside. In another bowl, combine the remaining cup of rice, 6 tablespoons of the melted butter, the saffron, and yogurt. Mix well and spoon onto bottom of a metal mold about 7 × 3 inches, such as a charlotte mold. Pack down with the back of a spoon. Add grated lemon rind and Syrian Mixed Spices or allspice to the rice and walnut mixture and spoon a layer of this on top of the yogurt-saffron rice. Place half the dried fruit and half the diced chicken over this in 2 layers. Spoon 1 tablespoon of the reserved fruit liquid and 1 tablespoon of the reserved melted butter over all. Repeat until all is used up. Pack down firmly. Cover top with foil and bake on bottom shelf of oven for 40 minutes. When ready to serve, place mold in cold water for a few minutes and then invert and unmold onto a serving dish. The top should be golden and crusty.

New Orleans "Dirty" Brown Rice with Chicken Giblets
Serves 6

2	tablespoons butter
1	tablespoon peanut oil
1	medium-size onion, finely chopped (about ⅔ cup)
1¼	cup ground chicken gizzards, with some hearts and liver included (about ¾ pound)
1	cup long grain brown rice
2¼	cups Chicken Stock (see Index)
2	tablespoons finely minced scallions, green part only
2	tablespoons finely minced parsley
1	clove garlic, finely minced
⅛	teaspoon black pepper
	pinch of allspice

Preheat oven to 350°F. Heat the butter and oil over medium-high heat in a large oven-to-table heat-proof casserole. Add the onion and saute for 4 to 5 minutes, stirring until lightly browned. Add the giblets and stir and cook for a few minutes until the pink color is gone. Stir in the rice and cook, while stirring, for 2 minutes and then add the chicken stock. Bring to a boil and stir in all the remaining ingredients. Cover casserole with lid or foil and transfer to oven. Bake for 40 minutes. Remove and let stand for 10 minutes until all liquid is absorbed. Fluff with a fork before serving.

Brown and Green Rice with Snow Peas
Serves 6

1	cup parsley
4	large shallots, peeled
2½	cups water
1	cup long grain brown rice
2	tablespoons butter
1	tablespoon tamari soy sauce
1	10-ounce package frozen tiny peas, thawed
	pinch of cayenne pepper
12	fresh Chinese snow-pea pods

Chop the parsley very fine and set aside. Mince the shallots and combine with water, rice, and butter in a saucepan. Place over medium heat, bring to a boil, stir once, and then cover and simmer for 25 minutes, or until most of the liquid is absorbed. Remove from heat and add the parsley, tamari, peas, and cayenne. Fluff with a fork, cover pot, and simmer for 5 minutes more. Remove from heat and let stand for 10 minutes. Mound rice on a platter and place snow peas around the edges like the spokes of a wheel.

Baked Rice and
Herb Stuffed Tomatoes
Serves 6

6   medium-size tomatoes
1   cup cooked short grain
    brown rice
1   clove garlic, finely minced
2   tablespoons finely minced
    parsley
1   teaspoon finely minced
    oregano, or ½ teaspoon
    dried oregano
2   teaspoons finely minced
    basil
4   tablespoons olive oil
¼   teaspoon black pepper
    curly parsley sprigs for
    garnish

Cut a thin slice from the top of each tomato and reserve. Core the center, scoop out pulp and juice, chop coarsely, and place in a medium-size bowl. Add rice, garlic, parsley, oregano, basil, 2 tablespoons of the olive oil, and the black pepper and mix well.

Preheat oven to 400°F. and place tomato cups in a medium-size oven-to-table baking pan so that they almost touch (this prevents them from falling over). Spoon filling into each tomato cup. Top with reserved top slice, drizzle olive oil over tomatoes in the pan, and bake for 25 minutes. Serve at room temperature with pan juices spooned over each tomato. Garnish each with a sprig of curly parsley.

Brown Rice and
Onion Puree au Gratin
Serves 6

5   tablespoons butter
2   large sweet Bermuda
    onions, chopped (about
    1½ pounds)
¾   cup short grain brown rice
3   cups Chicken Stock (see
    Index) or water
⅛   teaspoon cayenne pepper
⅓   cup light cream
½   cup shredded Gruyere
    cheese

In a large skillet, melt 4 tablespoons of the butter and slowly saute onions until soft and golden. Stir occasionally.

While onions are cooking, cook the rice in the chicken stock or water for 25 to 30 minutes, or until very tender. Then puree rice in a food processor or blender. When onions are cooked, puree in a food processor or blender and then combine with the pureed rice.

Add cayenne, cream, and remaining 1 tablespoon of butter. Spoon into a heavy au gratin oven-to-table dish, sprinkle top with cheese, and slip under broiler until cheese is melted and flecked with brown.

Black Beans and Brown Rice with Three Kinds of Peppers
Serves 6

1	cup sweet red peppers, seeded and cut into strips
1	cup light green sweet frying peppers, seeded and cut into strips
1	small fresh hot pepper, seeded and finely minced
2	cloves garlic, finely minced
2 or 3	scallions, thinly sliced (about ¾ cup)
1	tablespoon oregano leaves
1	teaspoon thyme leaves
1	bay leaf, crushed
2	cups cooked black beans (rinsed with cold water and drained)
¼	cup red wine vinegar and lemon juice mixed together
½	cup olive oil
3	cups hot, cooked long grain brown rice
¼	cup finely minced parsley

Place red and green peppers into a strainer and then set into a bowl. Pour boiling water over peppers and let steep for 30 seconds. Lift peppers out and rinse in cold water. Dry on paper towels and place in a large bowl.

Add all the remaining ingredients except the hot rice and parsley and mix together. Let marinate at room temperature for 1 hour. Then add the hot cooked rice (which can be prepared while peppers are marinating) and half of the parsley and mix together. Sprinkle remaining parsley on surface for garnish. Serve at room temperature or heat in oven at 375°F. for 10 minutes.

Celery-Orange Brown Rice
Serves 6

3	tablespoons butter
1	cup diced celery with leaves
¼	cup minced scallions
2	tablespoons minced parsley
1½	cups water
	grated rind of 1 orange
1	cup orange juice
1	cup long grain brown rice
¼	teaspoon black pepper

This rice dish is particularly good with duck and pork; also works well with chicken.

Melt butter in a heavy skillet. Add celery and scallions and saute for 5 minutes. Stir in parsley. Add water, orange rind, and juice and bring to a boil. Slowly stir in rice, cover and reduce heat and cook for 40 minutes. Remove from heat and let stand for 5 minutes. Sprinkle with pepper and fluff with a fork before serving.

Brown Rice and Mixed Vegetable Casserole with Cheese and Hot Chili Pepper
Serves 6

3 cups cooked long grain brown rice (cooked in chicken stock)
1 small carrot, shredded
⅓ cup sliced scallions
1 tablespoon tamari soy sauce
1 or 2 jalapeno peppers, seeded and whirled in a blender with 2 tablespoons water, or ¼ teaspoon red pepper flakes
¼ teaspoon ground cumin
3 cups bite-size pieces cauliflower
2 cups bite-size pieces broccoli
½ cup sliced celery
2 medium-size zucchini, sliced ½ inch thick
1 cup mushrooms, cut in quarters
12 whole cherry tomatoes lemon juice
5 slices Monterey Jack cheese, cut diagonally
5 slices cheddar cheese, cut diagonally
2 tablespoons pine nuts toasted in a tiny bit of butter

Preheat oven to 350°F. and butter a large, shallow casserole. Place cooked rice in a bowl and toss with carrot, scallions, tamari, hot pepper liquid, and cumin. Then layer rice mixture on bottom of casserole.

Place the cauliflower, broccoli, celery, and zucchini in a steamer and steam for 5 to 6 minutes. Add the mushrooms to the steamer and steam for 1 minute more. Attractively arrange these vegetables over the rice and tuck in the whole tomatoes. Sprinkle vegetables with lemon juice. Arrange the cheese on top, alternating the triangular slices of Jack cheese and the cheddar cheese in an overlapping pattern. Bake, uncovered, for 10 to 15 minutes or until cheese is bubbly and melted and vegetables and rice are hot. Sprinkle with toasted pine nuts and serve at once.

Green Lentil and Brown Rice Salad with Red Onion and Parsley
Serves 6

1   cup dried green lentils
1   cup hot, cooked long grain brown rice
¾   cup finely minced red sweet onion
1   clove garlic, finely minced
½   teaspoon ground cumin
¼   teaspoon black pepper
1   teaspoon grated lemon rind
¼   cup finely minced parsley
5   tablespoons lemon juice
6   tablespoons olive oil

Garnish:

tomato wedges
curly parsley

Soak dried lentils in enough cold water to cover for 1 hour. Drain and pick over. Cook in 4 cups boiling water for 10 minutes, or until they are tender but still retain their shape. Drain. (There should be 2 cups of cooked lentils.) Add to hot cooked rice and toss with a fork.

Add all remaining ingredients and toss again. Let stand for 1 hour at room temperature. Mound up on a serving dish and ring with tomato wedges and curly parsley when ready to serve. Do not serve ice cold; the flavors will be lost.

Walnut and Brown Rice Timbales
Serves 6

4   cups hot, cooked short grain brown rice
¾   cup grated walnuts
4   tablespoons butter
⅛   teaspoon grated nutmeg
safflower oil for greasing custard cups

Mix hot rice with grated walnuts. Heat butter in a small skillet until browned, but do not allow to burn. Pour over rice and nut mixture. Sprinkle mixture with nutmeg and press tightly into 6 individual custard cups that have been well oiled. When ready to serve, unmold to make 6 mounds. If you wish to prepare ahead of time, rice cups can be covered with foil and heated in oven for 10 minutes before unmolding.

Note: Walnuts should be fluffy, and this is best accomplished with a Mouli grater. Nuts can also be grated in a blender but will not be as light in texture.

Swiss Chard Stuffed with Brown Rice, Ricotta Cheese, and Almonds
Makes 12 pieces

These bright green packets enclose a lemony rice and cheese stuffing and are crunchy with chopped almonds. This dish can be prepared in advance and baked before serving.

12	large Swiss chard leaves
3	tablespoons butter
¼	cup chopped almonds
2	tablespoons peanut oil
2	medium-size onions, finely chopped
1	cup short grain brown rice
2	cups Chicken Stock (see Index)
1	tablespoon finely minced celery leaves or lovage
1	tablespoon finely minced basil
¼	cup finely minced parsley
¼	teaspoon black pepper
⅛	teaspoon nutmeg
3	tablespoons lemon juice
1	teaspoon grated lemon rind
1	pound ricotta cheese
2	tablespoons butter
¼	cup grated Parmesan cheese
½	cup water

Garnish:

paprika
lemon wedges

Fold Swiss chard leaves in half and, with a sharp knife, cut out the rib about halfway into each leaf. Reserve the ribs. Place leaves in the sink and gently run hot water over them to wilt. Lay paper towels on counter and carefully layer leaves between them to dry. Slice part of the ribs finely (about 2 cups), reserving remaining ribs for another use.

Melt the butter in a large skillet and add the almonds. Stir and toast until they start to color and then remove and set aside. Add the oil to the same skillet and saute the onions for 2 minutes. Then add the sliced chard stems and cook for 5 minutes more. Add the rice and stir to coat. Then add the chicken stock and bring to a boil. Lower heat, cover skillet, and cook for 30 minutes.

Remove from heat, stir in the celery leaves or lovage, basil, and parsley, and let cool. When cool, stir in the pepper, nutmeg, lemon juice, lemon rind, ricotta cheese, and almonds.

Preheat oven to 350°F. and butter a large oven-to-table casserole that can accommodate the rolls. To prepare rolls, remove 1 leaf at a time and overlap the cut end. Place ⅓ cup of the filling on this end. Fold over once, and then fold in sides. Continue to roll until stuffing is enclosed, and lay seam side down in prepared casserole. Repeat until 12 rolls are prepared. Then dot each with butter and sprinkle with Parmesan cheese. Add the ½ cup of water in bottom of pan. Cover with foil and bake for 20 to 25 minutes. Sprinkle paprika on lemon wedges for a touch of color and distribute wedges between rolls. Serve 1 or 2 per person, depending upon appetite and whether it is served as a main course or a side dish.

Risottos and Pilafs

It is no exaggeration to say that, given a cup of rice and whatever can be found in the kitchen cupboard or refrigerator—and using the basic recipes and techniques for *risotto* or pilaf—we can produce a lavish meal indeed, far more lavish than the sum of its humble parts.

Risotto is a unique method or technique of cooking rice Italian style. A true *risotto* is not just rice boiled in chicken stock. On the contrary, risottos are always creamy in texture and always prepared with short grain rice. Traditionally, the Northern Italian cooks who have always considered *risottos* "the pasta of Northern Italy" use a short grain rice grown in the Po Valley called *arborio* rice.

We find that short grain brown rice is most acceptable for the *risotto* method of cooking, and there is the added plus of a lovely nuttiness that brown rice offers.

Although many things can be added to the rice—seafood, chicken livers, vegetables, dried mushrooms, herbs, cheese, and, in Italy, even paper-thin slices of fresh white truffles—all classic *risottos* are produced by using one basic method of cooking the rice.

The principle of this method is to have the rice absorb the stock a bit at a time until the grains swell and a creamy tender union is formed between the rice and stock. The quantity of stock is approximate, since more or less may be needed to achieve the desired result. The idea is to add only a bit at a time, stir and allow the liquid to be absorbed. This is not a dish you can leave unattended on the stove; it must be watched very carefully to achieve a creamy rice texture with grains that are tender but firm, or *al dente,* to the tooth. Short grain brown rice may require additional liquid and cooking time; therefore, the amount of liquid is approximate since the brown rice grains themselves vary a bit in shape and size according to the variety available in your area.

Pilaf, pilaff, pulao, pellao—only a few of the many ways of spelling the name of this rice dish known throughout India and the Middle East. Pilafs, unlike *risottos,* are always prepared with long grain rice, and the cooking methods differ completely from *risotto.* The long grain raw rice is tossed and toasted in butter until it is completely coated and just begins to color. Then boiling stock is added, the pot covered tightly, and the rice steamed either on top of the stove or in the oven until all the liquid is absorbed. This allows the grains to become separate and fluffy, but still retain their texture.

What follows here are basic methods for a classic *risotto* and a simple pilaf with suggested additions and variations to create an endless repertoire of rice recipes.

Basic Risotto with Parmesan Cheese and Parsley
Serves 6

¼ teaspoon saffron, crushed into ½ cup water and steeped for 10 minutes

8 to 10 cups simmering Chicken Stock (see Index), or 5 cups stock and the rest boiling water

6 tablespoons butter

½ cup finely minced onions (1 large onion)

1½ cups short grain brown rice

½ cup grated Parmesan cheese

¼ teaspoon black pepper

2 tablespoons finely minced parsley

Prepare saffron. Place half the simmering stock and the saffron in a large saucepan. Melt 4 tablespoons butter slowly and when it begins to bubble, add the onions, stirring until they just begin to turn color, or are wilted. Add the rice and stir with a wooden spoon until grains are well coated. Stir in a soup ladle full of simmering chicken-saffron stock and cook, stirring occasionally, for 5 minutes, or until liquid is absorbed. Cover pot and simmer for 5 to 10 minutes. Then add another ladle full of stock (about ⅔ cup at a time), using as much of the remaining chicken stock as necessary. Bite-test a grain. If it is tender but firm, and the rice is creamy, not soupy, it is done.

Stir in the remaining 2 tablespoons butter, Parmesan cheese, and the pepper. Sprinkle with parsley and stir once. Serve immediately.

Note: *Arborio* rice takes less time and liquid to cook. Brown rice takes about 1 hour and 15 minutes cooking time to reach the desired creamy doneness and approximately 10 cups of liquid. *Arborio* cooks in about 35 minutes with 6 cups of liquid for the same amount of rice.

Variations:

1. *Risi e Bisi—Risotto* and Peas: Add 1½ cups fresh green peas, or 1 10-ounce package of frozen peas during the last 15 minutes of the cooking time.

2. *Risotto con Funghi Secchi—Risotto* with Dried Italian Mushrooms: Soak 1 ounce dried Italian mushrooms in lukewarm water for 30 minutes. Strain liquid in a strainer lined with piece of paper towel in case the liquid is gritty. Rinse softened mushrooms well and cut into small pieces. Add the mushroom liquid to the cooking stock and stir in the softened mushrooms after 15 minutes of cooking time.

3. *Risotto* with Asparagus Tips: Slice 1 pound of asparagus diagonally and discard tough ends. Boil for 5 minutes. (Use cooking liquid as part of stock when cooking risotto.) Add the asparagus for last 5 minutes of cooking.

4. *Risotto Primavera:*   Instead of ½ cup of minced onions, replace with 6 to 8 shallots, if you like. Add ¼ cup finely minced basil; ¼ cup finely minced parsley; ¼ pound cooked string beans, cut diagonally into 1-inch pieces; 1 tomato, skinned and cubed; and 1 small zucchini, steamed and cut into strips. Stir in the above for the last few minutes of cooking.

5. *Risotto Verde:*   Add 1½ cups shredded raw spinach and 1 tablespoon toasted pine nuts for the last 5 minutes of cooking.

6. *Risotto* with Shrimp: Add 2 cloves minced garlic when onion is added. Cook 1 pound shrimp in 1 cup of

[*Continued on next page*]

water for 5 minutes. Use liquid mixed with stock for cooking rice. Shell shrimp, devein, and cut each in half. Toss with rice before serving. Do not add cheese.

7. *Risotto con Pomodoro—Risotto* with Tomato: Use half tomato juice and half stock to cook rice and sprinkle with 1 tablespoon finely minced basil.

Leftover *Risotto?*

1. Beat 2 eggs and mix with 1½ to 2 cups leftover *risotto*. Melt 3 tablespoons butter in an omelette pan. Flatten into a "cake" with a spatula and cook over low heat for 10 minutes. Loosen bottom with spatula, allowing some butter to drip down sides of pan and under cake. Invert on dish, slide back into pan, and cook until reverse side is golden.
2. Or—mix with 1 egg, form into cakes, and deep fry as for croquettes.

Basic Long Grain Rice Pilaf
Serves 6

6	tablespoons butter
1	medium-size onion, finely minced
1	clove garlic, finely minced
1½	cups long grain brown rice
3 to 4	cups Chicken Stock (see Index)
¼	teaspoon black pepper (optional)

Melt butter in a heavy saucepan, *not* lined with SilverStone this time. Add onion and garlic and saute over medium heat for 1 minute, stirring until translucent. Stir in rice and cook, while stirring, until grains are coated with butter (about 2 to 3 minutes). Add the stock and bring to a boil over high heat. Cover tightly with foil and reduce heat as low as possible. Cook for 40 minutes. Don't peek until time is up, then remove cover, and fluff rice with a fork. For a drier pilaf, partially cover rice with foil again and allow rice to steam over low heat or flame tamer until serving time.

If a golden crust forms on the bottom, that's fine. In the Middle East, no pilaf is served without this crust. To serve, fluff rice again and turn out onto a hot serving platter. Scrape off bottom crust and use to garnish rice.

Note: Pilaf can also be baked in the oven. After stock boils, cover rice, and bake in a 375°F. preheated oven for 30 minutes. Remove cover, fluff with a fork, cover loosely, and return to oven, with heat off, until serving time.

Variations:
1. Turkish Pilaf: Add ½ cup of the very thinnest pasta broken into small pieces and 1 tablespoon pine nuts to the raw rice, and coat with butter. Proceed with the recipe.

2. Indian Pilaf: Add ¼ cup dried currants before adding stock. Sprinkle with 2 tablespoons toasted cashews or almonds and 1 tablespoon grated orange rind.
3. Pilaf with an Herb Bouquet: Tie with a string for easy removal: 1 bay leaf, 2 sprigs each of parsley and thyme. Add to rice when stock is added and remove when serving.
4. Prune and Lemon Pilaf: Grate lemon rind and squeeze juice of 1 large lemon. Then add both to stock. Tuck 10 pitted prunes into rice when stock is added.
5. Cumin and Pepper Pilaf: Add 1 cup finely diced red and green sweet peppers to onion and saute. Then add ½ teaspoon ground cumin to chicken stock before adding to rice mixture.
6. Saffron Pilaf: Add ½ teaspoon crushed saffron to chicken stock before adding to rice. When cooked, garnish with a sprinkling of 1 tablespoon minced parsley.
7. *Mejedrah*—Brown Rice and Lentil Pilaf with Fried Onions and Yogurt: Soak ½ cup green lentils overnight. Cook for 10 minutes in stock or water until they're tender, but still retain their shape. Drain and toss with pilaf. Top with 3 large onions, sliced and fried crisp in 2 tablespoons olive oil or chicken fat. Pass yogurt in a bowl at the table.

Almost any single chopped fresh herb, about 1½ tablespoons, can be added to the basic pilaf recipe—dill, basil, mint, parsley, tarragon. Simply stir it into the hot rice before serving.

Try dried spices as well, about 1 teaspoon stirred into the pilaf—cumin, curry, anise, cinnamon, allspice.

Any leftover pilaf can be used to stuff vegetables (tomatoes, zucchini, peppers) or poultry.

Rice Ring with Mushrooms, Cashews, and Chicken Liver
Serves 6

6   tablespoons butter
⅔   cup finely minced scallions
½   pound mushrooms, very
      finely chopped
1   2-ounce chicken liver
⅛   teaspoon black pepper
1   teaspoon finely minced sage
½   cup chopped cashews
1   cup short grain brown rice
2   cups Chicken Stock (see
      Index) or water
¼   cup finely minced parsley

Fill the center of this ring with minted green peas and you will have the perfect complement to broiled chicken.

Melt 4 tablespoons of the butter in a heavy skillet and add the scallions and mushrooms. Stir for 1 minute and push to one side of the skillet. Add the chicken liver and cook, turning, for 2 to 3 minutes, or until firm and the pink color is lost. Remove liver with a slotted spoon to cool, and turn off heat under skillet. Cut liver into very small pieces and add to the skillet with the mushrooms. Stir in pepper and sage and set aside.

In a SilverStone-lined pot, melt the remaining 2 tablespoons of butter and add the cashews. Stir and cook for 1 to 2 minutes, or until nuts just begin to turn color. Add the rice and chicken stock or water and bring to a boil. Stir in mushroom mixture, lower heat, cover pot, and simmer for 30 minutes, or until most of the liquid is absorbed.

Preheat oven to 350°F. and generously butter a 9½-inch ring mold. Sprinkle bottom of mold with parsley and spoon mushroom-rice mixture into ring. Bake for 30 minutes more, or until rice is tender and liquid is absorbed. Let cool for 10 minutes in pan on a wire rack. Then loosen and unmold onto serving plate.

Spinach and Rice Salad with Blue Cheese Dressing
Serves 6

½   cup cottage cheèse
1   ounce blue cheese, crumbled
3   tablespoons milk
2   tablespoons apple cider vinegar
¼   teaspoon black pepper
1   tablespoon finely minced scallions
10   ounces spinach leaves, shredded

1½   cups long grain cooked brown rice
6   large mushrooms, very thinly sliced
½   cup thinly sliced red onions
      (cut slices in half)
2   hard-cooked eggs, cut into quarters,
      for garnish

This salad can be served as a meal or as an accompaniment to broiled fish or chicken.

To prepare dressing, combine cheeses, milk, cider vinegar, pepper, and scallions. Refrigerate for at least 1 hour to allow flavors to develop.

In a large bowl, combine spinach, rice, mushrooms, and onions. Add dressing and toss until well coated. Pile into a glass bowl and decorate with egg wedges.

Baked Orange Rice Custard with Dates and Honey
Serves 6

2 tablespoons soft butter
1 cup cooked short grain brown rice
1 cup pitted dates, cut in half
1 navel orange, peeled and sliced paper thin, about 8 or 9 disks
⅓ cup plus 2 tablespoons mild honey
3 cups milk
1 tablespoon grated orange rind
½ teaspoon vanilla extract
3 eggs, beaten
⅛ teaspoon cinnamon, optional

Preheat oven to 325°F. and butter a 6-cup baking dish (a souffle dish does nicely). Dot the bottom of the dish with the remaining butter. Set dish in a larger pan and have a kettle of boiling water ready.

Spread cooked rice evenly on bottom of baking dish and then arrange the dates in a layer to cover the rice. Layer the orange slices over dates. Trickle 2 tablespoons of honey over the orange slices and set aside while preparing the custard.

Scald milk slowly in a SilverStone-lined pot until a skin forms on the milk. Add the remaining ⅓ cup honey, the orange rind, and vanilla extract to the milk and let cool for 15 minutes. When cool, whisk the beaten eggs into the milk and pour over rice and fruits. (The orange slices will float to the top.) Place in oven, pour ½ inch of boiling water into bottom pan, and bake for 1½ hours, or until center is firm. Sprinkle surface with cinnamon, if desired, and serve warm or cold.

Ginger Peach Creamy Rice Pudding
Serves 6

2 quarts milk
⅔ cup sweet glutenous brown rice
1 teaspoon grated ginger root
⅓ cup mild honey
6 peaches, peeled and sliced (about 3 cups)
⅛ teaspoon ground cardamom
¼ teaspoon cinnamon
1 teaspoon vanilla extract

Bring milk to a boil. (Use a 5-quart SilverStone-lined pot for easy cleanup.) Slowly add the rice, stirring constantly. When milk boils again, lower heat and cover pot. Simmer for 30 minutes. Then remove pot lid and simmer for an additional 45 minutes, stirring occasionally with a wire whisk. Add ginger root, honey, peaches, cardamom, cinnamon, and vanilla. Stir and simmer for 15 minutes more. Serve warm or cold in a large glass bowl.

Brown Rice Cream
with Cottage Cheese
and Candied Lemon Slices
Serves 6 to 8

This is a moist, thin, cakelike dessert—very light and delicate, with a lemony sweet taste.

4 tablespoons soft butter
½ cup mild honey
3 eggs, separated
1½ cups creamed large curd cottage cheese
3 tablespoons lemon juice
⅓ cup Basic Brown Rice Cream (see recipe in this section)
½ cup raisins
pinch of cream of tartar

Preheat oven to 350°F. and butter an 8-inch springform pan. Using a food processor, cream the butter, then add the honey and process until combined. Add the egg yolks and combine well.

Place the cottage cheese in a large bowl and add the lemon juice. Stir in the rice cream and raisins. Then add the butter-honey-egg mixture, half at a time. (The cheese should remain in curds.)

Beat the egg whites in another bowl with the cream of tartar until stiff. Fold into the cheese mixture. Spoon into the prepared pan and bake for 40 minutes. Cool on a wire rack for 15 minutes, then top with Candied Lemon Slices. Loosen from the sides of the pan by running a knife around the edge. Place on serving dish and remove side of springform. Serve directly from base of springform pan while slightly warm.

Candied Lemon Slices:

3 tablespoons mild honey
3 tablespoons water
8 paper-thin center slices of lemon, seeds removed

Mix honey and water in a skillet and bring to a boil. Lower heat to simmer and place lemon slices in 1 layer in skillet. Simmer for 5 minutes, carefully turn slices, and simmer for 5 minutes more, or until lemon slices are transparent and syrup is almost evaporated. Let stand for 5 minutes before placing on top of dessert.

Orange Pecan Rice
"Sweet Nothings"
Makes 24 muffins

     2 tablespoons butter
    ½ cup mild honey
     1 egg
     1 cup buttermilk
     1 teaspoon vanilla extract
     1 cup plus 2 tablespoons
            brown rice flour
    ½ teaspoon baking soda
     2 teaspoons baking powder
     1 tablespoon rice bran
     2 tablespoons rice polish
     1 tablespoon finely minced
            orange rind
    ¼ cup finely chopped pecans
    24 pecan halves

Preheat oven to 400°F. Have ready nonstick, small-cup (1¾-inch diameter) muffin tins. Melt butter with honey and cool. Set aside.

Beat egg with a whisk until lemon color and light. Then whisk in buttermilk and vanilla and set aside.

Sift together rice flour, baking soda, baking powder, rice bran, and rice polish and combine with wet ingredients. Stir in orange rind and chopped pecans. Put a scant tablespoon of batter into each cup, top with a pecan half, and bake for 12 to 15 minutes. Cool in pan for 10 minutes and then remove muffins to wire rack.

Rye: Comin' through the . . .

Rye is another of those remarkable grains that started its career as a lowly weed, only to become a "star" of the European bread world. It is, possibly, the hardiest of grains, since it can thrive in poorer soils, colder climates, and wetter conditions than any other cultivated grain. It was first discovered in Turkey and ancient Greece, pushing its way into the fields of cultivated grains with stubbornness and persistence. The European wheat farmers in the Middle Ages finally harvested the grains together and ground them into a flour called "maslin." It soon became the choice of cooks and bakers all over the continent. Rye had arrived!

Because of its tolerance of colder climates, it is grown and used all over Eastern Europe and Russia, in the Scandinavian countries, and in Germany in much greater quantities than here in the United States. European visitors to these shores find the bread that we call "rye" quite unlike the hearty, crusted, heavy loaf made from unsifted flour in their own countries. We, in turn, really taste rye bread for the first time as it should be baked when we travel east to Europe. Pumpernickel bread in Germany, for example, is dark and thick and quite heavy in texture, unlike our supermarket, caramel-colored, chemically treated bread carrying the same name. Consequently, when we get a yen for pumpernickel we bake our own.

We like to use rye in our bread baking because of its strong, distinctive flavor. It is high in protein but low in gluten, so we suggest that if you do use it in your own baking, you measure about 30 percent rye flour to 70 percent wheat flour in order to strengthen the gluten content and help the breads to rise.

The Forms of Rye

Whole Rye Berries or Groats: They can be sprouted for use in salads, soups, or breads, or they can be ground in a mill and then used as a cereal or for baking. Keep in mind, though, that rye berries are comparatively soft, and they may clog a stone mill. However, if you have steel blades in your mill, they'll work quite well, and the rye berries can be ground easily.

Rye Flakes or Rolled Rye: Groats that are pressed or rolled between high-pressure rollers, very much like rolled oats. Can be cooked and eaten as a morning breakfast, or soaked and used to top breads as a nutritious decoration.

Rye Meal: A pumpernickel-type rye, whole ground to the consistency of cornmeal. Blend it with other flours in your baking.

Rye Flour: Whole ground into a finer consistency than rye meal (pumpernickel flour). You will probably find rye flour sold as white, medium (the most common), or dark. It makes excellent bread, sourdough rolls, and crackers, but it should be blended with wheat flours because of its low gluten content.

Rye Grits: Whole rye cracked into six or eight separate pieces, free of flour. They are used as a cereal or can be mixed with other grains or finer ground meal for bread. They are not easily obtained in certain parts of the country, but can be ordered by mail (see Mail-Order Sources).

Basic Whole Rye Berries or Groats

Yields 2¼ cups

1 cup whole rye groats
2½ cups water

Pick over dry grain, removing any foreign matter. Rinse in cold water, drain, and soak overnight in 2 cups of water. When ready to cook, drain soaking water and measure. Add enough fresh water to make 2½ cups. Bring water to boil and add groats. Bring to a boil again, stir, lower heat, cover pot, and simmer for 45 minutes. Let stand, covered, with a piece of paper towel under pot lid to absorb moisture.

Basic Rye Flakes

Yields about 3 cups

1 teaspoon butter, or corn oil
1 cup rye flakes
3 cups boiling water

Melt butter or heat oil in a skillet and add rye flakes. Toast, while stirring, until flakes are light tan and begin to smell nutty and aromatic. Set aside.

Boil water and slowly add the toasted flakes, stirring constantly without disturbing the boil. Lower heat and cover pot. Simmer for about 15 minutes, or until liquid is almost absorbed. Let stand for 5 minutes.

As a breakfast cereal, serve with warmed milk, nuts, seeds, and raisins.

Hungarian Rye and Cabbage Boards

Makes 24 6 × 2-inch pieces

½ small head cabbage (about 1 pound)
1 medium-size onion
2 tablespoons butter
2 teaspoons mild honey
¼ teaspoon paprika
¼ teaspoon black pepper
1 cup rye flour
¾ cup unbleached white flour
1 teaspoon baking powder
6 teaspoons soft butter, cut into pieces
2 tablespoons sour cream
1 egg yolk
1 whole egg
1 teaspoon water

Shred cabbage and onion very fine in a food processor (or by hand). Melt butter in a large skillet and stir in honey. Add the cabbage-onion mixture and simmer, uncovered, until browned (about 25 to 30 minutes), stirring occasionally. Add the paprika and pepper and cool in the refrigerator for 15 to 20 minutes.

Sift and mix the flours together with the baking powder. Add the butter and process in a food processor (or cut butter into flour mixture with a pastry blender) until it resembles crumbly coarse cornmeal. Then turn out into a large bowl.

Mix the sour cream and egg yolk together and beat with a wooden spoon for a few strokes. Then add the sour cream-egg yolk mixture and the cooled cabbage mixture to the flour mixture. With floured hands and work surface, knead dough for 5 minutes. (More flour may be necessary but dough should be slightly damp and soft.) Wrap and chill in the refrigerator for 1 hour. Then preheat oven to 375°F. and butter 2 or 3 baking sheets.

Divide dough into 4 pieces for easier handling. Chill the ones not being worked on. Flour a piece of waxed paper and a rolling pin and roll dough ¼ inch thick. Cut into 6 × 2-inch pieces. Carefully peel off paper and place on baking sheet. Repeat until all dough is used up.

Mix egg and water together and brush this glaze on the surface of each board. Bake for about 15 minutes, or until golden. Cool slightly on a wire rack. The boards should be flexible and eaten warm.

Cabbage, Beet, and
Tomato Borscht with Rye Groats

Serves 6 to 8

1¼	pounds short ribs of beef, bone in, cut into 1½- to 2-inch pieces.
2	large onions, coarsely chopped (about 1¼ cups)
3	cloves garlic, coarsely chopped
1	2-pound head green cabbage, coarsely chopped (about 12 cups)
¼	teaspoon paprika
¼	teaspoon black pepper
2	cups cooked tomatoes
2	cups tomato juice
8	cups water
½	cup rye groats, picked over and washed
½	pound beets, peeled and sliced (about 1 cup)
1	bay leaf, crumbled
1	teaspoon oregano, or ½ teaspoon dried oregano
⅛	teaspoon ground cloves
⅓	cup lemon juice (about 2 lemons)
3 to 4	tablespoons mild honey

In a large, heavy pot, sear meat on all sides over medium-high heat. Remove pieces of meat with a slotted spoon and set aside. In the same pot, add onions and garlic. Saute, while stirring, for 5 minutes and then add the cabbage. Stir and cook for 5 minutes more and then add the paprika and pepper.

Return the meat to the pot and add all the remaining ingredients, except the cloves, lemon juice, and honey. Bring to a boil, then lower heat and simmer, with lid slightly ajar, for 2 hours. Mix the cloves, lemon juice, and honey together and stir into the soup just before serving.

Rye Sprouts, Mushrooms, and Raw Cabbage Salad
Serves 6

Dressing:

¼ cup safflower oil
1 tablespoon tarragon vinegar
  juice of ½ lemon
1 tablespoon tamari soy sauce
1 teaspoon Dijon-style
  mustard
¼ teaspoon paprika
¼ teaspoon black pepper
2 tablespoons finely
  chopped pimiento

Prepare dressing first. Combine all ingredients and whisk together. Let stand for 30 minutes to develop flavors.

Salad:

2 cups rye sprouts (whole rye
  groats, sprouted)
¼ pound mushrooms, thinly
  sliced
2 cups finely shredded green
  cabbage
1 cup finely shredded red
  cabbage
½ green pepper, seeded and
  cut into thin strips
2 scallions, cut diagonally into
  ¼-inch pieces

Toss all salad ingredients together in a glass bowl and chill. When ready to serve, toss again with dressing.

Cumin Seed Rye Crisps
Makes about 36 crisps

1½ cups rye flour
½ cup unbleached white flour
1 teaspoon baking powder
2 teaspoons whole cumin seeds
1 teaspoon brewer's yeast (optional)
½ cup corn oil
½ cup milk

Mix together both flours, baking powder, cumin seeds, and brewer's yeast, if desired. Make a well in the center. Combine oil and milk in a cup and add slowly in the center, stirring to add the flour toward the liquid center. Then flour hands, gather dough into a ball, and knead until smooth (5 or 6 times). Wrap and chill dough for 20 minutes.

Preheat oven to 375°F. and butter 2 baking sheets. Flour a work surface and rolling pin and roll the dough, half at a time, about ¼ inch thick. Cut into 2 × 3-inch pieces and place on prepared baking sheet. Prick all over with a fork and bake for about 20 minutes, or until just golden. Cool on wire rack and then store in an airtight container.

Double Rye and Caraway Seed Dinner Muffins
Makes 12 muffins

1½ cups rye flour
⅔ cup gluten flour
¼ cup toasted rye flakes
1 tablespoon baking powder
⅛ teaspoon pepper
2 teaspoons caraway seeds
1½ cups potato water
1 egg, beaten
1 tablespoon mild honey
2 tablespoons butter, melted, or corn oil

Preheat oven to 375°F. Combine rye flour, gluten flour, rye flakes, baking powder, pepper, and caraway seeds in a large bowl and set aside. In another bowl, mix remaining ingredients together. Add liquid ingredients to dry ingredients and stir just until moist. Spoon batter into greased muffin tins, bake for about 20 to 25 minutes, and serve at once.

Finnish Hardtack—
Rye Flatbread Wheels
Makes 2 flatbreads

In Finland, these flat, hard, crunchy crisp breads are traditionally strung on a broom handle and hung to dry until all the moisture is gone. Then pieces are broken off and used to make open-face sandwiches.

1 package dry yeast
   (¼ ounce)
1 cup warm water
2½ cups sifted rye flour

Dissolve yeast in water and let stand for 10 minutes. Place sifted flour in a large mixing bowl and make a well in the center. Add the liquid (yeast and water) and with a small rubber spatula or a fork, begin to incorporate the flour into the liquid until a ball of dough forms. Thoroughly flour your hands and a surface for kneading, since dough is sticky. Knead for a few minutes until elastic. Oil a bowl and add the dough, turning it so that the entire surface is coated with oil. Cover bowl and let dough rise for 1 hour in a warm place.

Divide dough into 2 pieces. Roll each on a floured surface into an 8½-inch circle, ½ inch thick. Preheat oven to 450°F. and butter and flour a baking sheet. Cut a 2-inch circle from centers of each larger circle. Prick wheels with a fork in a pattern. Drape over rolling pin and transfer to prepared cookie sheets. Let rest for 15 minutes or more and then bake for 10 to 15 minutes.

Remove by sliding off cookie sheet onto a wire rack. (They will still be pliable when removed.) Turn off heat and return to oven on wire racks. Leave for several hours, or overnight, to dry properly. Or do as the Finns do; if you live in an area with not too much humidity, string on a broom handle and hang for a few days until dry and crisp. Store in an airtight container.

We have written quite a lot about the nutritional value of whole grains, but the remarkable thing about these underutilized foods is that *they taste good, too!*

We began to believe that our pet birds were singing so well because of the good-tasting millet we'd been feeding them. We are now convinced that one reason America's cattle look so content is that they eat the sorghum America's people ignore. We baked the Milo Currant Cake and sat down for the ultimate test of all recipes: the tasting. The first bite told us the verdict, and we looked at each other and smiled. The *taste* of sorghum is superb.

The sorghum family is an amazing species, extremely resistant to drought, grown where the climate is too hot and dry for wheat or rice. Thus, it has become the most important grain for over 300 million people who live in the developing countries of Africa, East Asia, and India. In the areas of China and Japan that are too dry to grow rice, sorghum has become the staple grain, with much of it being grown for wine in sections of the Chinese mainland. Recently, the crisis of drought in northeastern Brazil has made the government aware that the poor farmers of the area would be better off planting drought-resistant sorghum in their desiccated cornfields. The yield from those fields would more than double as a result.

Grain sorghum (milo) is now a part of our pantry stock. Though the ancient recipes are for simple foods like pancakes or porridge or basic puddings, ours are more unusual, but easy to make, and very, very tasty.

Some Savory Secrets of Sorghum (Milo)

The Forms of Grain Sorghum

Milo Flour: Grain sorghum (milo) flour is now easily obtainable by mail order from Walnut Acres (see Mail-Order Sources).

Whole Grains: Since everyone agrees that sorghum is nutritionally good and that it tastes just marvelous, we thought that there would be countless commercial suppliers anxious to display the grain in the local natural foods stores. Actually, as of this writing, the only way to obtain the whole grain is to live near a rural feed store, where you can purchase the milo type of sorghum in bulk. If you do buy it, however, make sure that the grains you purchase have not been treated with pesticides.

Breads

Milo Herb and Cheese Loaves
Makes 6 miniature loaves

2   cups milo flour
2   cups buttermilk
2   eggs
1   teaspoon baking soda
1   teaspoon dried *fines herbes*
        (blend of tarragon,
        thyme, chives, chervil,
        and parsley)
6   tablespoons grated
        Parmesan cheese
2   tablespoons minced chives

Preheat oven to 450°F. and oil 6 mini loaf pans. In a saucepan, cook milo and buttermilk over low heat for 5 to 10 minutes, or until very thick. Remove from heat and let cool.

Beat eggs in a bowl and then add the cooked milo. Sprinkle baking soda over milo and eggs and mix well. Add all remaining ingredients and mix until well combined. Pour into prepared pans and bake for about 30 minutes, or until cake tester inserted in center comes out clean. Let cool for 10 minutes before removing from pans. Serve a half loaf or a full loaf per person.

Milo Muffins with Mixed Dried Fruit and Nuts
Makes 12 large muffins

2   cups milo flour
2   cups buttermilk
2   eggs
1   teaspoon baking soda
2   tablespoons mild honey
½   teaspoon vanilla extract
1   cup coarsely chopped
        mixed dried fruit
½   cup finely chopped pecans

Preheat oven to 450°F. and oil a 12-cup muffin tin. In a saucepan, cook milo and buttermilk over low heat until thick (about 5 to 7 minutes). Set aside and let cool.

Beat eggs in a mixing bowl and add cooled milo. Sprinkle the baking soda over eggs and milo and blend well. Add remaining ingredients and mix well. Pour into prepared cups and bake for about 20 minutes, or until cake tester inserted in center comes out clean. Let cool for 10 minutes before removing from cups.

Sorghum **Roti** *with Poppy Seeds* *and Toasted Onions*

A quick flat bread baked on a griddle.

Makes 18 *rotis*

2⅓ cups water
2 cups sorghum (milo) flour
¼ cup poppy seed
¼ cup instant toasted onions
pinch of cayenne pepper

Bring water to a boil in a SilverStone-lined pot and sift flour over water, stirring constantly. Cook for a few minutes until very stiff.

When cool to the touch, turn out onto a floured surface and press dough into a rough circle with floured hands. Sprinkle with poppy seeds, onions, and cayenne and then knead for about 3 to 4 minutes to make a ball of dough. With hands, roll into a thick cylinder about 2½ inches in diameter. Cover and let rest for 15 minutes. When ready to bake, cut cylinder into 18 even pieces and roll each piece into a ball between the palms of your hands. Cover the rest while working. Roll each ball out about ¼ inch thick.

Heat a nonstick-surface griddle and cook 3 or 4 rotis at a time over medium-high heat. Press each one down with a spatula for a few seconds and turn several times back and forth to prevent burning. They should rise slowly, forming 2 separate layers inside. The steam forms in the center, causing them to puff up slightly and bake through. They are baked when mottled with brown specks and puffy in center. Keep warm in foil and when all are ready, serve hot with butter or cheese. Fold in half to eat.

_____ **Dessert**

Milo Currant Cake

Makes 1 8-inch cake

2 cups buttermilk
2 cups milo flour (sorghum)
2 eggs
½ cup date sugar
½ teaspoon cinnamon
¼ teaspoon nutmeg
1 teaspoon vanilla extract
1 teaspoon baking soda
1 cup currants
18 pecan halves

Preheat oven to 350°F. and generously butter an 8-inch springform pan. Combine buttermilk and milo flour in a medium-size saucepan and cook over medium heat for 5 to 7 minutes or until thick. Remove milo mixture from heat and let cool.

In a small bowl, lightly beat eggs and add to cooled milo. Add all the remaining ingredients except currants and pecan halves, and mix well. Pour half of the mixture into prepared springform pan. Sprinkle all the currants evenly over mixture. Spoon remaining mixture evenly over currants. Arrange pecan halves in a circular pattern on the top and bake for 30 minutes. (Cake is done when cake tester inserted in center comes out clean.)

Remove from oven and place on wire rack. While hot, run a sharp knife around the edges of the cake to separate from pan sides. Remove springform sides and let cool. Can be served warm or at room temperature.

Tricks for Triticale Treats

We count ourselves as old friends of triticale (pronounced trit-i-*kay*-lee), and our relationship with the unusual and tasty grain dates back to the time when Mel was researching his book *Bread Winners.* Not only did it introduce us to a new, protein-rich grain in our bread baking, but it also brought us into contact with new friends like triticale-growers Ron Kershen and Bernard Hartman down in Canyon, Texas, and with Frank Ford of Arrowhead Mills, all of whom were enthusiastic and encouraging in our early experiments. We have come a long way since that time, and the more we cook with the grain, the more enamored we become, both with its "ryelike" or "nutlike" flavor and with its nutritional characteristics.

The name triticale comes from the Latin terms *triticum* for wheat and *secale* for rye—and it is exactly that, a combination of both grains, but with a much higher protein content and a better balance of essential amino acids than either one. If the combination of rye and wheat should occur in nature, the resultant strain would be a hybrid, sterile, and thus incapable of reproducing itself. However, this problem was overcome as early as the 1930s, making triticale a true man-made grain.

Its acceptance was moderately slow at first—but when have we ever accepted a new food with any degree of speed? Even today, we have to pronounce the name at least twice for friends of ours who read about triticale in our books. However, in the past few years, we have begun to find it in natural foods stores across the country—not only in the large cities like New York and San Francisco and Boston, but even in Bozeman, Montana, and in Visalia, California. If triticale is not readily available in your own area, you can order it by mail (see Mail-Order Sources).

When you bake with triticale you'll find that its very low and delicate gluten content will probably dictate that you add some high-gluten flour or unbleached white flour, as we do in the recipes that follow. On the other hand, the triticale berries (groats) have become a staple in our bread baking, and we generally add as much as ¾ cup (cooked) to our batter to add crunch and nutrition.

Most of all, we love the taste. We have described it previously as "ryelike" or "nutlike." You may have your own description after you've tasted it. And, when your dinner guests look up in a questioning glance as they wonder about the unusually good flavor of your bread or cake or muffins or soup, just pronounce it slowly— twice: trit-i-*kay*-lee.

The Forms of Triticale

Whole Triticale Berries or Groats: The whole berries can be cracked just like wheat berries in order to shorten the cooking time. Cooked whole, they are delicious in pilafs, or they can be added to bread or soups.

Triticale Flakes: These are made by a process similar to that used to make rolled oats. The flakes can be added to baked goods, or they can be cooked as a breakfast cereal.

Triticale Flour: Remember that the gluten content is very low and you may need to add unbleached white or gluten flour for lightness in baked goods. If you like, you can use it in combination with whole wheat flour, but the result will be much more dense.

Basic Whole Triticale Berries or Groats

Yields 2½ cups

1 cup triticale berries
2¼ cups water

Soak berries in water overnight. The next morning, drain soaking water and measure. Add enough fresh water to make 2¼ cups. Bring to a boil, add drained plumped berries, cover pot, lower heat, and simmer for about 40 minutes. Bite-test a kernel for tenderness. Place paper towels between pot and lid to absorb excess moisture and let stand for 5 minutes. Use in breads, as a cereal, or in various other dishes in this section.

Note: Whole triticale berries can be cracked in a mill or blender and cooked for 20 to 25 minutes.

Basic Triticale Breakfast Cereal

Yields 4 cups

2½ cups water
1⅓ cups triticale flakes

Bring water to a boil and slowly add triticale flakes, stirring constantly. Cover pot, lower heat, and simmer for about 10 minutes. Place a paper towel under pot lid and let stand for 5 minutes. Serve with butter, small bowls of raisins, sunflower seeds, and a pitcher of maple syrup to pass at the table. (We also use any cooked leftovers in our breads.)

Note: As of this printing, Arrowhead Mills is the only source we know of for triticale flakes.

Soup

Kale, Leek, and Triticale Berry Soup

Serves 6

1 tablespoon chicken fat
2 cups well washed, coarsely chopped leeks, white part only
1 small dried hot pepper
½ pound kale, trimmed and coarsely chopped (about 8 cups)
6 cups Chicken Stock (see Index)
2 medium-size carrots, shredded (about 1½ cups)
⅔ cup cooked triticale berries
1 tablespoon red wine vinegar

Melt chicken fat in a heavy pot. Add leeks and saute until wilted, stirring occasionally. Add hot pepper and kale. Stir and cook for 5 minutes. Then add the chicken stock. Bring to a boil and simmer, covered, for 20 minutes. Remove hot pepper, add the carrots and triticale berries, and simmer for 15 minutes more. Just before serving, stir in the vinegar. Serve hot.

Whole Wheat Walnut Cookies—Three Ways   For this recipe, see page 200

Pasta Tutto Giardino— *The Whole Garden*   For this recipe, see page 249

Frank Ford of Arrowhead Mills

Frank Ford is now an old friend, and a most unusual man. We first got to know him and the people at Arrowhead Mills some years back when we first began our research on triticale. We have remained in contact ever since, though we have yet to make our first trip down to Hereford, Texas, where Arrowhead is located. The invitation is always open, he reminds us, and one day we will take him up on it.

He is, above all, a man of the land. "I was born on the worst sandstorm day in the history of the dust bowl," Frank recounts. It was the depth of the depression and the worst of times for the American farmer. So, when he started Arrowhead Mills with Henry Turner and George Warner in 1960, he already understood the nature of struggle, the battle against odds. Fortunately, Arrowhead has always been able to produce high-grade wheat, for it is in Deaf Smith County, the heart of the hard red winter wheat area. "Our major problem," recalls Frank, "was in getting grocery stores to allow me to leave bags of stone-ground whole wheat on consignment. Anyone smart enough to run a store *knew* that wheat should be white!"

Sales in 1965 were about $28,000, and gradually the company grew, based on its philosophy of selling "whole foods grown on fertile soil, without pesticides or chemical fertilizers . . . and getting it to the customer as fresh and at the best prices we can . . . and keeping our life simple." Frank tells of visitors who came "thinking that Arrowhead was a big corporation and were quite shocked to find that it was a warehouse that Turner and I had sort of helped lay block by block, pouring the roof by hauling water up and mixing material for the roof ourselves. We had a railroad car for an office!" The company grew as people became more interested in natural foods, and in the seventies, the natural foods revolution became a fact.

And where do we—all of us—go from here? Frank Ford sees the inordinate waste in a system that supplies a nation through long lines of transportation. "Food supply lines have to be shortened," he states. "People who live in apartments in the big cities have to develop ways of growing some of their own food by having rooftop gardens, a sprouting system in their kitchens, indoor window-sill herb gardens, and if they have a backyard they should have a garden."

On the subject of the decline of the small family farmer, Frank Ford snorts, "Some people say that the multinational corporations will buy all the land, put it on the computer, and that food prices will go down because of all this efficiency. Well, if big companies and their computers are so efficient, I can't help but wonder why the price of oil being sold by all those big companies isn't going down!" Frank still knows how to ask the big questions.

Triticale Berries, Zucchini, and Three Cheeses

Serves 6

2 tablespoons olive oil
1 medium-size onion, chopped (½ cup)
1 clove garlic, finely minced
¼ cup diced green pepper
1 pound zucchini, sliced ¼ inch thick (about 3 or 4 small zucchini)
1½ cups cooked triticale berries
4 eggs
½ cup milk
1 teaspoon Dijon-style mustard
⅛ teaspoon black pepper
1 teaspoon finely minced marjoram, or ¼ teaspoon dried marjoram
¼ pound Jarlsburg cheese, thinly sliced
¼ pound Monterey Jack cheese, thinly sliced
6 cherry tomatoes, cut in half
¼ cup grated Parmesan cheese
1 tablespoon finely minced parsley for garnish

Preheat oven to 400°F. In a large skillet, heat oil and add onion, garlic, and green pepper. Stir over medium heat until wilted, but not brown. Add the zucchini and stir. Cook for 2 minutes, stirring constantly. Then add the triticale berries and stir. Remove from heat and put into a 14-inch, flat oven casserole.

In a bowl, beat eggs with milk, mustard, and black pepper. Stir in herbs and pour mixture over vegetables. Cover with slices of Jarlsburg and Jack cheese and bake for 15 minutes. Remove from oven and ring casserole with the cherry tomatoes. Sprinkle the Parmesan cheese over the tomatoes and on top of the vegetable mixture. Slip under broiler for 3 to 4 minutes, or until cheese is dappled with brown. Sprinkle with parsley before taking to the table.

Sour Cream, Fresh Dill, and Triticale Berry Yeast Bread
Makes 1 loaf

1 package dry yeast (¼ ounce)
¼ cup warm water
1 tablespoon soft butter, cut into small pieces
1 cup sour cream
1 tablespoon mild honey
1 egg, lightly beaten
2 tablespoons finely minced onions
1½ tablespoons finely minced dillweed
1 cup triticale flour
1½ cups whole wheat flour
1 cup gluten flour
½ teaspoon baking soda
½ cup cooked triticale berries
1 egg white, beaten until foamy
1 teaspoon dill seeds

Dissolve yeast in water and let stand for 10 minutes until bubbly. Pour into a large mixing bowl and add butter, sour cream, honey, egg, onions, and dillweed. Mix well with a wooden spoon.

In another bowl, mix the three kinds of flour and baking soda together. Stir in the cooked triticale berries. Add the dry ingredients to the liquid ingredients, and stir with a wooden spoon until dough starts to form.

Flour hands and a work surface and knead dough for 5 to 10 minutes, or until dough feels elastic. (If dough feels too damp, knead in a bit more gluten or whole wheat flour.) Oil a large bowl and rotate dough in bowl to cover surface with oil. Cover with a cloth and let rise in a warm place for 1 hour.

Turn out on floured surface and knead again for 8 to 10 strokes, then return to bowl again for a second rising (about 50 minutes). Shape into a loaf and turn into a buttered 9 × 5 × 3-inch loaf pan. Cover with cloth again and let rise for 30 more minutes. Preheat oven to 350°F. Bake for 45 to 50 minutes. Five minutes before the loaf is done, remove from oven and quickly brush surface with beaten egg white. Scatter dill seeds over surface, return to oven, and complete baking until golden.

Triticale Gorgonzola Buttons
Makes about 40 buttons

4 tablespoons butter, cut into small pieces
¼ pound Gorgonzola cheese
1 cup triticale flour
½ cup unbleached white flour
1 teaspoon baking powder
¼ cup nonfat dry milk
⅛ teaspoon cayenne pepper

Cream butter and cheese in a food processor. Add all remaining ingredients and mix until dough is formed. Roll with hands into a long cylinder, 11 inches long by 1 inch thick, wrap with foil, and chill for at least 1 hour. (It can be chilled overnight as well.)

When ready to bake, preheat oven to 350°F. and line a baking sheet with foil. Sterilize a 25-cent coin by boiling in water for 10 minutes. Lift out with tongs and dry on a piece of paper towel until cool. Slice roll in ¼-inch-thick slices and place, closely spaced, on prepared baking sheet. Press coin down in center of each cracker. This will form a raised border. Prick with a small 2-pronged fork in the center and bake for 10 to 12 minutes, or until golden. Cool on wire racks.

Triticale, Apple Cider, Fruit, and Nut Yeast Cake

Makes 1 cake

1½   cups apple cider, at room temperature

2   packages dry yeast (½ ounce)

¼   pound butter, melted and cooled, or ½ cup bland oil

⅔   cup mild honey

3   eggs

1   teaspoon vanilla extract

2   cups triticale flour

1   cup unbleached white flour

1   tablespoon grated orange rind

¼   teaspoon ground cardamom

½   cup coarsely chopped walnuts

¼   cup raisins

¼   cup black figs, cut into ½-inch pieces

½   cup pitted dates, cut into ½-inch pieces

1   cup soft pitted prunes, cut into ½-inch pieces

¾   cup soft dried apricots, cut into ½-inch pieces

Heat ½ cup of the cider until lukewarm. Place in a small bowl and sprinkle yeast over cider. Mix well and let stand for 10 minutes.

Mix butter and honey together with a wire whisk and then beat in eggs, one at a time. Add the vanilla, the yeast mixture, and the remaining cider. Beat well and set aside.

Sift the flours together and then add all the remaining ingredients to the flour mixture, stirring well to mix. Combine with the liquid ingredients, beating well with a wooden spoon. Butter a 9-inch springform pan, pour in batter, and cover with a cloth. Let stand in a warm place for 1 hour.

Preheat oven to 350°F. and bake for 1 hour. Cool completely on a wire rack before removing sides.

Note: If you let cider stand at room temperature for a few days, it just begins to turn and get tingley. Pour some additional cider over the baked cake for extra moisture and flavor.

Triticale Carrot Spice Cake
with Maple Walnut Frosting
Makes 1 cake

1½ cups triticale flour
½ cup whole wheat pastry
      flour
2 teaspoons baking powder
1 teaspoon baking soda
½ teaspoon nutmeg
½ teaspoon ground cloves
2 teaspoons cinnamon
½ cup raisins
½ cup coarsely chopped
      walnuts
¾ cup maple syrup
½ cup butter, melted, or oil
2 eggs
1 teaspoon vanilla extract
3 or 4 carrots, grated (about
      2 cups)
1 teaspoon grated lemon rind

Preheat oven to 350°F. and butter an 8½-inch spring-form pan. In a large bowl, mix all the dry ingredients together. Add the raisins and walnuts and set aside.

In another bowl, mix the maple syrup with the melted butter and beat in eggs 1 at a time. Stir in the vanilla, carrots, and lemon rind. Then add all the dry ingredients to the liquid ingredients, beating well. Pour into prepared pan and bake for 45 to 50 minutes. Let cool and remove sides of springform pan, leaving the cake on the base. Frost the top of cake only with the frosting below.

Maple Walnut Frosting:

1 package soft cream cheese
      (3 ounces)
1 tablespoon soft butter
¼ cup maple syrup
2 tablespoons chopped
      walnuts

Beat all ingredients, except walnuts, until smooth. Spread on top of cake and sprinkle with chopped nuts.

Wheat:
The Amber
Waves of Grain

We remember a trip by train through the American Midwest too many years ago, in the days before an airplane could whisk us from New York to Los Angeles in less time than it takes to bake a good sourdough bread. The golden, waving fields of grain never seemed to end—they stretched from horizon to horizon. And, as the train rolled on, new and vast acres of rich, ripe wheat unfurled before us, like a wind-swept carpet. When darkness fell, and still there was no end, we realized anew just how bountiful this beautiful country is.

In filming for the National Council of Farmer Co-operatives years later, we never could set our cameras quite high enough to capture the brilliant panorama of the wheat fields. No barn roof seemed lofty enough to use as a camera platform. Out of desperation, we finally took to the air in small planes to move across the land and capture the endlessness of the wheat fields.

No doubt about it, wheat is the grain with which Americans are most familiar. Our grammar school geography books and our singing of "America, the Beautiful" at assemblies had us equating the Great Plains with "amber waves of grain" before we really understood what "amber waves" were! Possibly the most widespread cereal crop in the world, wheat dates back about 8,500 years to Iraq. Many of us who bake bread know well the story of how the Egyptians accidentally discovered a method for levening their wheat dough almost 6,000 years ago. Writers of cookbooks frequently use wheat as the comparative measure of nutrition—"amaranth has more protein than wheat," for example. It has become the scale by which we measure other grains. It is a golden grain, a nutritious grain, *when* we use it in its original form.

Unfortunately, wheat is also the grain that has been the victim of the most tampering, the most processing, the most draining of its food value in turning it from kernels of nutrition into bleached, refined, and all-purpose flour. It is almost as though the processors were Draculas,

180

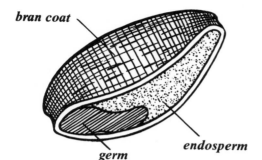

bran coat

germ

endosperm

refrigerator or in a cool, dry place, where it will keep well for months.

The Forms and Varieties of Wheat

Some Wheat Terminology

Sometimes wheat is referred to as being either *winter* or *spring* wheat. The designation refers to the time of planting. Winter wheat is planted in the fall, matures over the winter, and then is harvested in late spring and into summer, depending upon the climate. Spring wheat is planted in the spring and harvested in late summer and into fall.

Wheat varieties are also designated as *hard* or *soft* wheat. This merely refers to the gluten content. Hard wheat has a high gluten content and an ability to absorb more water, thus making it perfect for baking breads; while soft wheat has a low gluten content and is generally used for pastry, cakes, or cookies.

Whole Wheat Berries: The name for the whole grains of wheat. The berries can be soaked and cooked and left whole for pilafs, soups, or stews, or they can be added to baked goods. We use them frequently in our breads to add nutrition and crunch. When they're sprouted, wheat berries can be made into croquettes or added to salads and baked goods.

Whole Hulled or Peeled Wheat Berries: Sometimes called *frumento* or *kuta*. They're pale golden in color with only the outermost hull removed. They can be used in desserts and cakes or eaten as pilaf or morning cereal. The hulled berries can also be added to baked goods or soups. They have a gelatinous quality when they're cooled.

Whole Green Wheat Berries: Sometimes called *gruenken*. They are wheat kernels picked while still unripened, and then dried. They can be steamed and used for pilaf, but they are more commonly used for soups, stews, and casseroles. Green wheat berries can also be ground into flour. If they are not available in your neighborhood, they can be ordered by mail (see Mail-Order Sources).

taking a perfectly healthy kernel of wheat and sucking from it every last drop of its natural goodness. However, the use of whole wheat flour and the other forms of the grain has been enjoying a revival, as more and more people discover that it is not only healthier, but the end product tastes a lot better! Mel discovered it when he was testing *Bread Winners,* and both of us found that whole wheat flour added a tasty flavor to seafood, and the results are in our book *The Fish-Lovers' Cookbook.*

Most of the wheat grown in the United States and Canada still goes into the milling of the white, unbleached, or bleached (all-purpose) varieties of flour. This product has about 20 percent less protein than whole wheat flour, 55 percent less calcium, and 74 percent less potassium. Overall, the extraction process leaves 20 to 30 percent of the vitamins and minerals of the original wheat kernel. The starchy endosperm that remains gives breads a puffy, high-rise look, but without the nutrition offered by the whole grain. Certainly, the milled all-purpose flour is not nutritionally worthless, but one would hardly single it out as very worthwhile!

In our recipes, we use the whole grain in its various forms, whether as whole berries, cracked wheat, or wheat flour. Keep in mind that the germ of the wheat berry contains a large amount of oil, so we suggest that you purchase smaller amounts than you would if you were buying the processed, longer-shelf-life, white flour. If you have any whole wheat left over, store it in the

Cracked Whole Wheat: Whole wheat berries that literally have been cracked into four to six pieces. Use them for cereals, casseroles, or soups, or as a chopped-meat extender.

Whole Wheat Grits: Whole wheat berries that are cracked into six to eight pieces. The same process used for cracking the whole wheat (above) is also used here. Since this form is finer, it cooks more quickly.

Cream of Wheat: Sometimes called farina. It is finely ground, hulled wheat which still contains the germ. Only the outer bran layer is missing. Cream of Wheat is used for desserts, dumplings, and cereal.

Whole Wheat Flakes or Rolled Wheat: Wheat berries that are heated and pressed in the same manner as rolled oats. They are fast cooking and can be used as a cooked cereal or in baked goods.

Puffed Wheat: The whole berry heated and then puffed up with air. It is ready to eat as is and requires no cooking. The puffed wheat can be used as a breakfast cereal or added to baked goods and candy. Just remember, when you buy wheat in this form, a part of your purchase price is going for air, and you get less nutrition per dollar as a result.

Shredded Whole Wheat: Manufactured commercially in several forms, including large biscuits and small bite-size morsels. Look carefully at the ingredients list on the package—shredded wheat products usually contain both salt and sugar. They are ready to eat as snacks or cereal, or they can be made into a candy.

Whole Unprocessed Pure Bran Flakes: The outer layer of the hard wheat kernel or berry. They're used to add extra fiber and enrichment to baked goods or they're sprinkled on cold or hot cereals. Buy them *unprocessed,* which is not the same as "ready-to-eat-bran-cereals."

Wheat Germ: The untreated natural embryo of the wheat berry. It's ready to eat, either raw or toasted, and it can be used for breading poultry, meat, or fish, as an extender of meat, or for nutritional enhancement. Sprinkle some on yogurt or on any cooked or ready-to-eat cereals; put it in candies, cakes, cookies, breads, or desserts. Wheat germ must be refrigerated after opening, since the germ contains oils which will quickly turn rancid at room temperature.

Bear Mush: A finely milled, whole grain wheat hot cereal.

Wheat Grass: A young wheat plant cut at the moment when the embryo of the wheat grain is moving up from the roots through the stalk (about 20 days after sprouting). The plant is then about six to eight inches high. The wheat grass is similar to other leafy green vegetables, but it has a higher concentration of nutrients. It comes in handy at the times when you don't get enough green vegetables in your area, but you can also use it just to add flavor to food. If it's not available at your natural foods store, you can order it by mail in several forms: powder, tablets, or a vegetable seasoning to sprinkle on food (see Mail-Order Sources).

Wheat Flours

Whole Wheat (Stone Ground): Hard wheat flour available in fine or medium grind. The bran and the germ of the whole wheat berry are ground together into flour. Stone-ground whole wheat flour can be used to replace all white, refined flour in baking, though it doesn't contain as much gluten and the breads will not rise quite as high.

Whole Wheat Pastry Flour: A more finely milled flour. It is soft whole wheat, making it perfect to replace white flour in pies, cookies, cakes, waffles, and pancakes. Sift twice before measuring for lighter baked goods, then *put the bran left in the strainer back into the flour.* The only reason to sift whole wheat flour is to lighten it and keep it from packing down.

Graham Flour: Whole wheat flour in which the inner part of the kernel (the endosperm) is finely ground and the bran layers are returned to the flour and left coarse and flaky. Graham flour is excellent for bread and rolls. Just be certain you read the label before you buy, since there are times that the miller removes the germ to give the flour longer shelf life. If you should get such a product, simply add some wheat germ before using it.

Gluten Flour: Wheat flour with some additional gluten. Gluten is isolated by washing the starch from high-protein wheat flour; then it is dried, ground, and added to wheat flour. This flour is usually combined with low-gluten flours such as rye, barley, or triticale to produce a lighter finished product.

Basic Whole Wheat Berries

Yields 2¾ cups

1 cup whole wheat berries
(groats)
3½ cups water

Toast berries in a dry, heavy SilverStone-lined pot until fragrant and lightly toasted, and until they begin to pop slightly. Transfer to a bowl and soak overnight in 3 cups water.

In the morning, the berries will have doubled in size and absorbed some of the liquid. Drain soaking liquid and measure. Add enough cold water to make 3½ cups. Bring to a boil and add wheat berries. When liquid boils again, cover pot, lower heat, and simmer for about 50 minutes to 1 hour. Bite-test a kernel for tenderness. Let stand, covered, for 10 minutes with a piece of paper toweling between pot and lid to absorb moisture.

Basic Whole Hulled Wheat Berries

Yields 2¾ cups

1 cup hulled wheat berries
3 cups water
1 tablespoon butter

Pick over wheat berries to remove foreign matter and soak in water overnight. In the morning, the berries will have swelled to almost double in size.

Drain soaking water and measure. Add enough fresh water to make 4 cups. Return water, soaked wheat berries, and butter to a SilverStone-lined pot and bring to a boil. Lower heat and simmer for 1 hour and 10 minutes, stirring occasionally. The mixture should be tender and sticky. If you wish to use as a pilaf, follow the instructions for Basic Whole Wheat Berries (see recipe in this section).

Basic Cracked Whole Wheat

Yields 3¾ cups

1   cup cracked wheat
2½ cups water
1   teaspoon butter or sesame
    oil

Place wheat in a SilverStone-lined pan and toast for 4 to 5 minutes, shaking pan and stirring with a wooden spoon until the grains give off a toasted nutty aroma.

Meanwhile, in a tea kettle, boil 2½ cups water. When wheat is toasted, pour back into measuring cup and pour boiling water into the saucepan, adding the butter or oil to the water. Bring to a rolling boil and gradually add the cracked wheat to the boiling water, stirring all the while. Cover pot, lower heat to very low, and cook for 15 minutes. Place paper towels between pot and lid and let stand for 5 minutes. Fluff with a fork before serving.

Basic Whole Wheat Flakes

Serves 6

4   cups water
1⅓ cups wheat flakes

Bring water to a boil. Slowly sprinkle wheat flakes over water without disturbing the boil and stir constantly with a wooden spoon. Then lower heat, cover pot, and simmer for 20 minutes. Remove from heat and let stand for 5 minutes before serving.

Note: Wheat flakes can also be used uncooked in baked goods.

Double Apple Spiced Cracked Wheat Cooked in Apple Juice
Serves 6

1½ cups dried apple slices
½ cup boiling water
4 tablespoons mild honey
3 tablespoons butter
1 cup cracked wheat
4 cups boiling apple juice
¾ teaspoon ground cinnamon
¼ teaspoon ground cardamom

Place apples in a small bowl and pour boiling water over them. Stir in honey and let steep. Melt the butter in a SilverStone-lined pan and add the cracked wheat. Stir to coat with butter and toast, stirring constantly, for about 2 minutes. Add the boiling apple juice and spices, lower heat, cover pot, and simmer for 15 minutes. Remove from heat and let stand, covered, for 5 minutes. Spoon out into individual bowls and top with honey apple slices. Pass a pitcher of milk at the table to pour on top.

_____Appetizer

Mini Sprouted Wheat, Pecan, and Onion Croquettes
Makes about 24 croquettes

2 cups finely chopped
     sprouted wheat berries
¾ cup finely ground pecans
1 cup whole wheat bread
     crumbs
1 cup finely grated onions
     (about 1 large onion)
2 tablespoons butter, melted
½ teaspoon baking powder
1 egg, beaten
1 tablespoon finely minced
     parsley
⅛ teaspoon allspice
¼ teaspoon black pepper
½ teaspoon grated lemon rind
     peanut oil for frying

Mix all ingredients together and form into balls the size of walnuts. Flatten into tiny cakes. Heat oil to 375°F. in a skillet and fry a few at a time, turning once until browned. Drain on paper towels. Serve hot.

If you prefer to bake them, use tiny muffin tins and bake at 350°F. for 35 minutes. Let stand for a few minutes before removing from tins. Serve with drinks or as a snack.

Egyptian Hulled Wheat Berry, Chicken, and Chick-Pea Soup

Serves 6 to 8

1 cup whole hulled wheat berries (soaked overnight in 2½ cups water)
½ cup dried chick-peas (soaked overnight in 2½ cups water)
1 2½- to 3½-pound chicken, left whole
2 small beef marrow bones
½ teaspoon whole peppercorns
¼ teaspoon turmeric
2 large onions, quartered (about ¾ pound)
1 large clove garlic, peeled and left whole
2 small turnips, peeled and cut in half
2 stalks celery with leaves
2 small carrots, whole
6 sprigs parsley
1 teaspoon Syrian Mixed Spices (see Index), or 1 teaspoon allspice
1 tablespoon butter

Drain wheat berries and chick-peas, saving the water for the soup stock, and set both aside. In a large heavy pot, place the chicken and marrow bones. Measure the soaking liquid, add enough cold water to make 9 cups, and then add to the pot along with the peppercorns and turmeric. Bring to a boil, lower heat, and add the onions, garlic, and turnips. Tie the celery, carrots, and parsley together in a bundle with white string or thread and tuck into pot. Simmer, covered, for 1 hour and 15 minutes.

Lift out the chicken, the marrow bones, and the bundle of tied vegetables. Discard the bones and tied vegetables. Set chicken aside to cool. Strain the soup, pressing the onions, garlic, and turnips against the strainer. Return the stock to the pot and bring to a boil. Add the chick-peas and wheat, lower heat, and simmer for 45 minutes to 1 hour, or until grain and chick-peas are tender.

Meanwhile, when chicken is cool enough to handle, remove skin and bones and discard. When grain is tender, add half the chicken meat to the pot and heat through. Save the remaining half for another use. Melt the butter and Syrian Mixed Spices or allspice together. Dribble this mixture on the surface before serving. It will float on top, dotting the surface in a "polka dot" fashion.

Triple Wheat, Pork, and Apple Loaf with Herbs
Serves 6

Pork and tart-sweet apples are a perfect team in this meat loaf.

1 slice whole wheat bread, crumbled
½ cup milk
1 teaspoon tamari soy sauce
1½ pounds lean ground pork
¼ cup wheat germ
½ cup cooked cracked wheat
1 egg, lightly beaten
¾ cup finely chopped unpeeled apples
¾ cup finely chopped celery and leaves
½ teaspoon dried sage
1 clove garlic, finely minced
¼ teaspoon fennel seeds
2 tablespoons minced parsley
1 teaspoon minced basil
¼ teaspoon dried thyme
⅛ teaspoon nutmeg
½ teaspoon black pepper

Heat oven to 350°F. Place the crumbled bread in a small bowl and pour the milk and tamari over it. Let stand until bread absorbs the liquid.

Mix all the remaining ingredients together and add the moistened bread and soaking liquid. Shape into a loaf, place in a shallow baking pan, and bake for about 1 hour. Let cool for 5 minutes before slicing.

Wheat Berry and Chive Pilaf Baked with Herbs, Wheat Germ, and Chicken Legs
Serves 6

Crusty chicken legs and herb-flavored whole wheat berries—an inexpensive dish, festively presented like the spokes of a wheel.

1 recipe Basic Whole Wheat Berries (see recipe in this section)
1 tablespoon butter
4 tablespoons finely minced chives
½ cup raw wheat germ
⅓ cup grated Parmesan cheese
½ teaspoon finely crushed dried rosemary
½ teaspoon onion powder
¼ teaspoon garlic powder
¼ teaspoon crushed dried thyme
½ teaspoon paprika
¼ teaspoon black pepper
½ cup buttermilk
12 chicken legs
large sprig of rosemary for garnish

Preheat oven to 325°F. Line a baking pan with heavily buttered foil and set aside. Mix cooked wheat berries with butter and toss with chives in a bowl and set aside.

Combine all remaining ingredients, except buttermilk and chicken legs. Place wheat germ mixture in one flat pie pan and buttermilk in another pie pan. Then roll chicken legs first in buttermilk and then in herbed wheat germ, coating completely with dry mixture. Place on prepared pan and bake for about 50 minutes, or until chicken tests done with point of knife. In the last 15 minutes of baking, wrap pilaf in foil and heat in oven. Then using a round warmed platter, mound the wheat berries in the center and arrange the chicken legs like the spokes of a wheel, around the pilaf. Place a sprig of rosemary in the center of pilaf.

Whole Wheat Pinwheel Roulade Stuffed with Spinach and Pine Nuts

Serves 6

Try this elegant dish for a vegetarian gourmet, or a Christmas holiday buffet. It is served at room temperature and, therefore, can be prepared ahead of time.

Roulade:

- 4 eggs at room temperature
- 1 cup whole wheat pastry flour
- ¼ cup clarified butter, cooled

Garnish:

curly parsley
sweet red pepper strips

Line a 10 × 15 × 1-inch jelly-roll pan with aluminum foil, leaving extra on either end. Butter surface of foil generously. Preheat oven to 400°F. Fold a piece of cheesecloth into 4 layers, dampen, and set aside.

In a medium-size bowl with electric hand beater, beat eggs for about 5 minutes, or until they are very thick and almost tripled in volume. Sift flour over eggs and then gently fold in to incorporate into eggs. Then fold in the clarified butter. Working quickly, spoon and spread batter evenly on prepared pan and bake for about 8 minutes, or until firm. Immediately place dampened cheesecloth over top and quickly invert onto counter top. Peel off foil and roll up tightly from long side, with the cheesecloth. Let cool for at least 30 minutes while preparing filling.

Filling:

- 2 tablespoons butter
- 2 cloves garlic, finely minced
- 1 cup finely sliced scallions (about 6 to 8 scallions)
- 1½ pounds spinach
- ¾ cup parsley leaves
- ¼ teaspoon pepper
- ¼ teaspoon nutmeg
- 1 tablespoon lemon juice
- 1 tablespoon grated lemon rind
- 2 tablespoon pine nuts
- 2 eggs, separated

Melt butter in a medium skillet and saute garlic and scallions until wilted. Set aside.

Steam spinach for 1 to 2 minutes, or until wilted, and drain. Line a kitchen towel with paper towels and place spinach on paper toweling. Roll up and squeeze several times until no moisture is left.

Using a food processor, mince parsley first and then add the spinach and chop together. Remove to a medium-size bowl and stir in the pepper, nutmeg, lemon juice and rind, spinach mixture, and pine nuts.

In another bowl, whip egg whites until stiff with an electric hand beater. Then add egg yolks and whip again for a few seconds. Fold into the spinach mixture.

To assemble: Carefully unroll roulade onto a large sheet of waxed paper for easier placement on serving platter. Remove cheesecloth and spread filling almost to the edges with a rubber spatula. Carefully reroll back into its shape, lift quickly with waxed paper onto large serving platter, slip out waxed paper, and decorate with curly green parsley and bright red pepper.

Fattoush—
Syrian Whole Wheat
Pita Bread Salad
Serves 6

Mint, lemon, and cucumber cool this salad. The whole grain bread absorbs the dressing.

2¼ cups toasted, cubed whole wheat pita (about 2½ breads)

3 medium-size tomatoes, diced

1 small green pepper, diced

4 scallions, thinly sliced

2 medium-size cucumbers (peel only if waxed), chopped (about 2 cups)

½ cup finely minced parsley

⅓ cup finely minced mint

1 small clove garlic

¼ teaspoon black pepper

⅓ cup fresh lemon juice

⅓ cup olive oil

2 tablespoons crumbled feta cheese or other dry goats'-milk cheese

Combine bread cubes, tomatoes, green pepper, scallions, cucumbers, parsley, and mint in a glass salad bowl.

In a small bowl, mix garlic, black pepper, and lemon juice, crushing garlic with the bottom of a knife handle or mortar and pestle. Pour over salad and toss well. Add olive oil and mix again. Sprinkle with cheese and serve.

Note: See *Bread Winners,* page 328, for recipe for whole wheat pita bread.

Romanian Cream of Wheat, Chive, Parsley, and Tomato Dumplings
Makes 14 dumplings

Feather-light and savory, these little dumplings can be eaten in soup or as a side dish with chicken. Prepare them just before cooking, so they puff up.

1 small tomato, finely chopped
2 tablespoons finely minced chives
1 tablespoon finely minced parsley
6 cups Chicken Stock (see Index)
¾ cup milk
¼ cup regular Cream of Wheat cereal (not instant farina)
1 tablespoon butter
1 egg, beaten
⅛ teaspoon white pepper

Mix together tomato, chives, and parsley in a small bowl and set aside. Bring chicken stock to a boil in a wide-based pot.

In a medium-size saucepan, bring milk to a boil and very slowly add the Cream of Wheat, stirring constantly with a wooden spoon. Lower heat and stir until quite thick. (It takes only a few minutes.) Remove from heat and stir in butter. Beat until butter is mixed in well and then add beaten egg and pepper. Beat again with wooden spoon and add the tomato-herb mixture. Wet a teaspoon, scoop dumpling batter by the rounded spoonful, and push off with finger into simmering stock. Cover pot and simmer for 10 minutes. Either lift out with slotted spoon and serve with chicken, or serve in the chicken stock.

_____ **Breads**

Graham Raisin Bran Sour Cream Muffins
Makes 12 muffins

1 cup graham or whole wheat flour
1 cup unprocessed bran (not bran cereal)
2 tablespoons wheat germ
1 teaspoon baking soda
1 tablespoon baking powder
½ teaspoon cinnamon
½ cup raisins
4 tablespoons soft butter
¼ cup date sugar
1 large egg, beaten
1 cup sour cream
¼ cup light molasses

Preheat oven to 400°F. and butter a 12-cup muffin tin. In a large bowl, combine flour, bran, wheat germ, baking soda, baking powder, cinnamon, and raisins and set aside.

In a food processor, beat butter and date sugar together until creamy. Add the remaining ingredients and beat again. Then add the liquid ingredients to the flour mixture, combining just until the dry ingredients are moistened. (The batter will be thick.) Spoon batter almost to the top of each muffin cup and bake for about 15 to 20 minutes. Remove from cups.

Mixed Wheat Irish Farm Bread
Makes 1 large loaf

3 cups whole wheat or
graham flour

2 cups unbleached white
flour

2 tablespoons baking powder

½ teaspoon baking soda

⅓ cup bran

¼ cup wheat germ

4 tablespoons soft butter,
cut into small pieces

⅓ cup whole wheat flakes
(rolled wheat)

¼ cup fine bulgur

½ cup whole wheat sprouts,
or cooked whole wheat
berries, or a combination
of both

2¾ cups buttermilk

1 tablespoon mild honey

Combine both flours, baking powder, baking soda, bran, and wheat germ in a large bowl. Crush butter into mixture with fingers until crumbly. Add all the remaining ingredients except the buttermilk and honey. Make a well in center and pour in buttermilk and honey. (More buttermilk may be needed if grains are very absorbent.) Flour hands and knead dough in bowl, revolving bowl and kneading 5 or 6 turns. Then turn out onto a floured surface and knead a bit more until dough feels well blended and elastic.

Preheat oven to 425°F. and butter a baking sheet. Place ball of dough on prepared baking sheet and flatten and shape into a 2-inch-thick circle with palms of hands. Dip a sharp knife into flour and cut a Y inside a triangle on the surface of the dough, about 1 inch into the bread. Bake for 25 minutes, then reduce heat to 350°F. and bake about 20 minutes more. Bread is done when a slight tap on bottom of loaf produces a hollow sound. Wrap well in foil to prevent drying out and set aside for 5 to 6 hours before slicing.

Note: If you prefer a less crusty loaf, wrap bread with a dampened tea towel and place it on its side to cool completely.

Whole Wheat
Cheddar Cheese Flowers

Makes about 40 crackers (depending on size of flower cookie cutter)

1 cup whole wheat pastry
   flour
⅛ teaspoon cayenne pepper
1½ teaspoons baking powder
4 tablespoons butter
½ cup grated cheddar cheese
3 tablespoons sour cream

Place flour, cayenne, and baking powder in a bowl and stir together. Cut the butter into cubes and add to the dry ingredients along with the cheddar cheese. Using a pastry blender, work the butter and cheese into the mixture until dry ingredients look crumbly. Add the sour cream and form dough into a ball. Wrap in waxed paper and chill for at least 1 hour. This facilitates rolling and keeps the dough flexible.

Lightly flour a flat surface and rolling pin and roll dough ⅛ inch thick. Cut into flower shapes with a cookie cutter. Preheat oven to 400°F. Reroll scraps and continue to cut until all dough is used up. Carefully place on ungreased cookie sheet and bake for 8 to 10 minutes, watching carefully to prevent burning. Lift with spatula and cool on wire racks. Store in an airtight container, but do not refrigerate or crackers will lose their crispness.

Variations:
1. Poppy Seed Chive and Cream Cheese Squares: Substitute 4 tablespoons cream cheese for cheddar cheese and add 2 tablespoons poppy seeds and 2 tablespoons finely minced chives. Roll out and cut into 1½-inch squares before baking.
2. Sesame Seed Cream Cheese Circles: Substitute cream cheese for cheddar cheese and add 2 to 3 tablespoons sesame seeds. Roll and cut into small circles.

Whole Wheat Cranberry Orange Bread
Makes 1 loaf

This bread is best the day after baking when the flavors develop sufficiently.

1½ cups cranberries
½ cup mild honey
2 large navel oranges
1 egg
4 tablespoons butter, melted and cooled
2½ cups whole wheat flour
1 tablespoon baking powder
½ teaspoon baking soda
½ cup coarsely broken walnuts

Coarsely chop the cranberries. If you use a food processor, this takes only 4 strokes. Place in a small bowl and add honey. Mix well and let stand for 1 hour, or until the honey and cranberries exude a liquid.

Meanwhile grate the rind of the oranges. (There should be 3 tablespoons.) Set aside and peel off the white bitter pith from the oranges. Then chop the pulp coarsely in a food processor. Mix the pulp, and whatever orange juice accumulates, with the honey-cranberry mixture. Then beat egg well and add melted butter. Add this to the same bowl and set aside.

Preheat oven to 350°F. and butter a 9 × 5 × 3-inch loaf pan. In a large mixing bowl, combine the flour, baking powder, baking soda, and walnuts and stir in the grated orange rind. Combine the liquid ingredients with the dry ingredients and spoon into the prepared pan. Bake for about 50 to 60 minutes, or until a cake tester inserted in center comes out clean. Cool in pan on a wire rack for 10 minutes. Turn out of pan onto a wire rack to cool completely. Wrap with aluminum foil and use the following day for the best flavor.

Whole Wheat Sprouts, Cheddar Cheese, and Apple Quick Bread
Makes 1 loaf

2½ cups whole wheat flour
2 teaspoons baking powder
    pinch of baking soda
2 tablespoons soft butter, cut into small pieces
1 cup chopped whole wheat sprouts
1 cup grated cheddar cheese
1 cup tart shredded apple with skin
⅔ cup milk
1 tablespoon mild honey
1 egg, beaten
½ teaspoon vinegar

Preheat oven to 375°F. and butter an 8-inch round cake pan. Mix flour, baking powder, and baking soda together in a bowl. Then add butter and rub between fingers into flour to a fine crumbly mixture. Then add sprouts, cheese, and apple and mix well.

In a second bowl, mix the milk, honey, egg, and vinegar and add to flour mixture. Mix into fairly thick dough and place in a buttered pan. Cut surface like a "tic-tac-toe" game and bake for about 45 minutes, or until a light brown and crusty surface is formed. This is a fairly dense bread, which will not rise too much. Remove from pan and cool on a wire rack. Break off chunks where the cuts were made and serve slightly warm with butter.

Whole Wheat Zucchini and Carrot Muffins
Makes 12 large muffins

2½ cups whole wheat flour
1½ tablespoons baking powder
5 tablespoons butter
⅓ cup mild honey
1 tablespoon grated orange rind
2 tablespoons orange juice concentrate
3 eggs
¾ cup milk
1 teaspoon vanilla extract
1 small carrot, shredded
1 medium-size zucchini, shredded
½ cup coarsely chopped walnuts

Butter a 12-cup large muffin tin and preheat oven to 325°F. Sift flour and baking powder together, return the bran left in sifter, and set aside.

In a small saucepan, combine butter, honey, orange rind, and orange concentrate and stir over low heat until butter is melted. Set aside to cool.

In a large bowl, beat the eggs with an egg beater until foamy and add the milk and vanilla. Then add the carrot, zucchini, and butter mixture. Stir in the flour mixture, half at a time, mixing only until dry ingredients are moistened. Then fold in the nuts. Spoon batter into prepared muffin cups, almost to the top, and bake for 45 to 50 minutes. Muffins are done when cake tester inserted in center comes out clean. Cool muffins slightly on a rack before removing them from their pans. They look lovely served in pleated paper cups.

Baked Whole Wheat Bread Pudding with Apple Meringue
Serves 6

4 slices whole wheat bread
5 tablespoons soft butter
4 egg yolks (reserve whites)
2 cups milk
⅓ cup date sugar
½ teaspoon cinnamon
¼ teaspoon nutmeg
1 teaspoon vanilla extract
½ cup raisins

Spread slices of bread with 4 tablespoons of the butter. Use the remaining tablespoon to butter a 1½-quart, deep souffle dish and preheat oven to 350°F. Cut bread slices into cubes, place in a bowl, and set aside.

Beat egg yolks with a wire whisk. Add milk, date sugar, cinnamon, nutmeg, and vanilla. Beat well until frothy. Pour over bread cubes, add raisins, and let stand for 5 minutes until some of the liquid is absorbed by the bread. Spoon into souffle dish and place in a larger pan containing enough boiling water to reach 1 inch up the side of the souffle dish. Bake for 1 hour and 10 minutes. In the last 10 minutes of baking, prepare the Apple Meringue.

Apple Meringue:

4 egg whites
¼ teaspoon cream of tartar
1 cup unsweetened applesauce
4 tablespoons maple syrup
½ teaspoon vanilla extract
½ teaspoon grated lemon rind

In a large bowl, beat the egg whites and cream of tartar with an electric beater or a hand eggbeater until very foamy and slightly stiff. Mix all remaining ingredients together and add ½ cup at a time to the egg whites, beating all the while. Continue beating for 10 minutes, or until very stiff. Spoon in large dollops on top of bread pudding and slip under a hot broiler for 30 seconds to 1 minute, or until the top is golden. Watch carefully to prevent burning. Serve hot, warm, or cold.

The **Pastiera** of Carmelo Borgone

When Carmelo Borgone speaks of his hometown of Agrigento in Italy, his eyes light with the memory of "the most beautiful town in Sicily, a jewel that overlooks the valley of the temples!" It was there that his family ran a local ice cream factory and bakery, and where Carmelo first learned to bake the indescribably delicious holiday cake, *pastiera,* made from the hulled wheat berries called *frumento.*

Carmelo has been a baker for 30 years, and he works just around the corner from where we live, as Chief Pastry Chef at Veniero's, a family landmark in our neighborhood since 1894, and one of the most famous Italian bakeries in New York City. For a week before the holidays of Easter, Thanksgiving, and Christmas, Carmelo and his crew bake *pastiera* for the shoppers who come from as far away as New England to purchase the specialty.

Acquiring Carmelo's recipe for *pastiera* was not an easy task, since he bakes between 40 and 60 cakes at one time. Each time he described an ingredient, he made huge circles with his hands, scooping up an imaginary tub of butter, while saying, " . . . then you add a little butter. . . ." As with all great chefs, the amounts are all unspecific. However, we have created a version of his *pastiera,* and the recipe follows.

Italian Pastiera: Hulled Wheat Berry and Ricotta Cake

Makes 1 cake

Rich and luscious, this dessert is baked only at Easter time and Christmastime in Sicily. Our version was concocted after a conversation with Carmelo Borgone, master baker at Veniero's in New York.

Basic Whole Wheat Crust (use for any filled pie):

- 1½ cups whole wheat pastry flour
- 1 teaspoon grated lemon rind
- ½ cup soft butter, cut into small pieces
- 1 egg yolk (reserve white)
- ¼ cup mild honey
- ¼ teaspoon vanilla extract

Mix flour and lemon rind together. Cut in butter until crumbly. Mix egg yolk, honey, and vanilla together and stir into flour mixture until a ball of dough forms. Wrap and chill for 1 hour.

Preheat oven to 400°F. Remove sides from a 9-inch springform pan and place a third of the dough on the ungreased pan bottom. Cover with a piece of floured waxed paper and roll. Then press dough with fingers to fit. Remove paper and prick surface with fork. Bake for 10 minutes, or until golden. Remove from oven and cool pastry. Butter the inner sides of the springform pan and fit over the cooled base. Roll out and then press the remaining two-thirds of the dough onto the sides of pan, patting and stretching dough to fit. If it tears, it can be patched, so don't worry—but it must be thin and must cover the inside completely, right up to the top rim of the pan.

Filling:

- 4 eggs, separated, plus leftover white from crust
- ½ cup mild honey
- 2 pounds ricotta cheese
- 2 tablespoons grated orange rind
- 1 tablespoon grated lemon rind
- 2 teaspoons orange flower water
- 1 teaspoon vanilla extract
- 2 cups Basic Hulled Wheat Berries (see recipe in this section)
- 2 tablespoons flour

Beat egg yolks in a food processor. Add honey and beat again. Add the cheese, half at a time, and beat. Then beat in the orange and lemon rinds, orange flower water, and vanilla. Remove to a large bowl and stir in the hulled wheat berries and flour.

Beat egg whites until stiff, fold into the cheese filling, and pour into pan. Raise the oven temperature to 475°F. and bake for 10 minutes. Then reduce temperature to 200°F. and bake for 1 hour and 15 minutes. (Cover with a tent of foil if top browns too quickly.) Turn off heat and let cake remain in oven for 15 minutes more. Then remove from oven and cool completely. As it cools, it solidifies and shrinks a bit. Refrigerate for a few hours before removing sides of springform pan. Serve at room temperature.

Whole Wheat Gingerbread Persons

Makes 30 cookies

½ cup soft butter
½ cup date sugar
1 tablespoon grated orange rind
2 tablespoons grated lemon rind
1 tablespoon grated ginger root
1 teaspoon cinnamon
¼ teaspoon ground cloves
½ cup light molasses
½ cup apple cider vinegar
1 egg
3 cups whole wheat pastry flour
1 teaspoon baking soda

Cream butter and date sugar together until light and fluffy. Add orange rind, lemon rind, ginger, cinnamon, and cloves and beat well.

In a small pot, slowly heat molasses to the boiling point. Remove from heat and add the vinegar. Cool for a few minutes, then add to the butter mixture, and beat until throughly blended. Then beat in the egg. Mix the flour and baking soda together and add to the mixture to make a smooth yet soft and pliable dough. Scrape out with a floured rubber spatula and wrap in waxed paper to chill for 1 hour.

Roll out dough ¼ inch thick on a floured board with a floured rolling pin. (Use only half the dough at a time for easier handling.) Cut with a person-shaped cookie cutter. Reroll scraps and continue cutting until all the dough is used.

Preheat oven to 350°F. and line 2 cookie sheets with aluminum foil. Carefully lift cookies with a spatula onto prepared pans and bake for 10 to 15 minutes, or until golden brown. Shift pans for even browning. Remove at once and cool on a wire rack. When completely cool, store in an airtight container. They are better the second day, but who can wait?

Note: If you wish, cut a hole in the top of the cookie for a string to pass through before baking. Decorate and hang on the Christmas tree.

Whole Wheat Walnut Cookies—Three Ways

Makes about 30 cookies

½ cup soft butter
⅓ cup date sugar
1 egg, separated
2 teaspoons vanilla extract
1 cup whole wheat pastry flour, sifted
1 cup finely chopped walnuts

Beat butter and date sugar together until creamy. (Use a food processor or hand electric beater.) Beat in egg yolk and vanilla and then mix in the flour until a ball of dough is formed. Wrap and chill in the refrigerator for 15 minutes.

Preheat oven to 375°F. Beat egg white with a wire whisk until foamy. Place about ¼ cup chopped nuts on a piece of foil. Use the dough to create cookies in 3 different shapes.

Variations:

1. Fingerprint Cookies Filled with Jam: Shape one-third of the dough into small balls (about 1 teaspoonful for each cookie). Dip into egg white and then into the ¼ cup chopped walnuts. Place on ungreased cookie sheet, 1 inch apart. Press a well in the center with index finger.
2. Aggression Cookies: Knead ½ cup walnuts into the remaining two-thirds dough until well incorporated. Divide in half and set half aside. Again roll into small balls and place on same cookie sheet, 2 inches apart. Dip the bottom of a glass in date sugar and then press down hard on each ball of dough. Sprinkle tops of each with remaining chopped walnuts.
3. Fork-Ridged Cookies: Roll remaining one-third of dough into small balls and place on cookie sheet, 1½ inches apart. Press deeply with tines of a fork that have been dipped in flour.

Bake all cookies for 10 to 12 minutes. Remove to wire rack and cool completely. Spoon a small amount of jam or Orange Date-Nut Butter (see Index) in each well left by your finger on the first batch of cookies.

"But the cost!"

Before we even begin to discuss wild rice, we might as well address the question of the price of this wonderful grain. If we were to begin by saying that wild rice is not a grain at all, but an aquatic grass seed *(Zizania aquatica),* resistant readers would not be deterred from their basic concern, and we'd hear, *"But the price!"* And should we tell of the hardships of the Chippewa Indians in Minnesota who harvest wild rice, the voices would still rise up as one with, *"It's so expensive!"*

Of course, we readily admit that the cost *per pound* is quite high, and those little four-ounce boxes of wild rice hardly seem to match the big figures rung up at the check-out counter. However, if you consider this tasty whole grain carefully, you realize that it can actually work out to be quite *inexpensive* on a per portion basis. The original volume of wild rice more than *triples* when it is cooked, which brings the cost per serving down to a reasonable range, even in these days of high prices and astronomical inflation. This, in addition to the fact that it is an unrefined, high-fiber food source, high in cereal protein, B vitamins, and essential minerals—and very low in fat—makes it worth looking into the next time you're preparing a dinner for the family or very special guests.

The history of wild rice is also the history of the Chippewa, the Sioux, the Fox, and the Winnebago Indians of the Upper Great Lakes Region. Even today, about three-quarters of all the wild rice comes from Minnesota. One of the few "grains" native to North America, wild rice is probably the major reason that in the earliest days the Indians of the area were able to survive those harsh, cold winters, when game became scarce and ice covered the fishing grounds. For the tribes who depended so much upon wild rice, it became known as *manomin* or "good berry."

The harvesting is still done in the traditional way in the north lake country of Minnesota, and

Wild Rice: The "Rolls Royce" of Grains

September is known as the "rice moon." In each boat or birch canoe, two occupants harvest an allotted section of the lake. One man pushes the craft through the tall rice with a long pole, while the second man pulls the plant down over the boat and beats out the grains with two sticks. The grain that falls into the water is the seed for next year's crop.

Commercial production of wild rice was almost unknown until a few years ago, and it is still a frustrating and difficult process. The growing states are rightfully concerned about protecting the interests of the Indian tribes who still depend upon the annual harvest for their income. Furthermore, even with modern technology, wild rice is a difficult crop to grow commercially, in part because so little is really known about it. George Moriarity of the Wild Rice Growers Association says, "Wild rice is today where corn and oats were a hundred years ago." It is vulnerable to the weather—a severe windstorm at harvesttime can destroy a crop by blowing the seeds into the water. Migrating birds, knowing a good dinner when they see it, can devastate a growing area. Insects, disease, and drainage can add to the toll.

The job of preparing a crop for market is still tedious and expensive. Formerly, the Indian braves danced on the wild rice in clean, new moccasins in order to loosen the grains from the hulls, and even today the traditional method includes putting the rice into bags and pounding it by hand with clubs. The women of the tribe then winnow the grain by using shallow birchbark trays, tossing the seeds into the air and letting the wind do the job. Newer developments include the addition of custom-built harvesters that skim the lake tops, shipment to market by aircraft, and ingenious methods of parching, hulling, and winnowing. Yet, it still takes two to three pounds of wild rice in the husk to obtain one pound of finished product.

As always, though, all the technical data gives way finally to one measure of judgment—the flavor. The chewy, nutty, smoky food has become a favorite of cooks all over America and Canada, and in the recipes that we include, we try to show you just how far this wonderful ricelike food can be stretched to lessen the cost per portion. In any case, we know that our recipes for wild rice are a vast improvement over the one given by the eighteenth-century fur trader, Peter Pond, who suggested that we "eat it with Bairs Greas and Sugar . . ."

The Grades of Wild Rice

Select (Short): Used where appearance is not a primary concern, since some of the grains may be broken or not of uniform length and size. The Select grade is perfect for use in baked goods such as muffins, in pancakes, or in soups.

Extra Fancy (Medium): The most popular grade of wild rice. The grains are of equal size and quality, and they're clean and unbroken. The Extra Fancy grade is usually used for salads, side dishes, and stuffings, and it can be used as an alternative for the Giant grade.

Giant (Long): The super deluxe grade of wild rice. Each grain is usually about one inch long, and naturally this is the most costly of the grades. It's usually reserved for use with wild game (pheasant, quail, venison).

Miscellaneous Grades: A variety of other grades, including some that are parboiled or otherwise processed, and the white and wild rice mixtures that you'll find on the supermarket shelves. However, the three grades listed above are the ones we strongly recommend for purity, flavor, and better food value.

Basic Wild Rice

Yields 2 cups, or about 6 servings

Although there are several accepted ways to pre-pare plain boiled wild rice, we find this method the easiest and fastest, and the one with consistently good results.

4 ounces wild rice
2¼ cups water

Pick over dry rice, removing any foreign material. Bring water to a boil in a 5-quart, flat-bottom, SilverStone-lined pan with cover. Rinse rice in a strainer under cold running water and drain.

When water boils, add rice, stir, and bring to a boil again. Lower heat, cover, and simmer for 45 minutes, or until rice grains open. Remove from heat and let stand with paper towels between pot and lid until any remaining liquid is absorbed. Then fluff with a fork. If some liquid still remains after standing, dry over low heat, shaking pan rather than stirring to prevent grains from becoming mushy.

Note: Usually, wild rice, unless purchased loose, is packaged either in 4-ounce or 6-ounce packages. There are various grades, but we have used the Extra Fancy medium or long grain (see Mail-Order Sources).

To cook 6 ounces wild rice, use 3 cups water and simmer for 45 minutes. This will yield 3½ cups, or about 8 servings.

The yields and cooking times for the Select (short) grade and the Giant grain will vary. The large size will, of course, take longer—from 20 to 30 minutes longer.

Cooked wild rice can be kept in the refrigerator for 1 week and freezes well.

Christmas Wild Rice
with Red and Green Peppers
and Mushrooms
Serves 6

4 tablespoons butter
1 medium-size onion, coarsely
   chopped
½ sweet red pepper, diced
½ green pepper, diced
12 medium-size mushrooms,
   thickly sliced
¼ teaspoon black pepper
1 teaspoon shredded lemon
   rind
2 cups cooked wild rice
   (4 ounces dry)

Heat butter in a large skillet and saute onion, while stirring, for 2 minutes. Add the peppers and mushrooms and continue cooking, while stirring, over medium heat until mushrooms give up their liquid and then reabsorb it.

Remove from heat and toss with remaining ingredients. Spoon into an oven-to-table casserole and cover with foil. When ready to serve, heat in preheated 350°F. oven for 15 to 20 minutes. Serve as an accompaniment to any poultry or pork dish, or use as a stuffing for baked chicken breasts.

Fennel, Endive, and
Wild Rice Salad
Serves 6

2 cups cooked wild rice
   (4 ounces dry)
1½ cups thinly sliced endive
   (⅛ inch thick)
1 cup sliced bulb fennel
   (⅛ inch thick)
2 tablespoons finely minced
   chives
1 tablespoon finely minced
   parsley
2 tablespoons diced pimiento
   or sweet red pepper
½ teaspoon finely minced
   lemon rind
⅓ cup mayonnaise
1 tablespoon milk
¼ teaspoon black pepper
   lettuce leaves for garnish

Mix all ingredients together lightly to avoid crushing grains. Mound salad on a bed of loose lettuce leaves and serve at room temperature.

Thanksgiving Wild Rice with Sausage, Acorn Squash, and Brussels Sprouts

Serves 6

Prepare this dish the night before, just reheat, and you can skip the additional vegetables and stuffing.

2   medium-size acorn squash (about 1½ pounds), quartered, seeded, and steamed for 15 minutes
½   pound very small Brussels sprouts, steamed for 8 minutes
½   pound Homemade Pork Sausage, crumbled (see Index)
1   medium-size onion, coarsely chopped (about ½ cup)
2   cups cooked wild rice (4 ounces dry)
2   sage leaves, finely minced, or ½ teaspoon dried sage
½   teaspoon finely minced marjoram, or ½ teaspoon dried marjoram
⅛   teaspoon black pepper
1   tablespoon butter, melted freshly grated nutmeg

Set aside the squash pieces and Brussels sprouts. In a large skillet, cook the sausage, stirring occasionally, for 10 minutes. Add the onion and cook, while stirring, for 10 minutes more. Drain off any accumulated fat and return skillet to heat. Stir in cooked wild rice, sage, marjoram, and black pepper. Spoon mixture into shallow oven-to-table casserole and top with pieces of squash. Fill each squash cavity with Brussels sprouts. Drizzle some butter and a few gratings of nutmeg over vegetables, cover with foil, and reheat in a 350°F. oven for about 15 minutes.

Wild Rice with Pecans and Tangerines
Serves 6

Try this side dish, instead of the usual orange sauce, with roasted duck.

2 tablespoons butter
½ cup pecans
3 tangerines
2 cups cooked wild rice
    (4 ounces dry)
1 teaspoon grated ginger root
½ cup finely minced celery
    leaves or lovage
1 tablespoon finely minced
    parsley

Melt butter in a skillet and add the pecans. Toast, stirring constantly, and then set aside.

Grate the rind of 2 tangerines and set aside. Then peel all 3 tangerines, pulling off the white particles, and divide them into segments.

Combine the nuts, grated rinds, and the tangerine segments with all the remaining ingredients, stirring gently. Transfer to an oven-to-table serving dish, cover with foil, and bake in a 450°F. preheated oven for 15 minutes just before serving.

Wild Rice Poultry Stuffing with Apples, Prunes, and Filberts
Yields 5 to 6 cups

Enough stuffing for a 10- to 12-pound turkey or goose, or for the center of a festive crown roast of pork.

4 tablespoons butter
½ cup finely sliced scallions
½ cup finely chopped celery,
    with leaves
¼ cup finely diced green
    peppers
½ cup coarsely chopped
    mushrooms
1 teaspoon crushed dried
    sage
¼ teaspoon black pepper
½ teaspoon dried thyme
2 cups coarsely chopped,
    unpeeled red apples
¾ cup pitted prunes, cut in
    half
¼ cup toasted, chopped
    filberts
3½ cups cooked wild rice
    (6 ounces dry)

Heat butter in a large skillet and saute scallions over medium heat for 1 minute, while stirring. Add the celery, green peppers, mushrooms, and sage and saute for 5 minutes, while stirring, until wilted. Add all the remaining ingredients and combine well.

Stuff about 4 cups of the mixture into the cavity of the bird and about 1 cup into the crop. Heat any leftover stuffing separately and serve with the carved bird.

Pasta Party Rolls with a Variety of Fillings   For this recipe, see page 286

Marinara Sauce   For this recipe, see page 233

We have tried throughout this book to maintain the integrity of the grains, to make them individual, and to introduce our readers to the taste, the nutrition, and the flexibility of each of them—one by one. But, as we look at the endless containers of grains, of grits, and of groats (to name but a few) in our kitchen we naturally begin to wonder, "What would happen if . . .?"

What would happen if we used millet with corn flour, oat flakes with rice flakes, bulgur with short grain brown rice, barley grits with corn germ? The inventor, the creator, the experimenter in all of us conjures up the image of a chef in his *toque blanche* surrounded by test tubes—mixing, adding, bubbling, tasting. It can, indeed, be done with grains.

Once we understand just how the individual grains are prepared, the idea of mixing them becomes eminently reasonable, and many grains can be used, one with the other, to prepare dishes that have *their* own distinctive flavors and textures.

There are several commercially prepared, packaged mixed grains available:

Mixed Grains: If One Is Good, Would Two Be Better?

Erewhon

- *Morning Cereal:* A combination of brown rice, whole wheat, whole oats, hulled barley, sesame seeds, and soybeans.
- *Infant Cereal:* The same combination as above, but more finely milled.

Arrowhead Mills

- *7-Grain Cereal:* A combination of wheat, oats, triticale, millet, soy, buckwheat, and corn.

Mixed Flaked Grain Granola with Dates, Prunes, and Raisins
Serves 6

The inclusion of several different grains, instead of using oats alone, adds a new dimension in taste to this breakfast favorite—a rewarding experiment for all grain lovers.

⅓ cup triticale flakes
1 cup rolled oats
2 tablespoons barley flakes
2 tablespoons rice flakes
⅔ cup boiling water
⅓ cup sunflower oil
⅓ cup mild honey
1½ teaspoons vanilla extract
⅔ cup sunflower seeds
½ cup chopped walnuts
½ cup flaked coconut
⅓ cup wheat germ
2 tablespoons unprocessed bran
½ cup plumped raisins
½ cup pitted dates, cut into small pieces
½ cup pitted prunes

Mix triticale, oats, barley, and rice together in a bowl. Add boiling water, stir, and let stand for 5 minutes.

Preheat oven to 325°F. Spread the moistened flakes in one layer in a 9 × 13 × 2-inch baking pan and toast in oven, stirring occasionally, for 20 minutes.

Meanwhile, in a small skillet, slowly heat oil and honey together. Stir in vanilla, sunflower seeds, walnuts, coconut, wheat germ, and bran, and then pour over flakes, stirring to distribute well. Toast for 10 minutes more, stirring occasionally so grains toast evenly. Mix remaining ingredients together and add to mixture after it is toasted. The fruits stay plump and moist and the grains are soft but cooked and nutty. Serve with milk.

Mixed Grain and Vegetable Soup with Bean Sprouts
Serves 6

2 pounds lamb bones, neck and shoulder (beef or veal bones can also be used)
9 cups water
¼ cup cracked dry corn (crack in blender)
¼ cup whole bulgur
¼ cup whole millet
2 tablespoons short grain brown rice
¼ cup whole rye berries
1 whole onion
5 whole cloves
1 clove garlic, peeled
2 carrots
2 stalks celery
1 small turnip, peeled
12 sprigs parsley
3 sprigs dillweed
  celery leaves or lovage
1 bay leaf
1 small dried hot pepper
6 tablespoons mung bean or soybean sprouts

In a 5-quart pot, place bones and water and bring to a boil. Lower heat and simmer for 5 minutes. Skim any scum from surface and discard.

Stir in corn, bulgur, millet, rice, and rye berries. Pierce the bottom of the onion with the point of a knife, insert cloves, and add to the pot along with the garlic, carrots, celery, and turnip, and simmer for 1 hour.

Place parsley, dillweed, celery leaves or lovage, bay leaf, and pepper in a piece of cheesecloth, tie ends, and add to the pot. Continue cooking for 1 hour more.

When ready to serve, use tongs to lift out cheesecloth bag, all the vegetables, and the bones. When cool, slice 1 carrot, remove any meat scraps from the bones, and return to the soup. Discard remaining vegetables and bones. Reheat soup before serving and top each bowl with 1 tablespoon of raw, crunchy sprouts.

Mixed Grain Pilaf with Herbs and Slivered Almonds
Serves 6

This pilaf is the perfect accompaniment to any meat or poultry dish; or you may add leftover cubed chicken or beef to it for a complete meal.

2 tablespoons butter
⅓ cup slivered almonds
2 tablespoons olive oil
⅓ cup whole bulgur
⅓ cup long grain brown rice
⅓ cup whole barley
1 clove garlic, finely minced
1 large onion, finely chopped (about ⅔ cup)
2 medium-size carrots, shredded (about 1½ cups)
2½ cups stock, either Chicken Stock or Vegetable Stock (see Index) or beef stock
1 teaspoon thyme, or ½ teaspoon dried thyme
1 teaspoon marjoram, or ½ teaspoon dried marjoram
⅓ cup finely minced parsley
4 teaspoons black pepper

Melt butter in large, flat, oval oven-to-table casserole and toss nuts over medium heat until golden in color. Lift out with a slotted spoon and reserve. Add olive oil to casserole, heat, and then add bulgur, brown rice, and barley. Stir to coat grains evenly with the oil and toast for about 1 minute. Add the garlic and onion and cook, stirring, until wilted.

Stir in the carrots, then add the stock and bring to a boil. Cover with foil and simmer for 35 to 40 minutes. Add all remaining ingredients, except reserved nuts, cover again, and let stand for 10 minutes. Before serving, toss with reserved almonds.

Mixed Grain Griddle Cakes
or Waffles

Makes about 32 small griddle cakes, 2 large waffles,
or 8 small waffles

1   cup whole wheat flour
1   cup rolled oats
½   cup yellow cornmeal
1   teaspoon baking soda
1   tablespoon baking powder
2   cups buttermilk
1   cup plain yogurt
¼   cup butter, melted
2   eggs, lightly beaten
2   tablespoons maple syrup

In a large bowl, mix flour, oats, cornmeal, baking soda, and baking powder together.

Combine buttermilk, yogurt, butter, eggs, and maple syrup in a second bowl and beat well. Then add dry ingredients to liquid ingredients, blending well. Let batter stand for 15 minutes before baking.

Preheat griddle or waffle iron. Drop by spoonfuls onto griddle and cook until surface is dry and bubbly before turning over to cook second side. If making waffles, follow directions of your particular waffle iron.

One-Rise 7-Grain Bread

Makes 2 medium-size loaves

This recipe uses Arrowhead Mills 7-Grain Cereal consisting of wheat, oats, triticale, millet, soy, buckwheat, and corn.

1½   cups boiling water
1   cup 7-Grain Cereal
2   packages dry yeast
     (½ ounce)
½   cup warm water
¼   cup mild honey
3   tablespoons corn oil
3   tablespoons butter, melted
     (lukewarm)
2   eggs, beaten
4½ to 5   cups whole wheat flour

In a large mixing bowl, pour boiling water over 7-Grain Cereal. Let cool to room temperature.

Dissolve yeast in warm water and honey. Stir and blend thoroughly.

Add yeast-honey mixture to cereal mixture. Then add corn oil, butter, and eggs and mix thoroughly with a wooden spoon. Add about 4 cups of flour, a bit at a time, stirring with wooden spoon. Mixture should be crumbly but damp. Turn out onto a lightly floured surface and knead in remaining flour until dough is smooth but slightly damp. Knead about 8 to 10 minutes. Divide in half, place each portion in a well-buttered, medium-size loaf pan, cover with a towel, and place in a warm spot to double (about 50 minutes to 1 hour). Preheat oven to 375°F. and bake for 50 minutes, or until breads test done.

Mixed Grain Mincemeat Tea Loaf
Makes 1 loaf

Vegetarian Mincemeat:

¼ cup raisins

¼ cup currants

¼ pound dried apples, coarsely chopped

½ teaspoon cinnamon

⅛ teaspoon ground cloves

½ teaspoon grated ginger root

1 tablespoon grated lemon rind

1½ cups apple cider

½ cup coarsely chopped walnuts

2 tablespoons soft butter (optional)

Mix all ingredients except nuts and butter together in a SilverStone-lined pan. Bring to a boil and then simmer, uncovered, stirring occasionally, for about 45 minutes to 1 hour, or until liquid is absorbed and mixture is very thick. Stir in nuts and butter, if used, and cool. There should be 2 cups.

Tea Loaf:

2 cups whole wheat flour

1 cup white cornmeal

½ cup rye flour

½ teaspoon baking soda

2 teaspoons baking powder

½ cup nonfat dry milk

1½ cups buttermilk, room temperature

2 cups mincemeat

Preheat oven to 350°F. and generously butter a 9 × 5 × 3-inch loaf pan. In a large bowl, mix all the dry ingredients together. Add the buttermilk and the 2 cups of mincemeat. Stir well with a wooden spoon. Pour into prepared pan, wet fingers, and smooth surface. Bake for 1 hour. Cool in pan for 15 minutes. Remove from pan and continue cooling on a rack for 15 minutes more before slicing. Delicious spread with ricotta cheese.

Upside Down Mixed Grain Skillet Cake with Ginger Pears and Cranberry Topping

Makes 1 skillet cake

Topping:

4	tablespoons butter
6	tablespoons mild honey
1	teaspoon grated ginger root
1	cup whole cranberries
4 or 5	small Bosc pears, peeled, cored, and coarsely chopped

In a 10-inch black cast-iron skillet, slowly melt the butter over low heat and then add the honey. Stir for 1 minute and then add the ginger root. Spread the cranberries around in this mixture, remove from heat, and spoon the chopped pears over the cranberries. Set aside.

Cake:

¼	cup yellow corn flour
¼	cup oat flour
½	cup whole wheat pastry flour
1	cup unbleached white flour
1	tablespoon baking powder
4	tablespoons soft butter
½	cup mild honey
2	teaspoons vanilla extract
2	eggs
⅔	cup milk

Preheat oven to 350°F. Sift flours and baking powder together and set aside.

In a mixer or food processor, beat butter until creamy. Add honey and vanilla and beat again. Then add eggs and continue to beat until light. Alternately add a third of the flours and a third of the milk, beating after each addition. Spoon batter evenly over fruit in the skillet and bake for 45 minutes, or until center of cake is done.

Invert at once over a serving dish. Keep skillet on cake for 5 minutes and then remove. Cool before serving.

Part III
Ah–the Pastas!

Pasta Perfect

One of the most exciting and satisfying film experiences we've ever had was an assignment for Alitalia Airlines to produce a documentary on the foods of Italy. It was called *Buon Appetito,* and we traveled the country from top to bottom, from the Alps through Sicily, from the hill towns around Rome to the islands of Ischia and Capri and Sardinia, first assembling the food of the region, then photographing it, and finally— eating what we had just filmed! Over three seasons of that year, we devoured all that the countryside had to offer. We enjoyed the fresh spring salads, the carefully chosen, lean cuts of tender veal, the wines that aged deep in the caves, the desserts of chestnut puree or fresh fruits and pungent cheeses, and the pastas. Ah, the endless surprise of pastas, in a hundred configurations bathed in as many different and surprising sauces.

Almost everyone we know is a "pastaholic." The mere mention of the name of this book brings a light to the eyes of our friends when we get to the last word. But, at the same time, there are many misconceptions about this "Italian Soul Food." In fact, one of our dear Italian friends, Libero Pilotto, used to ask incredulously, "Where did you Americans learn to cook Italian food? Did you *invent* it?" No self-respecting Italian cook would let a tomato sauce bubble on the stove all day long, especially one made with pieces of delicate seafood.

In Italy, pasta dishes are made quickly, many of them improvised by using seasonal or regional vegetables, cheeses, and herbs, plus some meat or fish for additional flavor. The sauces are an artist's palette of flavors and textures. One version might be light and subtle as a zephyr, another hearty and robust, earthy as the mother and father who run the little trattoria hidden on a hillside road in Tuscany. For them, a perfect pasta sauce is the result of a momentary whim, a creative gift for a hungry guest.

Another misconception about pasta and its sauces generally comes into the conversation after our friends reflect with envy on our culinary adventures in Italy, giving some small solace to themselves with the statement, "Yeah, but you must sure have gotten fat!" It is a measure of the American guilt complex that anything *that* good *must* be fattening.

We have already discussed the return of the lowly carbohydrate in our introduction to this book, and all types of grain foods—including pastas—are now recognized as foods that deliver more nutritional value than excess calories. Ounce for ounce, the complex carbohydrates give us the same amount of energy as protein, but without the large caloric intake of fat. Long-distance runners have changed their diets to include more grains, and so have other athletes, and so have today's dieters. And so have we.

It takes but a small amount of pasta to make up a "portion" in a recipe—as little as two to three ounces per person. An ounce of pasta is about 75 to 100 calories, a normal portion only 150 to 300.

Now we come to the next of the myths: the sauces. Only in this country do we inundate pasta in thick, heavy, long-cooked tomato sauces. In Italy, the sauce is but a part of the entire picture, a delicate balance of tastes and textures atop a myriad variety of pasta shapes. A small portion of pasta begins the lunch, followed by a small, lean piece of meat accompanied by a vegetable, a light and delicate salad, some coffee, and fresh fruit for dessert. And so, to the statement, "You sure must have gotten fat!" we can only answer that we actually *lost* weight over the year of making our film about the foods of Italy. And, my, *did we eat well!*

No matter that we generally equate the noble noodle only with the country of Garibaldi, the world of pasta is larger than all of Italy. At one time it was rumored that Marco Polo brought the first pastas back from his trip to China, but the story has been laid to rest by historians and food authorities. Ancient Etruscan bas-reliefs that long predate Marco Polo depict utensils used for making pasta—almost the same equipment you find today for making it in the home. A manuscript about the life of Blessed Hermit William, published about the year 1200, says, "He invited William to dinner and served macaroni." But most convincing of all, is the fact that ravioli was commonly eaten in the city of Rome *20 years* before Marco even embarked on his world tour!

Certainly, Marco Polo did bring some pasta home from China. The Chinese had been making noodles of flour and water since the Shang Dynasty (about 1700 B.C.). Even today their cuisine includes a wide variety of noodles made from corn, rice, and mung beans. It is quite possible, in fact, that forms of pasta developed simultaneously in various cultures around the globe, for it did not take much of a sophisticated technology to mix a grain flour with water and then dry it for future use. The Japanese use a pasta called *soba,* a thin noodle made of buckwheat. And some historians believe it was the Arabs who first made pasta from their flour, in order to keep it for long journeys. One of those trips may well have been into Sicily, where they began the long history of Italian pastas.

We have divided this section of the book into several parts, including "store-bought" pastas, how to make pastas at home, and the international versions of the noble noodle. Economical, healthful, tasty, imaginative, its shapes and varieties and the hundreds of sauces make pasta a food that never gets boring. If you are a "pastaholic" as we are, read on. Read on.

"Pasta Spoken Here"

The English translations for the names of the pastas are charming and whimsical—lady's legs, greedy priests, Venus's navel, fat little lambs, sparrow's tongues, little stars. In Italian, pasta names roll off the tongue like the silver tones of a Verdi opera—*fedelini, lingue di passeri, rigatoni, capelleti, tortellini, tubettini.* There are spirals and tubes; flat—thick and thin—ribbed, and rounded; seashells and stars and butterflies; turbans and fancy bows. Though the variety is confusing, once you learn to separate them into categories, a vast array of pastas can be used easily and interchangeably with many of the same sauces. The basic *shapes* of pasta will determine just which sauces it is best to use.

Whole grain pastas are being manufactured now, and they are becoming more available in our local supermarkets and natural foods stores. However, we also find that these have no real consistency of color, shape, or texture. Each brand is different. You'll have to experiment, as we did, to find the one that best suits your taste. As of this writing, the commercial whole grain pastas include rice, corn, buckwheat, and wheat, plus some combinations of spinach or tomato and whole wheat flour. Some of the fanciful shapes that we describe can only be manufactured with special machine dies, and many may not be available in whole grain versions. In fact, the vast majority of commercial pastas do not use whole wheat flour, but are made with semolina, in the more traditional way.

Some pastas can only be made at home—such as the barley noodles or some vegetable puree pastas (beet or carrot)—but you'll probably find that, in any case, *any* homemade noodles are lighter and better than the commercially manufactured ones. You'll have a new taste treat in store for you with homemade *agnoletti, tortellini,* or *farfalle.* Here, then, is our "Pasta Primer" to help you learn the language of pasta.

Pasta Primer

- Strings: Round, solid, straight rods, usually long.
- Tubes (macaroni/*maccheroni*): Hollow or pierced pasta, almost endless variations in this group.
- Sheets, Ribbons, and Cutout Shapes: Flat pasta, cut into ribbons (noodles) of varying widths and different shapes.
- Pastas Designed to Hold Sauces: Sometimes called "specialty pasta."
- Filled Pastas: Basically circles and squares of pasta that are filled before cooking.
- Soup Pastas *(pastina)*: Tiniest size of many varieties of pasta shapes. Some shapes are uniquely for soup, others for pilafs.
- Oriental Noodles: Chinese and Japanese varieties—egg, rice, and buckwheat in various widths.

Basic Terminology

Because pasta comes in so many different varieties, we include this outline of terminology.

Length: Pasta comes short and long. The Italian verb *tagliare,* to cut, is often used to indicate the shorter varieties of pasta. For example, *ziti tagliati* (cut *ziti*).

Surface Texture: Some pastas are smooth and some have grooves. The smooth-textured pastas are not usually defined. Grooved pastas are referred to as *rigati,* the Italian word for grooves. For example, *ziti rigati* (grooved *ziti*).

Shape: Some pastas have curly edges or pinked edges, and some are flat. This description usually applies to the sheet and ribbon categories of pastas. The Italian word used to describe the curly edge is *ricci.* For example, lasagna *ricci* (curly-edged lasagna).

Size: When talking about the "size" of pasta, we are referring to *thickness* of a string pasta, the *diameter* of a tube pasta, or the *width* of a sheet or ribbon pasta. The Italians refer to size with a diminutive or superlative ending tagged onto the pasta's basic name. In America, manufacturers are less poetic and resort to numbers to differentiate sizes. For example, elbow macaroni #1, #2, or spaghetti #8, #9, #10.

The endings to look out for in Italian are:

- Large size: -oni *(ziti/zitoni)*
- Small size: -ini, -ine, -ette, -ina (spaghetti/ *spaghettini; fettuce/fettucine; conchiglie/ conchigliette;* pasta/*pastina*)

Basic Forms

Strings: The most ubiquitous form of pasta, extruded by machine, available in many, many sizes, all of which are characterized as solid, straight, long round rods. Depending upon the manufacturer, different names, and sometimes numbers, are given to denote the differences in thickness.

For example: *spaghettoni,* thickest spaghetti; *spaghetti,* medium thickness; *spaghettini,* thin spaghetti.

- *Vermicelli* (small worms): Very thin spaghetti, sometimes sold in nests.

- *Fedelini* (the faithful): Very thin; also sold in clusters or nests.
- *Capellini* (hair): Thinnest form of spaghetti, also called *capelli d'angeli* or angel's hair.
- *Fusilli:* Spaghetti, of any thickness, that has been curled like a corkscrew. (Sometimes curled around knitting needles.)
- *Gemelli* (twists or twins): Two short strands of spaghetti twisted tightly together, like rope or embroidery thread, about three inches long.
- *Linguine* (thin tongues): Another form of extruded pasta, flattish or oval-shaped rods, ranging in different widths. "Linguine" usually refers to the medium-thick rod.
- *Lingue de passeri* (sparrows' tongues): Thinner than linguine.

gemelli

Tubes (Macaroni/*Maccheroni*): Hollow, pierced, extruded tube forms of pasta in countless variations.

Long Tubular Pastas: Macaroni

- *Spaghetti bucati* or simply *bucati* (pierced spaghetti): The thinnest variety of tubular pasta, long like spaghetti.
- *Perciatelli:* Thicker spaghetti, like *spaghettoni,* but pierced.
- *Ziti* (bridegrooms): Technically refers to a long-length, medium tube pasta; we are more familiar with *ziti tagliati,* the cut version of this long tube.
- *Fusilli bucati* (pierced, curled spaghetti): Just what the name says.

Short Tubular Pastas with Straight Cut Ends

- *Tufoli:* Largest tubes, generally used for stuffing.
- *Cannelloni* (large reed): Usually formed from homemade pasta squares or crepes, stuffed, and then rolled into tube form.

vermicelli

fusilli

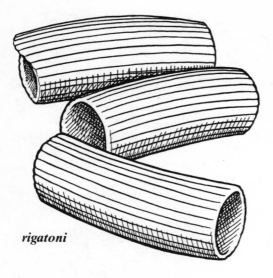

rigatoni

- *Rigatoni:* Large "grooved" pasta tubes.
- *Occhi di lupo* (wolves' eyes), *zitoni, denti di cavallo* (horses' teeth): Various names given to large-size tubular pastas.
- *Macaroni/maccheroni:* An almost generic name for all tubes, actually refers to medium tube pastas of 2- to 3-inch length, also called *ziti* or *mezzani* (medium).
- *Ditali* (thimbles): Small short tubes.
- *Tubetti* (little tubes).

Short Tubular Pastas with Diagonally Cut Ends

- *Manicotti* (muffs): Largest of these pastas, usually used for stuffing.
- *Penne* (quills, pens, or feathers): Medium-thickness tube (*pennone* is the larger version, and *pennine* is smaller).
- *Mostaccioli* (moustaches): Medium-thickness tubes, identical to *penne.*

Curved Tubular Pastas (Elbows): Made of any and almost all the forms of tubular pastas, ranging in thickness from thin, called *stivaletti* (little boots), to over ½ inch in diameter.

- *Cavatappi* (elbow twists): Ridged, corkscrew-shaped elbows.
- *Creste di galli* (cockscombs): Medium elbows with ruffled crest on the outside edge.
- *Capelli di prete* (priests' hats): Similar to above, but without crest.

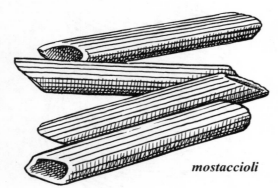

mostaccioli

cavatappi

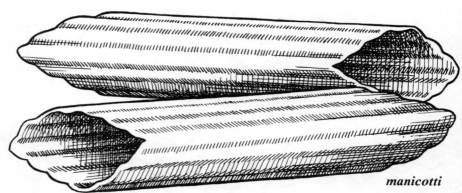

manicotti

Sheets, Ribbons, and Cutout Shapes

Sheets: Available only fresh or homemade, they are called *sfoglia* in Italian. They are the basic material for all forms in this category. Their thickness is pretty standard; the variations are in cutout shapes and sizes, widths of noodles, and edges that are pinked or curled.

Ribbons

- *Lasagna:* Broadest of the ribbons, sometimes with rippled edges.
- *Papardelle:* 1-inch-wide ribbon, often with pinked edges.
- *Tagliatelle:* ¾-inch-wide ribbon.
- *Fettuce:* ½-inch-wide ribbon; when edge is rippled it is called *mafalda.*
- *Fettucine:* ¼-inch-wide ribbon; when edge is rippled it is called *margherita,* sometimes called *mafaldina.*
- *Trenette:* ⅛-inch-wide ribbon, sometimes called *tagliarini.*

Cutout Shapes

- *Maltagliati* (badly cut): Rolled sheet of pasta, cut in different angular pieces.
- *Farfalle* (butterflies): Wide ribbons are cut, usually with a pastry wheel, making pinked edges, then cut again into short lengths, which are twisted or pinched in the middle to look like butterflies.

creste di galli

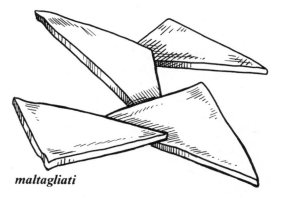

maltagliati

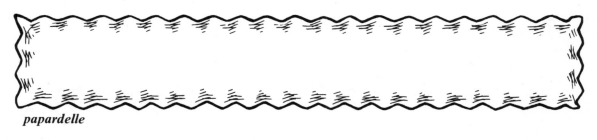

papardelle

mafaldina

triangoli

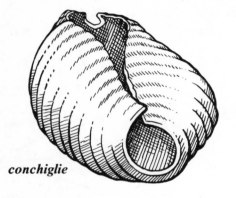

conchiglie

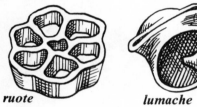

ruote   *lumache*

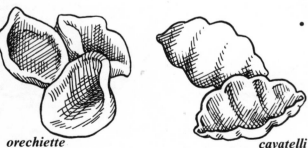

orechiette   *cavatelli*

gnochetti sardi

- *Cravatte* (bow ties), *nastrini* (ribbons or tapes): Cut from ribbons with a pastry wheel into short lengths, which are then pinched in the center to make bow ties. The ends are rounded on these.
- *Quadrucci* (squares): Sheets first cut into noodle strips and then down into little squares.
- *Triangoli* (triangles): Sheets cut into little triangles.

Pastas Designed to Hold Sauces (Specialty Pastas)

- *Conchiglie* or *maruzze* (shell): The name given to the largest conch-shaped pastas, which are generally stuffed. The smaller versions have diminutive endings, for example, *conchigliette*.
- *Lumache* (snail-shell shape): Another shell shape, available in several sizes.
- *Rotelle* (small wheels): Corkscrew spiral pastas usually about 2 inches long; also called *fusilli*.
- *Ruote/rote* (wheels): Cartwheel-shaped pastas in several sizes.
- *Orechiette* (little ears), *dischi volanti* (flying saucers), *vongole* (clam shells): Different names for similar small, round, indented pastas.
- *Gnochetti sardi* (little Sardinian shells): Long, narrow, grooved shells.
- *Cavatelli:* Short curled shells with a narrow, grooved surface; also called *gnocci*.
- *Margheritine* (small daisy).

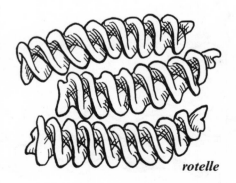

rotelle

Filled Pastas: Actually a variation of sheets (*sfoglia*). These are usually based on two basic shapes, the square and the circle. The sheet of pasta is rolled out, cut into either squares or circles, filled, and then shaped into a variety of forms before cooking.

Squares

- *Ravioli:* Little squares of stuffed pasta, usually sealed with pinked edges; commercial varieties are usually fresh or frozen.
- *Pansotti* (pot bellied): Squares folded diagonally over stuffing to form triangles, then usually sealed with pinked edges.
- *Capelleti* (little hats): Little triangles of stuffed pasta which are then curled around the finger and have the two ends joined to form a circle. The third side is not enclosed, but sticks up, forming a little tail.

Circles

- *Anolini:* Round or ring-shaped stuffed pasta.
- *Agnoletti* (fat little lambs): Circles of pasta folded in half over the stuffing to form semicircular pastas.
- *Tortellini:* Semicircular stuffed pasta, like the *capelleti,* also formed around a finger, with the two ends joined together to form a ring. Without the tail of the capelleti, it is said to look like "Venus's navel."

Soup Pastas *(pastina):* Characterized by being very, very tiny. The shapes come from every category of pasta previously described, and some unique to soup.

- *Acini di pepe* (peppercorns): Little round, rodlike pastas.
- *Anelli* (rings), *anellini* (little rings): Thinly sliced little tubes.
- *Tubettini, ave Maria-paternoster* (rosary beads): Short, small tubes.
- *Capelli d'angeli* (angel's hair): Very fine noodles, usually in clusters.
- *Alphabets:* Tiny letters of the alphabet.
- *Orzo* (grain): Tiny grain-shaped pastas.
- *Conchigliette, maruzzini* (tiny shells): Very tiny size shells.

- *Perline microscopici* (microscopic pearls): Tiny round "pearls" of pasta in different flavors—carrot, spinach, egg—often recommended for babies. Frequently sold as *pastina*.
- *Semi di melone* (melon seeds): Tiny pastas, shaped like melon seeds.
- *Stelle* (stars), *stellini* (little stars): Tiny star-shaped pastas.
- *Tripolini:* Tiny pinched pasta bows, smallest version of *cravatte*.

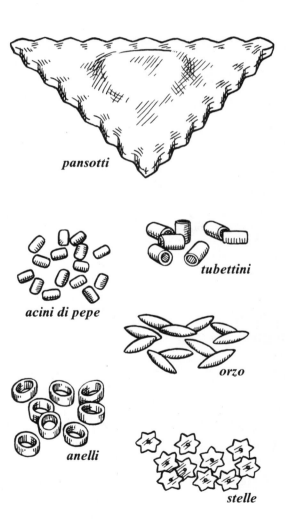

pansotti

acini di pepe

tubettini

orzo

anelli

stelle

Oriental Noodles

Chinese

- *Egg noodle varieties* are usually any noodles referred to as *mein,* such as *chow mein,* fried egg noodles, or *lo mein,* soft egg noodles. These are available fresh or dried, and sometimes in nests. Each Oriental country has its own name for the egg noodle variety.
- *Rice noodle varieties* are usually any noodles referred to as *fun.*

   Basic rice noodles *(fun):* Made from sheet dough and cut into different width noodles.

   Rice stick noodles *(fun):* The extruded variety, these are sometimes fine and opaque like Italian *vermicelli,* but also come in a range of thicknesses.

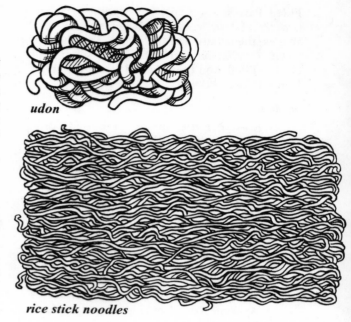

udon

rice stick noodles

Japanese

- *Somen:* Thin white noodles, sometimes made of buckwheat flour.
- *Soba:* Medium noodles usually of buckwheat flour.
- *Udon:* Thick wheat noodles.
- *Chuka-soba* or *ramen:* Crinkly wheat noodles, usually used in soup; they are quick-cooking.

Some Pasta Tips

Boiling the Bounty

The Pot: It takes a lot of water to cook pasta properly; with too little water the end result will be gummy and impossible to separate. Use a very large pot, but not too heavy in weight or it will take too long to boil the water. A large pot also allows you to use the proper amount of water without filling it to the brim. Use a pot with handles that will allow a good grip with pot holders.

The Method

- The correct amount of water for one pound of pasta is seven quarts. The pasta must "swim" around in the water.

- Make certain the water is boiling rapidly before you add the pasta.
- Add the pasta in small amounts, trying not to disturb the boil, stirring as you add each small batch. Stir with a wooden, long-handled fork and cook the pasta uncovered, occasionally stirring gently to distribute it evenly while it cooks. Should the water lose its boil when you add the pasta, cover the pot (leaving cover slightly ajar) only until water begins its rapid boil again. Then uncover and continue cooking.
- Timing depends upon the size and shape of the pasta. It is finished when it is *al dente* or "to the tooth"—neither soggy nor tough, but firm and cooked through. The cooking time will also vary, depending upon whether your heat source is gas, bottled gas, or electric, and it will vary from 8 to 20 minutes. Homemade pasta cooks fastest.
- A good rule to follow: Don't leave the kitchen while cooking pasta. The Italians have an apt saying that "pasta loves company." After five minutes (for small

pastas), lift out a piece and bite-test it for doneness. For freshly made and homemade frozen pasta, test after two minutes.

- For freshly made pasta, add two table-spoons of olive oil to the cooking water, since homemade noodles have a tendency to stick together. Stir with a wooden fork to keep the strands separated. Also use 2 tablespoons of olive oil for large pastas like lasagna and *manicotti.*
- The approximate cooking time for home-made pastas in this book is about four to six minutes for ½-inch, freshly made ribbon noodles, and six to eight minutes for dry pastas.
- The more adventurous test pasta for doneness by using a charming method that sounds like a joke, but works well. To find out if it's *al dente,* they throw a strand against the wall. If it sticks, it's ready; if it falls to the floor, it needs more cooking time. Some use the ceiling for testing.
- If you are going to use the pasta in a dish that will be baked afterward and covered by a sauce, undercook it a bit.
- When cooking pasta for a cold salad, rinse it in cold water as soon as it has been put in a colander and drained.
- Pour the finished pasta slowly into a colander placed in the sink. As it drains, shake the colander two or three times. Do not overdrain, since the pasta should not be too dry. We firmly believe in putting our faces directly into the steam of the draining pasta, to get what we call "The Sophia Loren Facial"—hoping that this maneuver might help to make us as beautiful as she is!
- Warm the serving dish and place a small piece of butter on the bottom, then spread it over the entire interior surface so that the hot pasta will not stick. Toss the pasta with additional butter so that it will not coagulate.
- Serve the pasta on hot plates—and remember that "pasta loves pepper!"
- One final rule: "The pasta should not wait for the guests. The guests should wait for the pasta!"

Selecting the Sauces

The hundreds of mind-boggling pasta shapes are equaled by the number of sauce possibilities. There are the traditional sauces, passed down from generation to generation. They vary only insofar as everyone's mother added a different ingredient, or a modified amount of one herb, or a secret incorporation of yet another, never to be divulged to posterity. In addition to the classic sauces, there are, of course, the sauces of serendipity, whipped up during an overwhelming stroke of imagination. There really is no formula, no set rule when it comes to pasta sauces. The sauce suggests the kind of pasta that should accompany it; sometimes it's vice versa. For example:

- *Homemade pastas*—freshly made flat strands or noodles—should use sauces that cling or are somewhat absorbed, such as the cream and cheese sauces.
- *Thick sauces* that have pieces of chopped meat or vegetables go well with shapes that catch and hold the sauce: shells, spirals, pastas with a hole in the middle, the short tubular pastas such as macaroni and *penne.*
- *Thin sauces* with an olive oil or seafood base are usually served with *spaghettini,* thin *linguine, vermicelli,* or *capellini.*
- With any sauce, as a general rule, allow about ½ cup sauce for each 4 ounces of pasta.

The Pleasures of Parmesan

It is expensive when you buy it by the pound, but a little bit of Parmesan goes a very long way when it's grated in a spice grinder or Mouli grater. Buy the best grade that you can get.

- Never buy ready-grated Parmesan cheese. It loses its flavor very quickly. Grate what you need, and then wrap and store the remainder of the bulk piece in an airtight plastic wrap in the cheese- or meat-keeper section of your refrigerator. It will keep for six months and the flavor will not be affected. If the cheese develops a slight mold while in storage, just scrape it off before grating.

- Tangy and full-flavored, aged Parmesan is the best cheese for grating and sprinkling on your pasta dishes. The best Parmesans come from the Reggio and Parma regions of Italy. An oval stamp with the manufacturer's name on the rind indicates a premium cheese.
- About two ounces of bulk cheese will yield ½ cup of grated Parmesan.
- To prevent any bulk cheese from crumbling, refrigerate it with the rind still on, then cut it into small pieces when you're ready to grate it, removing the rind at that time.
- For grating Parmesan cheese, a blender seems to do a better job than a food processor. You can also use the hand Mouli grater or your electric spice grinder. However, if you use the latter method, make sure the cheese is *dry,* since moist cheese will stick and break the blade. A spice grinder works beautifully if you use very small pieces.
- When preparing cheese sauces, use a heavy pan or a double boiler to reduce the amount of direct heat and melt the cheese slowly. This will also avoid stringiness.
- Strong cheeses like Parmesan are generally not used with seafood and delicate fish sauces, but since there are no rules anyway—and who's watching?—use whatever makes you happy.

Olive Oil Talk

It has been called "liquid gold." It was used to anoint priests and kings as a symbol of their divine origin. It is absolutely pure, has only nine calories per gram—and it has no cholesterol.

The finest olive oils are labeled "first pressing"—sometimes designated "extra-virgin." We always laugh at the labeling, since it would seem that being "virgin" would be quite sufficient! However . . . the "first pressing" is the oil that comes from the olive at the first breaking of the skin; and it is then filtered. The type of

filtering determines whether it will be a light oil or a full-bodied olive oil. Light olive oil has a delicate, pale golden color and a light texture—perfect for use with fish sauces, salads, vegetable and cheese sauces, and for most general, everyday cooking. On the other hand, the full-bodied oil—usually a green gold color—is more fruity and robust, more insistent in taste and texture, and it can be used with hearty sauces such as tomato or *pesto.* The flavor becomes even more intense when the oil is heated for frying.

We strongly recommend that you buy the "first pressing" or "extra-virgin" oil, trying small amounts at first, until you find the brand you like best. Superb olive oil is produced in countries such as Italy, France, Spain, and Greece. Should you decide to buy the lesser grades, keep in mind that some of these have an unpleasant aftertaste and an acidy flavor. A label reading "100% Olive Oil" or "Pure Olive Oil" is *not* a first pressing—just 100% olive oil. It might be a combination of pressings that includes the pits, pulp, and a chemically extracted residue oil. You may find, however, that some of the second pressing "virgin" oils suit your taste and your pocketbook.

- Olive oil does not have to be kept in the refrigerator, even though it does not age gracefully. In fact, refrigerated oil will turn cloudy, though flavor will not be affected. The oil keeps best in a tightly capped bottle stored in a cool, dark place.
- If you do not open the original can until you need the oil, it will keep just as it is until you uncap it. Then transfer it to a glass bottle or jar.
- Since we use a great amount of olive oil—especially in testing sections of a book such as this—we find that there are great savings to be had when we buy the largest amount offered by the brand. The cost is, of course, high—but it only hurts for a moment, and it also saves shopping time.

Notice that the title of this section promises only *some* of our favorites. If our editor had let us have our way, and if space were not a problem, this might well have turned into a pasta book, with *some* of our favorite grain recipes!

The pleasure has been in sifting through our files and our memories to choose the very best taste experiences with pasta to share with you. These are the cream of the crop. We selected them with several reasons in mind: some for ease of preparation, some for variety, some for their uncommon combinations, some for their fame or their proven ability to please a crowd. In many cases, all of these criteria are met in a single recipe. We know every one of these intimately, and we love them all. Cook, *mangia*, and enjoy!

Some of Our Favorite Recipes

General Cooking Tips for Sauces

Improvisation is the key to cooking sauces for pasta. Within a few minutes time, using almost any kind of vegetables, leftover meats, a few fresh herbs, and some cheese, a superb pasta dish can be created on the sport. A crisp salad and fruit for dessert complete the meal. Here are a few secrets to insure success.

- A pasta sauce is only as good as its ingredients. So use the best olive oil you can afford; most vegetable oils have little flavor, and they cannot replace good olive oil.
- Grow fresh herbs on a sunny window-sill and use them rather than dried herbs, whenever possible. Their fresh bouquet and consistently true flavors have a cleaner taste.
- Many sauces use sauteed onion and/or garlic as a base. Slow cooking of onions gives a mild sweet flavor to tomato sauces. Onions cooked quickly over high heat are better for meat and vegetable sauces when a more robust flavor is desired. Garlic must be treated gently. Browned or burned garlic is unpleasant and bitter and can throw off the taste of a sauce completely. Do not overcook garlic. For a light touch, crush a whole clove, cook lightly in oil and butter and then remove and discard.
- Fresh tomatoes in their full, seasonal, ripe glory are gorgeous additions to all dishes calling for them; but those hard, tasteless knots sold in supermarkets out of season are not acceptable substitutes; it is better to use canned, drained plum tomatoes. When quickly cooked, tomatoes retain their sweetness; when cooked too long, they develop a sour taste.

Quick Sauces
Lemon Cream Sauce with Pine Nuts
Serves 6

1 cup heavy cream
2 tablespoons grated lemon rind
2 tablespoons finely minced parsley
2 tablespoons butter
2 tablespoons grated Parmesan cheese
3 tablespoons toasted pine nuts
black pepper to taste

Heat cream over very low heat. Add lemon rind and parsley.

Cook pasta, drain, and toss with butter and Parmesan cheese. Pour cream sauce over pasta and toss again. Sprinkle with pine nuts and black pepper and toss once more. Use with any homemade fresh pasta or thin noodle such as *capellini*.

Pesto Genovese—
A Fresh Basil and Nut Sauce
Yields enough sauce for 1 pound pasta

3 cups loosely packed basil leaves
1 cup loosely packed parsley leaves
2 or 3 cloves garlic
1 teaspoon butter
12 blanched almonds, or
   1 tablespoon slivered almonds
12 walnuts
1 tablespoon pine nuts
   pinch of red pepper flakes
½ cup full-bodied olive oil
2 tablespoons soft butter
½ cup grated Parmesan cheese
2 tablespoons Romano cheese

This basil and nut sauce can only be prepared with fresh basil. However, it freezes beautifully and can be used in many ways.

Chop the basil and parsley very fine in a food processor or blender. Remove and set aside. Then mince garlic very fine and leave in the food processor.

Melt 1 teaspoon butter in a skillet and add all the nuts. Toss and toast over low heat for 1 to 2 minutes. Add nuts to the garlic and process until finely minced. Add the basil and parsley mixture and red pepper flakes to food processor. Slowly add the olive oil while food processor is in motion. Transfer to a bowl. Before serving over cooked, drained pasta, stir in 2 tablespoons soft butter and the cheeses. When pasta is cooked, take out ½ cup of the cooking water before draining and add it to the sauce to dilute it to the proper consistency.

Note: To freeze, do not add the butter and the cheese. Spoon into ice-cube trays, and when frozen, remove cubes and put in a heavy plastic bag. The butter and the cheese added to ¾ cup of defrosted cubes before serving will make the correct amount of sauce for 1 pound of pasta. The cubes can be added to minestrone soup, or they can top fish or chicken to make a sensationally delicious sauce.

Use this sauce with *linguine, spaghettini, tortellini, fusilli,* or *margherita.*

Variation #1: *Pesto* with Fresh Tomatoes
Yields enough sauce for 12 ounces pasta

1 tablespoon olive oil
2 cups cubed tomatoes
¾ cup *Pesto Genovese* (without cheese)
¼ cup warm pasta water
Parmesan cheese and black pepper to taste

Place oil in a warm serving bowl and add the tomatoes. Dilute the *pesto* with water and set aside. In a warm serving bowl, toss half the *pesto* at a time with cooked, drained pasta *(rotelle, penne,* or *orechiette)* to distribute evenly. Add cheese and pepper to taste. Can be served at room temperature.

Variation #2: *Pesto* with Roasted Sweet Red Peppers
Yields enough sauce for 12 ounces pasta

Since fresh tomatoes are not always at their best year-round, follow directions for Variation #1, substituting 3 roasted, peeled, and seeded peppers for tomatoes. Toss with cooked, drained *gemelli* twists or *pennine.*

Variation #3: *Pesticino—Pesto* with Mint and Cream
Yields enough sauce for 12 ounces pasta

2 tablespoons *Pesto Genovese* (without cheese)
3 tablespoons finely chopped mint, or 2 tablespoons dried, crushed mint
¼ cup heavy cream
2 tablespoons hot Chicken Stock (see Index), or water

Mix all ingredients together and toss with cooked, drained pasta *(fettucine, linguine,* or homemade thin noodles).

Note: This *pesticino* can also be added to fresh tomato or green pea soup for a delightfully soothing taste.

Variation #4: *Pesto* with 3 Cheeses
Yields enough sauce for 1 pound pasta

1 ounce blue cheese at room temperature
1 ounce soft cream cheese
4 tablespoons soft butter
3 tablespoons *Pesto Genovese* (with cheese)
2 tablespoons hot Chicken Stock (see Index)

Cream the cheeses and butter together in a food processor. Add *pesto* and then thin with stock. Use with any ribbon pasta.

Trifolati Sauces

These quick sauces are based on olive oil, or butter, garlic, hot pepper, and parsley. The Italian word _Trifolati_ was on every Italian menu at almost every Italian restaurant we ate in. A waiter gave us a rough translation . . . "anything, particularly vegetables, that are sliced thinly and cooked with garlic, oil, and parsley . . ."

Basic Olio e Aglio _(Oil and Garlic),_ a **Trifolati** _Sauce with Pasta_
Serves 6

  1 pound pasta, cooked and drained
  ½ cup olive oil
4 or 5 cloves garlic (or more, if desired)
  1 small dried hot red pepper
  2 tablespoons butter
  1 tablespoon finely minced parsley

Garnish:

grated Parmesan cheese
freshly grated black pepper

Heat olive oil slowly. Then add the garlic and hot pepper. When garlic begins to color, remove with a slotted spoon, along with the hot pepper. Allow oil to cool for a few minutes (or it will make the pasta gummy). Toss cooked, drained pasta with butter in a warmed serving dish, add flavored oil and parsley, and toss again. Garnish with cheese and pepper.

Note: Use part butter with olive oil if you wish.

Variation: Follow recipe for _Olio e Aglio_ sauce. However, after removing garlic and hot pepper, add any of the following shredded vegetables, and ½ cup chicken stock. Cover pot and simmer for 2 to 4 minutes, until vegetables are tender-crisp. Pour over pasta, add parsley, cheese, and pepper, and toss.

Use: 3 cups of finely cut broccoli florets or shredded rape (a turnip green type vegetable), shredded fresh spinach, 2 cups of thinly sliced mushrooms, or 2 sprigs of fresh rosemary to flavor the oil. Try 2 cups of coarsely shredded carrots or a puree of artichoke bottoms and a few tablespoons of cream.

Tomato-Based Sauces

Fresh Homemade Tomato Paste
Yields about 18 half pints

48 large, very ripe tomatoes
  3 sweet red peppers, seeded and chopped
  2 bay leaves, crumbled
  1 clove garlic, finely minced
  ¼ teaspoon mild honey (optional)

Combine tomatoes, peppers, and bay leaves in a large, heavy pot and cook, uncovered, over low heat for 1 hour.

Puree mixture in a food mill and then through a fine sieve. Add the garlic. Then add honey, if necessary. Return to pot and continue to cook slowly until thick enough to be mounded on a spoon. Stir often while cooking to prevent tomatoes from sticking to the bottom of pan. (Use a flame tamer to control slow cooking.) Spoon into half-pint containers and freeze (or freeze in ice-cube trays for small amounts). Defrost before using.

Marinara Sauce

Yields 3 cups

A pureed tomato sauce that is at its best when seafood is added. Use with _linguine_ or _spaghettini._

2 tablespoons olive oil
2 small onions, chopped (about ½ cup)
2 small carrots, shredded
1 large clove garlic, finely minced
¼ teaspoon or more black pepper
2 pounds very ripe plum tomatoes, peeled and diced, or a 1-pound, 12-ounce can of Italian plum tomatoes
1 small bay leaf, crumbled
¼ teaspoon crushed dried thyme
1 tablespoon butter
⅛ teaspoon dried hot pepper flakes
1 teaspoon grated lemon rind
2 tablespoons finely minced parsley for garnish

Heat oil in large skillet and saute onions, carrots, and garlic until soft (about 5 minutes). Add the pepper, tomatoes, and herbs. Cook, uncovered, over low heat for 15 to 20 minutes, stirring often.

Puree in a food mill and discard seeds. Then add the butter. (If seafood is used, add it at this point and cook for 8 to 10 minutes, depending upon thickness of the fish.) Add the red pepper flakes and lemon rind while seafood is cooking. Spoon sauce over cooked, drained pasta and sprinkle with parsley. Do not garnish with grated cheese if seafood is added to the sauce.

Fresh Uncooked Tomato, Herb, and Mozzarella Sauce

Yields 3 cups

1½ pounds ripe tomatoes,
     skinned and coarsely chopped
1 tablespoon minced shallots
   (about 1 or 2 shallots)
2 cloves garlic, finely minced
2 tablespoons finely minced parsley
1 tablespoon finely minced oregano

This classic Neapolitan sauce is prepared at least 2 hours before serving to allow the flavors to blend completely.

2 tablespoons finely minced basil
1 teaspoon grated lemon rind
½ cup olive oil
1 tablespoon capers
⅛ teaspoon red pepper flakes
⅛ teaspoon black pepper
½ cup finely diced mozzarella cheese

Mix all ingredients together in a medium-size bowl and let stand for a minimum of 2 hours at room temperature. There should be about 3 cups of sauce.

Pour over 1 pound cooked, drained pasta, toss, and serve at room temperature. Pass Parmesan cheese and a pepper mill for freshly grated black pepper at the table. Serve with *rigatoni, ziti, perciatelli,* or spaghetti.

Ragu Bolognese

Yields 3 cups

1 tablespoon olive oil
2 tablespoons butter
2 tablespoons finely minced
   shallots, or 1 small onion,
   finely chopped
¼ cup finely chopped carrot
   (1 small carrot)
¼ cup finely chopped celery
   (1 stalk celery)
½ pound lean ground beef
¼ pound chicken livers, cut
   into small pieces
1 cup light cream
2 tablespoons tomato paste
2 cups peeled and diced plum
   tomatoes, or 2 cups
   canned, drained, and
   crushed plum tomatoes
1½ cups beef stock or water
¼ teaspoon black pepper
¼ teaspoon nutmeg

Heat oil and butter in a large, heavy pot. Add shallots or onion, carrot, and celery and saute until soft, stirring frequently. Add the beef and chicken livers and cook, while stirring, until they just begin to lose their color. Stir in ½ cup of the cream and continue stirring until the meat absorbs it and becomes creamy in texture.

Add the tomato paste and tomatoes and stir for 1 minute more. Then add the beef stock or water and pepper. Cover pot and simmer over very low heat for 35 minutes (use a flame tamer). Add remaining cream and nutmeg and simmer until heated through. Serve with *tortellini, agnoletti,* ravioli, *rotelle,* or *margherita.*

Sicilian Tomato and Mushroom Gravy
Yields 6 cups

½ ounce Italian dried mushrooms (see Mail-Order Sources)
1½ cups hot water
3 tablespoons olive oil
¼ cup finely minced shallots
2 stalks celery, finely minced (about 1 cup)
1 large carrot, finely minced (about ½ cup)
½ cup finely minced parsley
½ teaspoon finely minced rosemary, or ¼ teaspoon crushed dried rosemary
1 teaspoon thyme leaves, or ½ teaspoon dried thyme
½ teaspoon finely minced sage, or ¼ teaspoon dried sage
⅛ teaspoon red pepper flakes
1 28-ounce and 1 14-ounce can of Italian plum tomatoes plus liquid

Pungent with Italian dried mushrooms. Sometimes cubed beef or pork is added for extra flavor. Use with *fusilli, perciatelli,* or spaghetti.

In a small bowl, pour hot water over mushrooms and let steep for 30 minutes. Strain liquid, rinse softened mushrooms, and cut up into small pieces. Set both liquid and mushrooms aside.

In a large, heavy pot, heat olive oil and saute the shallots, while stirring, for 1 minute, or until wilted. Add the celery and carrot, stir, and cook for 3 to 4 minutes. Stir in the parsley, herbs, and pepper flakes and continue to cook for 2 minutes more, stirring frequently. Then add the reserved mushroom liquid and the tomatoes and bring to a boil. Lower heat and simmer for 45 minutes. Puree in a food mill, discard seeds, and return to pot. Add chopped mushrooms and continue to cook for 30 minutes more.

Note: This sauce can be used with baked pasta dishes, such as *Conchiglie*—Giant Shells Stuffed with Sausage, Spinach, and Ricotta (see Index). It freezes well and can be refrigerated for several days if there is no meat in it.

Tomato Beef Sauce

Yields 1½ to 2 quarts

¼ cup olive oil
1¼ cups chopped onions
    (1 large onion)
1 large clove garlic, finely
    minced
1 carrot, grated
1 pound lean chopped beef
2½ pounds ripe plum tomatoes,
    peeled and cut up, or
    1 2-pound, 3-ounce can
    of Italian plum tomatoes
3 tablespoons tomato paste
    pinch of hot pepper flakes
1 teaspoon oregano, or
    ½ teaspoon dried oregano
¼ teaspoon black pepper
2 tablespoons finely minced
    parsley

Heat olive oil in a large, heavy pot and add the onions. Stir and cook for 5 minutes. Add the garlic and carrot. Continue to cook for 2 minutes and then add the chopped beef. Stir until the meat begins to lose color.

Add the tomatoes and crush them with a wooden spoon. Stir in all remaining ingredients except the parsley. Cover pot and simmer for 45 minutes, stirring occasionally. Add parsley and taste to adjust seasoning. This sauce freezes well and can be used for baked lasagna for 6 to 8 people.

Tomato and Cream Sauce

Yields 3 cups

6 tablespoons butter
⅓ cup finely minced onion
    (1 small onion)
¼ cup finely minced carrot
¼ cup finely minced celery
1 pound ripe plum tomatoes,
    peeled and cut in half, or
    1 14-ounce can of Italian
    plum tomatoes
½ teaspoon dried thyme
1 cup heavy cream
1 tablespoon tomato paste
¼ teaspoon white pepper
⅛ teaspoon freshly grated
    nutmeg
⅓ cup finely minced parsley
    for garnish

A delicate, creamy, light tomato sauce. Best on *tortellini* and any thin, fresh ribbon pasta.

In a heavy skillet, melt butter slowly over medium heat. Add the onion and saute for 1 minute, while stirring. Then add the carrot and celery and cook until wilted (about 3 minutes). Add the tomatoes, crushing them with a wooden spoon. Stir in the thyme, lower heat, cover pot, and simmer for 45 minutes. Remove from heat and cool slightly.

Puree sauce in a blender (not a food processor). Return pureed sauce to pot and whisk in the cream, tomato paste, pepper, and nutmeg. Heat slowly over low heat to prevent curdling. Add parsley before serving.

Tomato, Eggplant, and Sausage Sauce with Peppers and Onions
Yields 4 cups

¾ to 1   pound eggplant
2   large cloves garlic
10   sprigs parsley
2   tablespoons olive oil
2   tablespoons butter
½   pound onions, diced into ½-inch cubes (2 medium-size onions)
½   teaspoon black pepper
½   pound Italian sweet sausage, removed from casing and crumbled
2   green peppers, seeded and cut into thin strips
2½   cups ripe plum tomatoes, peeled and cut into ½-inch pieces, or 1 2-pound, 3-ounce can of Italian plum tomatoes
¼   teaspoon fennel seeds
1   tablespoon finely minced basil
    Parmesan cheese

This sauce is best when made with fresh tomatoes, eggplant, and peppers picked at the peak of the season. Use with medium tubular pasta, *rigatoni, ziti,* or *mostaccioli.*

Trim but do not peel eggplant, cut into ½-inch cubes, and set aside. Chop garlic and parsley together very fine and set aside.

In a large skillet with deep sides, heat the oil and butter together, add the onion and black pepper, and saute over medium heat, stirring occasionally, until golden. Add the sausage and stir for 1 minute. Sprinkle with the garlic-parsley mixture, stir, and cook for 1 minute more. Stir in the green peppers, tomatoes, eggplant, and fennel seeds. Cover pot and simmer for 30 minutes.

While sauce is simmering, cook pasta and drain. (Allow 2 ounces uncooked pasta per person.) Serve in heated dish with 3 cups of sauce spooned over pasta. Sprinkle with minced basil and pass Parmesan cheese and extra sauce at the table.

Meat, Poultry, and Seafood Sauces

Fresh Fennel, Sausage, and Cream Sauce

Yields 2½ cups

Try this sauce with *orechiette, gemelli* twists, *rotelle, penne,* or any spinach pasta. The cream and sausage make a pale sauce that suits green pasta.

1 tablespoon butter
1 tablespoon olive oil
1 small onion, chopped (about ½ cup)
½ pound Italian-style sausage, removed from casing and crumbled
2 cups thinly sliced bulb fennel (reserve feathery tops)
¼ cup diced pimiento
½ teaspoon finely minced sage, or ¼ teaspoon dried sage
  pinch of red pepper flakes
¼ teaspoon black pepper
1 cup heavy cream

Heat butter and oil in a large skillet. Saute onion for 2 minutes and then add the sausage and fennel. Cook, stirring occasionally, over low heat for 5 minutes. Add all the remaining ingredients except the cream and continue to cook for 5 minutes more. Stir in the cream and let heat through slowly.

Frutte di Mare *Sauce*
with Pasta
Serves 6

The heat of the pasta warms this unusual sauce that
is prepared in advance.

1   cup water
½   pound rock lobster tail,
      defrosted and cut into
      small pieces
½   pound shrimp, shelled,
      deveined, and cut into
      small pieces
½   pound squid, cleaned and
      cut into thin rings
6   shallots, finely minced
      (about ¼ cup)
¼   cup finely minced celery
      and leaves
1   clove garlic, finely minced
3   pimientos (or 3 roasted
      sweet red peppers),
      rinsed, dried, and diced
      (about ¾ cup)
⅓   cup fish stock
1   tablespoon minced oregano,
      or 1 teaspoon dried
      oregano
⅓   cup finely minced parsley
1   tablespoon minced basil,
      or 1 teaspoon dried basil
1   teaspoon grated lemon rind
2   tablespoons olive oil
2   tablespoons lemon juice
      freshly ground black pepper
      to taste
1   pound *spaghettini* or
      linguine
2   tablespoons olive oil

Bring water to a boil and add lobster. Cook for 1 minute
and then add shrimp and squid. Cook for 1 minute and
remove from heat. Lift out seafood to a bowl with slotted
spoon. Strain cooking liquid and reserve ⅓ cup if you do
not have fish stock on hand.

Add all the remaining ingredients, except pasta and
2 tablespoons of olive oil. Stir and let stand at room
temperature for 20 to 30 minutes to develop flavors.

Cook pasta and drain. While hot, toss in warmed serving
bowl with 2 tablespoons olive oil. Spoon the sauce over the
pasta and toss well. Serve at once, or at room temperature.

Green Pasta with Chicken, Mushroom, and Tarragon Cream
Serves 6

Try this pale creamy sauce with spinach *fettucine* or homemade green noodles of any width. The contrast is lovely.

¾	cup Chicken Stock (see Index)
¾	pound boned and skinned chicken breast
¼	cup dry vermouth
12	ounces spinach pasta
3	tablespoons butter
2	tablespoons olive oil
6 to 8	white pearl onions, peeled and chopped
¼	cup finely minced celery
¼	pound small whole mushrooms
1	cup heavy cream
¼	teaspoon white pepper
½	teaspoon crumbled dried tarragon
2	ounces Gruyere cheese, grated

Garnish:

¼	teaspoon freshly grated nutmeg
2	tablespoons thinly shredded carrot

Heat chicken stock in a medium-size skillet and poach the chicken for 5 minutes on each side. Let cool in stock for 10 minutes, then lift out with tongs and cut into ½-inch cubes. Strain the stock, add the vermouth to it, and set aside.

Cook pasta and drain.

Wipe out the skillet and heat the butter and oil. When hot, add the onions and celery and saute over medium heat for 2 to 3 minutes, while stirring, until soft. Add the mushrooms, stir, and cook for 1 minute. Add the chicken, cream, pepper, tarragon, and stock. Simmer for 5 minutes and then add the cheese. Cook until heated through. Spoon over hot spinach pasta, grate nutmeg on top, and sprinkle with the shredded carrot.

Frutte di Mare *Sauce with Pasta*   For this recipe, see page 239

Green Lasagna Ricci—*Northern Italian Style*   For this recipe, see page 257

Pasta all'Amatriciana—
Pasta with Crisp Pork, Red Pepper, and Tomato Garnish
Serves 6

2 tablespoons butter

3 tablespoons olive oil

½ pound pork, cut into thin slivers (either cooked or uncooked)

1 medium-size onion, finely chopped (about ½ cup)

1 sweet red pepper, seeded and cut into thin strips

¼ teaspoon rosemary, or pinch of dried rosemary

½ teaspoon oregano, or ¼ teaspoon dried oregano

⅛ teaspoon red pepper flakes

¼ cup dry white wine

½ cup Chicken Stock (see Index)

12 ounces pasta *(rotelle, fusilli, bucatini,* or *cavatelli)*

2 large tomatoes, diced

4 tablespoons grated Parmesan cheese

Heat butter and oil in a large, heavy skillet. Add the pork and cook over high heat, stirring occasionally, until pork is brown and slightly crisp (about 5 to 8 minutes). Stir in the onion and cook for 1 minute. Then add the red pepper, herbs, and red pepper flakes. Stir and cook for 1 minute more. Then add the wine to deglaze the pan, stirring constantly to incorporate the brown bits on bottom of pan. Add the chicken stock, cover pan, and simmer for 5 minutes.

Cook pasta, drain, and toss in a heated serving dish with the pork and peppers. Top center with tomatoes and sprinkle with parsley and grated cheese. Toss again at the table before serving.

Salsa di Fegatini—
Chicken Liver and Onion Sauce
Yields about 2½ cups

Use this sauce with *papardelle, tagliatelle,* or *fettucine.*

3 tablespoons butter
2 tablespoons olive oil
2 medium-size onions, finely
    chopped
8 chicken livers, quartered
3 tablespoons whole wheat
    pastry flour (for dredging)
¼ cup lemon juice
2 sage leaves, minced, or
    ¼ teaspoon dried sage
3 sprigs oregano, leaves only,
    minced, or ½ teaspoon
    dried oregano
1½ cups hot Chicken Stock
    (see Index)
    black pepper to taste
¼ cup finely minced parsley
    for garnish

Heat butter and olive oil together in a large skillet. Add onions and saute over low heat, stirring occasionally, until onions are golden brown. Dredge the pieces of chicken liver in the pastry flour and add to the pan. Increase the heat to medium and saute the livers for about 2 minutes. Add lemon juice, herbs, chicken stock, and pepper. Lower heat again and simmer, stirring occasionally, for about 10 to 15 minutes. The sauce should be fairly smooth with just a few pieces of liver that have not disintegrated. Garnish with minced parsley.

Squid, Mushroom, and Egg Sauce with Seashell Pasta
Serves 6

The actual cooking time for this delicate and unusual sauce is less than 5 minutes. Try it with medium-size seashell pasta.

10 ounces seashell pasta
      (*conchiglie* or *maruzze*)
3 tablespoon butter
¼ cup finely minced shallots
      or white part of scallions
¼ pound small mushrooms,
      thinly sliced
2 cloves garlic, crushed and
      mashed to a paste with
      bottom of knife handle
½ cup fish stock
½ pound green string beans,
      ends trimmed and sliced
      very thin lengthwise
½ cup heavy cream
1 tablespoon finely minced
      chives or scallions
1 tablespoon finely minced
      chervil
1 teaspoon finely minced
      tarragon, or ¼ teaspoon
      crushed dried tarragon
2 tablespoons finely minced
      parsley
1 teaspoon grated lemon rind
¼ teaspoon black pepper
1½ pounds squid, cleaned (cut
      the bodies into thin rings
      and the tentacles into
      small pieces)
2 egg yolks
1 teaspoon lemon juice

While pasta is cooking, prepare the sauce. In a large skillet, melt butter and saute shallots for 1 minute, while stirring. Add the mushrooms, stir, and cook for 1 minute more. Add the garlic paste, fish stock, green string beans, cream, herbs, lemon rind, and pepper. Cook over medium-high heat for 1 minute, stirring constantly. Then add the squid and cook, while stirring, for 1 minute more, or just until squid loses its transparency and becomes opaque. Remove from heat and push solids to one side. Pour off the sauce into a saucepan and let cool slightly while draining the pasta.

Beat the egg yolks with a whisk. Slowly add to the sauce, whisking over medium heat until sauce thickens. Stir in the lemon juice. Spoon the squid mixture over the pasta and the egg sauce over all. Serve at once.

Vegetable, Cheese, and Egg Sauces

Green Pasta with Four Cheeses
Serves 6

6	tablespoons butter
¼	pound Bel Paese cheese, cut into small cubes (about ¾ cup)
¼	pound Gorgonzola cheese, crumbled
¼	pound Fontina cheese, cut into small cubes
1	cup heavy cream
⅛	teaspoon nutmeg
¼	teaspoon black pepper
1	pound ribbon spinach pasta *(tagliarini* or *fettucine)*
½	cup grated Parmesan or Asiago cheese

Melt butter in top of a double boiler over low heat. Add the Bel Paese, Gorgonzola, and Fontina cheeses and stir with a wire whisk until melted. Add the cream, nutmeg, and black pepper and continue to simmer, stirring occasionally, until smooth and hot.

Meanwhile, cook pasta. When ready to serve, pour sauce in bottom of large warmed serving bowl. Drain pasta, add to sauce, and toss to coat. Sprinkle with Parmesan cheese and toss again very thoroughly. Serve at once, while hot, on warmed serving plates. Pass a pepper mill at the table.

Spinaci e Ricotta— *Spinach, Ricotta, and Pine Nut Sauce with Pasta*
Serves 6

Use this sauce with any tubular pasta, such as *penne,* or with short pasta twists, such as *rotelle.*

1	teaspoon butter
3	tablespoons pine nuts
1	10-ounce package fresh spinach or 1 10-ounce package frozen chopped spinach, thawed
2	tablespoons butter
⅛	teaspoon nutmeg
1	teaspoon black pepper
12	ounces pasta, cooked and drained
1	cup ricotta cheese
¼	cup milk
	pinch of red pepper flakes
¼	cup grated Parmesan cheese

In a small skillet, melt 1 teaspoon of butter and toast pine nuts, shaking pan, until they are golden. Set aside.

Steam spinach in a steamer until just wilted (about 1 to 2 minutes). Let cool and chop in a food processor. Add 2 tablespoons of butter, nutmeg, and black pepper and toss with cooked, drained pasta. Dilute cheese with milk, add to pasta and toss again. Sprinkle with pine nuts and red pepper flakes. Pass Parmesan cheese at the table.

Paglia e Fieno—
Straw and Hay

Serves 6

1 tablespoon olive oil
3 tablespoons butter
½ pound Italian-style sausage, removed from casing and crumbled
1 small onion, finely minced (about ¼ cup)
½ pound mushrooms, thinly sliced
8 ounces green spinach *fettucine*
8 ounces wheat *fettucine*
1½ cups shelled green peas, or 1 10-ounce package frozen peas, thawed
1 teaspoon finely minced oregano, or ½ teaspoon dried oregano
¼ cup Chicken Stock (see Index)
¾ cup heavy cream
¼ cup finely minced parsley
⅓ cup grated Parmesan cheese
black pepper to taste

Heat oil and butter in a large skillet. Add sausage and stir until pink color is lost. Add onion and cook, while stirring, for 5 minutes more. Then add the mushrooms and cook over medium heat, stirring, for 2 to 3 minutes. While pasta is cooking, add the peas, oregano, and chicken stock to sausage mixture. Lower heat to simmer and cook for 2 minutes. Add the cream and half the parsley and continue to cook over low heat while you drain the pasta. When ready to serve, place half the sauce in a warm serving bowl, sprinkle with half the cheese, and add the hot drained pasta. Toss to coat and top with the remaining sauce, the rest of the cheese, and a few grindings of black pepper. Toss again and serve at once.

Pasta with Broccoli, Tomatoes, Cheese, and Green Peppercorns
Serves 6

1 pound *pennette, ziti, tagliati, rigatoni,* or *rotelle*

1½ tablespoons butter

1 tablespoon flour

1½ cups milk

1 cup finely diced mozzarella cheese (4 ounces)

½ cup thinly sliced scallions

1 teaspoon finely minced oregano, or ½ teaspoon dried oregano

1 teaspoon finely minced basil

½ teaspoon green peppercorns, finely crushed

3 cups broccoli florets, steamed for 1 minute and refreshed under cold water

2 cups cherry tomatoes, cut in half

¼ cup finely chopped parsley

Cook pasta. Meanwhile, melt butter in top of a double boiler over medium heat. Add flour and stir with a whisk for 2 minutes. Stir in milk and cook for 5 minutes. Then add ricotta and mozzarella cheeses. Stir constantly for about 2 minutes with a wooden spoon and then add the scallions, oregano, basil, and green peppercorns. Continue to stir constantly and cook over low heat. The cheese sauce will be stringy at first and then change to a smooth consistency. When it becomes smooth, remove from heat. Toss hot drained pasta in a warm serving bowl with the broccoli and tomatoes to heat them through. Pour the sauce over all and toss again. Sprinkle with parsley and serve at once.

Pasta Tutto Giardino—
The Whole Garden
Serves 6

1½ cups bite-size broccoli
      florets
2 cups snow peas
1 cup sliced zucchini
6 thin asparagus spears, cut
      diagonally into 1-inch
      pieces
½ cup shelled green peas
3 tablespoons olive oil
3 teaspoons finely minced
      garlic
¼ cup finely minced parsley
½ teaspoon black pepper
12 small cherry tomatoes, or
      2 medium-size tomatoes,
      cubed
18 small whole mushrooms,
      or 10 larger mushrooms,
      thickly sliced
1 pound _linguine_ or
      spaghettini
1 cup light cream
½ cup Chicken Stock (see
      Index)
6 tablespoons soft butter
½ cup grated Parmesan
      cheese
½ cup finely minced basil
⅓ cup toasted pine nuts

Mix broccoli, snow peas, zucchini, asparagus, and green peas together in a large bowl. Pour boiling water over them and let stand for 4 to 5 minutes. Drain and refresh under cold water and set aside.

In a very large skillet, heat olive oil and saute garlic for a few seconds. Add the parsley, pepper, and tomatoes and cook, while stirring, for 3 minutes. Add the mushrooms and cook for 1 minute more. Then add the blanched vegetables. Cook over very low heat until warmed through.

Meanwhile, while pasta cooks, place cream, chicken stock, butter, Parmesan cheese, and basil in a large warmed serving bowl and gently heat in a low oven until butter is melted. Toss with hot drained pasta. Then add all the vegetables in the skillet and toss lightly once more. Sprinkle with pine nuts and toss again. Serve with additional Parmesan cheese in a separate bowl.

Piselli e Conchigliette—
Peas and Shells
Serves 6

12 ounces tiny pasta
   (conchigliette, stellini,
   or *tripolini)*
 5 tablespoons butter
 2 tablespoons olive oil
 1 small clove garlic, finely
   minced
 1 medium-size onion, finely
   minced
 3 cups shelled green peas, or
   2 10-ounce packages
   frozen small peas, thawed
 1 cup Chicken Stock (see Index)
 1 tablespoon butter
 1 teaspoon finely minced
   fresh mint
 3 tablespoons finely minced parsley
   black pepper to taste
   Parmesan cheese

Cook pasta. Meanwhile, melt 4 tablespoons of butter and the oil in a large skillet and saute garlic and onion until wilted. Add peas and chicken stock and stir. Lower heat, cover pan, and cook for 2 minutes for frozen peas and 3 to 5 minutes for fresh peas, or until tender (do not overcook). Drain pasta and toss with the 1 tablespoon of butter and then the peas. Transfer to a warm serving dish and toss again with the mint, parsley, and black pepper. Pass the Parmesan at the table.

Spinach Pasta
with Gorgonzola Cheese and
Sweet Red Peppers
Serves 6

¼ pound Gorgonzola cheese,
   crumbled
½ cup milk
 3 tablespoons butter
⅓ cup heavy cream
 1 pound spinach pasta, cooked
   and drained
 2 small roasted sweet red
   peppers, seeded and
   diced (¾ cup), or 2 pimientos
 2 tablespoons finely minced parsley
⅓ cup grated Parmesan cheese
   black pepper to taste

Use flat ribbon spinach pasta, such as *fettucine* or *tagliarini.*

In a medium-size saucepan, add Gorgonzola, milk, and butter and cook slowly, while stirring, until smooth. Stir in cream and simmer until heated. Pour this sauce over cooked, drained pasta and toss. Add peppers and remaining ingredients and toss again.

Vegetable Carbonara _with Egg Sauce_
Serves 6

3 tablespoons olive oil

¼ pound Italian hot sausage, removed from casing and crumbled

5 scallions, sliced diagonally into 1-inch pieces

1 cup small broccoli florets

½ sweet red pepper, cut into thin strips (about 1 cup)

1 cup green string beans, split in half and then into 1-inch pieces

1 carrot, coarsely shredded

⅛ teaspoon black pepper

1 teaspoon finely minced oregano, or ½ teaspoon dried oregano

1 teaspoon finely minced basil, or ½ teaspoon dried basil

½ cup Chicken Stock (see Index)

1 pound pasta _(spaghettini_ or _linguine)_

2 tablespoons butter

3 eggs, well beaten

¼ cup finely minced parsley

⅓ cup plus 1 to 2 tablespoons grated Parmesan cheese

¼ teaspoon black pepper

The beaten eggs and cheese form a cream sauce that coats this colorful pasta dish. Traditionally, _carbonara_ is prepared with Italian bacon _(pancetta)._ We like this version even more.

In a large skillet, heat oil and slowly saute sausage, while stirring, for 2 to 3 minutes. Turn up heat to high, add scallions, stir, and cook for 30 seconds. Add the broccoli, red peppers, and string beans. Cook, while stirring, for 1 minute. Stir in the carrot, herbs, and chicken stock. Lower heat, cover pot, and simmer for 1 minute. Set aside.

Cook pasta. Meanwhile, heat a serving bowl until warm and then add the butter to it. In a small bowl, beat the eggs with parsley, cheese, and black pepper.

When ready to serve, drain the pasta (but not completely dry) and quickly add to the warm bowl with the butter. Pour the eggs over the pasta and toss well to coat. Add 1 to 2 tablespoons of additional cheese and continue to toss and coat the pasta. (The heat of the pasta should partially cook the egg.) Add the reserved sauteed vegetables and toss once more. Serve in large, deep, warmed plates.

Pasta with Zucchini and Parmesan Cheese Sauce
Serves 6

1 pound pasta (*fusilli, lingue di passeri, linguine,* or thin spaghetti)

4 tablespoons butter

2 or 3 cloves garlic, finely minced
pinch of red pepper flakes

1 pound zucchini, finely shredded (use shredding blade on food processor)

½ cup heavy cream

⅓ cup finely minced parsley

⅓ cup grated Parmesan cheese
few grindings of black pepper

Cook pasta. Meanwhile, in a large, heavy pot, heat the butter, garlic, and red pepper flakes until garlic begins to color (about 30 seconds—no longer or it will burn and be bitter). Quickly drain the cooked pasta and toss with the garlic butter over medium-low heat. Add the zucchini and continue to toss for another 30 seconds. Then add the remaining ingredients, tossing for about 1 minute, or until the sauce forms and coats the pasta. Serve at once with a few grindings of black pepper and extra Parmesan cheese if you wish.

Pasta and Beans
Minestrone for a Crowd
Serves 10 to 12

Every region in Italy has some version of this hearty soup. In the north, the Milanese replace the pasta with rice. In Genoa, *pesto* is added. This version adds beef, making it a complete meal in itself.

2	tablespoons olive oil
1	cup finely chopped onions (1 large onion)
2 or 3	cloves garlic, finely minced
1½	pounds beef shank, with bone in, cut into slices
12	cups water
2	cups peeled and cubed tomatoes
2½	cups coarsely chopped cabbage
1	cup chopped celery
1	cup chopped carrots
1	cup cubed potatoes
¼	teaspoon red pepper flakes
1	tablespoon finely minced oregano, or 1 teaspoon dried oregano
1	sprig rosemary, or ½ teaspoon dried rosemary
1	cup green string beans, cut into ½-inch lengths
2	cups unpeeled zucchini, cut into ¾-inch slices
2	cups cooked white kidney beans *(cannellini)*
4	ounces small tubular pasta (*tubetti* or elbow macaroni), cooked and drained
⅛	teaspoon black pepper
¼	cup finely minced parsley Parmesan cheese for garnish

Heat olive oil in a 7-quart heavy pot and saute onions and garlic, while stirring, until soft. Add the beef and bones and cook until meat loses its color. (Turn pieces over while cooking.) Add the water and bring to a boil. Skim foam from surface, lower heat, and simmer for 1 hour.

Lift out pieces of bone and meat with tongs; cut meat into cubes and return to pot. Discard bones. Then add the tomatoes and cabbage and simmer for 15 minutes. Stir in the celery, carrots, potatoes, red pepper flakes, oregano, and rosemary. Continue to cook for 15 minutes and then add all remaining ingredients except the parsley and Parmesan cheese. Cook for about 10 minutes more, or until zucchini is tender. Stir in parsley. Sprinkle with Parmesan cheese at the table.

Pasta and Beans

Papa Giovanni's Pasta e Fagioli
Serves 6

This recipe was given to us by the grandfather of a Sicilian friend. He claims it goes back 1,000 years and was passed on from father to son. It is the only thing he knows how to cook. This dish was also a favorite of the colorful former mayor of New York City, Fiorello La Guardia. He, along with millions of other Italians, called it by its dialect name — *pasta fazool.*

1½ cups navy pea beans, soaked overnight
½ cup olive oil
10 cups water
3 large cloves garlic
1 large onion
1 sprig rosemary
2 sprigs oregano
6 sprigs parsley
1 bay leaf
1 small dried hot red pepper
6 ounces pasta (small elbows, *ditalini,* or *tubetti*)
¼ teaspoon black pepper
1½ tablespoons tomato paste
1 tablespoon finely minced basil
Parmesan cheese for garnish

Drain beans and mix with olive oil in a large, heavy pot. Add water, garlic, and onion and bring to a boil. Skim off any foam and lower heat.

Tie rosemary, oregano, parsley, bay leaf, and red pepper with heavy white sewing thread and add to pot. Simmer, covered, for 1 hour and 15 minutes, or until beans are tender.

Meanwhile, cook pasta, drain, and set aside.

Remove onion and herb bouquet from beans and discard. Mash garlic in pot and leave with beans. Stir in tomato paste, add cooked pasta, and simmer for a few minutes until hot. Sprinkle with minced basil and serve. Pass a bowl of grated Parmesan cheese at the table to be sprinkled on top of soup.

Pasta with Lentils, Onions, and Tomatoes
Serves 6

2 tablespoons olive oil
1 cup finely chopped onions
    (1 large onion)
2 cloves garlic, finely minced
1 cup uncooked lentils,
    picked over and washed
2 cups Vegetable Stock (see
    Index)
1 cup chopped plum
    tomatoes
2 tablespoons tomato paste
1 tablespoon minced
    oregano, or ½ teaspoon
    dried oregano
¼ teaspoon red pepper flakes
6 ounces tubular pasta
    (elbow twists, *ziti,* or
    mostaccioli), cooked
    and drained
1 teaspoon lemon juice, or
    few drops of mild vinegar

Heat oil in a SilverStone-lined 5-quart pot and saute onions and garlic for 5 minutes, stirring constantly, until they are soft and begin to brown. Add lentils and vegetable stock. Bring to a boil, lower heat, cover, and simmer for 15 minutes. Then stir in tomatoes, tomato paste, oregano, and red pepper flakes. Cook for 15 minutes more, or until lentils are soft. Toss with cooked, drained pasta. Sprinkle with lemon juice or vinegar and toss again. Serve hot. A crisp, raw cabbage slaw is a perfect accompaniment.

Al Forno *(Baked): Layered, Filled, and Stuffed Pastas*

Conchiglie — *Giant Shells Stuffed with Sausage, Spinach, and Ricotta*

Serves 6

½ pound Italian-style sausage, removed from casing and crumbled very fine

1 small onion, finely chopped (about ¼ cup)

1 clove garlic, finely minced

1 10-ounce package frozen chopped spinach, thawed and squeezed dry (reserve liquid for vegetable stock)

1 tablespoon finely minced parsley

1 teaspoon finely minced oregano, or ½ teaspoon dried oregano

¼ teaspoon black pepper

1 cup ricotta cheese

1 egg, beaten

¼ cup grated Parmesan cheese

25 or 26 *conchiglie* (jumbo #95 shells)

3 cups Sicilian Tomato and Mushroom Gravy (see Index)

In a medium-size skillet, cook sausage until it loses pink color. Remove and drain on paper towels. In the same skillet, saute onion and garlic until wilted, stirring occasionally (about 1 to 2 minutes). If sausage is not fine, crumble after cooking into very tiny pieces and return to skillet. Add spinach, parsley, oregano, pepper, ricotta cheese, egg, and Parmesan cheese and combine well.

Cook shells while filling is cooling. Drain at once and spread out on waxed paper. Fill each shell with about 1 generous teaspoon of the filling. Spoon 1½ cups of the tomato and mushroom gravy on bottom of a 9 × 13 × 2-inch oven-to-table baking pan. Lay stuffed shells evenly over gravy. Spoon the remaining gravy over shells and sprinkle each shell with a pinch of Parmesan cheese. Cover with foil and refrigerate until baking time. Bake in a preheated 350°F. oven for 30 to 40 minutes, covered with foil. During the last 5 minutes of baking, remove foil and spoon some of the bottom gravy on top of each shell and continue to bake until done. Serve at once.

Green Lasagna Ricci —
Northern Italian Style
Serves 6

Meat Sauce:

3½ to 4 cups Tomato Beef Sauce or
          Ragu Bolognese (see
          Index)

Bechamel Sauce:

  8 tablespoons butter
  4 tablespoons whole wheat
     pastry flour
1¾ cups milk
  1 cup Chicken Stock (see
     Index)
  2 tablespoons heavy cream
  2 tablespoons white wine
  ⅛ teaspoon hot pepper sauce
  8 ounces green _lasagna ricci_
  ½ cup grated Parmesan cheese
     freshly grated black
        pepper to taste

Prepare the meat sauce the day before and assemble the casserole a few hours before serving time. This light version of lasagna is even lighter when you use homemade pasta.

Using a double boiler and low heat, melt 6 tablespoons of butter slowly over simmering water. Stir the flour into the butter with a wire whisk and cook, while stirring, for 3 to 5 minutes. Slowly add the milk, chicken stock, cream, and wine. Whisk for 5 to 10 minutes, or until sauce thickens. Continue to simmer for 5 to 10 minutes more, so that flour cooks properly. Stir in the hot pepper sauce and set aside. There should be 3 cups.

Cook pasta with 2 tablespoons olive oil. Drain, rinse under cold water, and then spread out on a tea towel and cover with waxed paper so pasta doesn't dry out.

To Assemble: Spoon 1 cup of meat sauce on the bottom of a 9 × 13 × 2-inch oven-to-table pan. Place 1 layer of pasta on top of sauce, overlapping a bit. Then spoon about 1½ cups of meat sauce over pasta. Over this, spoon 1½ cups of the _bechamel_ sauce. Sprinkle with half the Parmesan cheese and then add another layer of meat sauce, a layer of pasta, another layer of meat sauce, and the remaining 1½ cups of _bechamel_ sauce. Sprinkle with the remaining grated Parmesan. Dot with 2 tablespoons of butter and grind some pepper over the surface. Cover with foil and refrigerate until baking time. When ready to bake, preheat oven to 450°F., remove foil, and bake in top part of oven for 10 to 15 minutes, or until a dappled brown crust forms. Let rest for 10 minutes before cutting.

Note: If brown crust doesn't form, slip under broiler for a few minutes until it does.

Manicotti *Stuffed with Spinach and Cheese*

Serves 6

6   *manicotti* tubes, cooked
      with 2 tablespoons olive
      oil, drained, and spread
      on a tea towel
2   tablespoons butter
¼   cup finely chopped scallions
1   10-ounce package frozen
      spinach, thawed and
      squeezed dry (save liquid
      for vegetable stock)
2   eggs plus 1 egg white
1½ cups ricotta cheese
4   ounces mozzarella cheese,
      diced (about ¾ cup)
3   tablespoons grated
      Pecorino Romano cheese
1   tablespoon finely minced
      parsley
¼   teaspoon nutmeg
¼   teaspoon black pepper
2   cups Tomato Beef Sauce
      (see Index)
2   tablespoons grated
      Parmesan cheese

While *manicotti* tubes are draining on a tea towel, prepare filling. Melt butter in a medium-size skillet and saute scallions for 30 seconds, stirring with a wooden spoon. Add the spinach and cook, while stirring, for 30 seconds more. Remove from heat and cool.

Beat eggs and egg white with an eggbeater until light and foamy. Stir into spinach. Then add ricotta cheese, mozzarella cheese, Romano cheese, parsley, nutmeg, and pepper and mix well. Carefully stuff tubes with a long-handled iced tea spoon until full.

Butter a 9 × 13 × 2-inch oven-to-table baking pan. Spoon 1 cup of tomato beef sauce on bottom of pan and preheat oven to 350°F. Carefully place the filled *manicotti* tubes on the sauce. Spoon the remaining sauce over the centers of the tubes, sprinkle with Parmesan cheese, and bake for 15 minutes.

Seafood and Vegetable Timballo

Serves 6 to 8

Seafood and vegetables are tossed with special seasoning and layered with spinach pasta and a lovely pink-tinged tomato *veloute* sauce. Assembled in advance, it is baked before serving.

Timballo:

- 8 ounces spinach *lasagna ricci*
- 3 cups uncooked mixed seafood, cleaned and diced (a combination of shrimp, white flesh fish, lobster, and squid in any proportion)
- 4 cups diced vegetables (green string beans, zucchini, and broccoli florets)

Butter a 12-inch round pan and set aside. Cook and drain lasagna and then spread on a tea towel. Set aside. Put seafood in one bowl and vegetables in another and set aside. Then prepare Seafood and Vegetable Seasonings.

Seafood and Vegetable Seasonings:

- 1 tablespoon butter
- 1 tablespoon olive oil
- ¼ cup finely minced shallots
- 1 clove garlic, finely minced
- 2 tablespoons finely minced parsley
- 1 teaspoon thyme leaves, or ½ teaspoon dried thyme
- 1 teaspoon oregano, or ½ teaspoon dried oregano
- 2 teaspoons grated lemon rind

Melt butter and oil and quickly saute shallots and garlic until wilted. Mix remaining ingredients together. Divide the seasoning and toss half with the seafood and half with the vegetables. Then prepare the Tomato *Veloute* Sauce.

Tomato *Veloute* Sauce:

- 6 tablespoons butter
- 4½ tablespoons whole wheat pastry flour
- 1 cup fish stock
- 1 cup heavy cream
- 1 cup milk
- 2 tablespoons tomato paste
- ¼ teaspoon white pepper

In the top of a double boiler over medium heat, melt butter and whisk in flour. Stir and cook for 2 minutes. Mix the fish stock, cream, and milk together and whisk into the flour-butter mixture. Cook, while stirring, for 10 to 15 minutes, or until thickened and smooth with no floury taste. Stir in the tomato paste and pepper.

To Assemble: Using half the pasta, make a layer on the bottom of the pan. Then layer all the seafood over the pasta. Pour half the *veloute* sauce over the seafood. Make another layer of pasta, and then a layer of all the vegetables. Pour the remaining sauce over the vegetables. At this point, refrigerate or bake.

Preheat oven to 450°F. Cover pan with aluminum foil and bake for 10 minutes. Remove foil and bake for 10 minutes more. Let rest for 10 minutes before cutting into pie-shaped wedges.

Pasta Salads

Pasta Salad with Mozzarella Cheese, Broccoli, and Sweet Red Peppers

Serves 6

Rotelle is the pasta to use with this garlic vinaigrette dressing. Serve at room temperature for best flavor.

Garlic Vinaigrette:

- 4 tablespoons Dijon-style mustard
- 4 tablespoons fresh lemon juice
- 4 large cloves garlic, finely minced
- ½ cup olive oil
- ¼ teaspoon black pepper

Mix all ingredients together in a food processor or blender and set aside while preparing salad.

Salad:

- 8 ounces *rotelle,* cooked and drained (medium-size shells or twists may be substituted)
- 1 large sweet red pepper, seeded and finely diced
- 2 cups broccoli florets, separated into tiny pieces
- 1 pound mozzarella cheese, cut into very small cubes
- ⅓ cup toasted pine nuts

Mix the cooked, drained pasta with the red pepper in a medium-size bowl. Steam the broccoli for 1 minute and then refresh under cold water. Drain and then add to the bowl along with the mozzarella cheese. Toss with the garlic vinaigrette dressing and sprinkle with toasted pine nuts.

Pasta Salad Pescara
with Red Onion and Oranges
Serves 6

6 ounces small pasta shells
   (conchigliette, lumache,
   or *tripolini),* cooked and
   drained
1 cup water
2 tablespoons white wine
   vinegar
6 black peppercorns
1 bay leaf
¼ teaspoon anise seeds
2 small dried hot peppers
1 pound rock lobster tail, in
   shell, defrosted
½ pound shrimp, in shells
1 pound squid, cleaned
¼ cup finely minced parsley
2 tablespoons small capers,
   rinsed and drained
1 teaspoon finely minced
   oregano, or ½ teaspoon
   dried oregano
1 medium-size red onion,
   sliced paper thin and
   separated into rings
   (about 1 cup)
1 cup thinly sliced celery
1 large naval orange, peeled,
   membranes removed,
   and cut into cubes
   (about 1 cup)
2 teaspoons grated orange
   rind
2 tablespoons lemon juice
6 tablespoons olive oil
1 tablespoon red wine vinegar
   black pepper to taste
   sprig of parsley for garnish

Place cooked, drained pasta in a large bowl. In a large saucepan, mix the water, white wine vinegar, peppercorns, bay leaf, anise seeds, and hot peppers together and bring to a boil. Add the lobster tail, cover pot, lower heat to medium, and cook for 8 minutes. Add the shrimp and squid and cook for 2 minutes. Remove from heat and cool in broth.

Remove the 2 hot peppers, cut into very tiny pieces, and add to pasta. Lift out seafood and discard liquid. Shell and devein shrimp and then cut into small pieces. Cut the squid bodies into thin rings and the tentacles into halves. Shell and cube the lobster. There should be about 3 to 4 cups of seafood. Add to pasta along with the parsley, capers, oregano, onion, celery, orange, and orange rind and toss lightly.

Mix the lemon juice and olive oil with a whisk, pour over the salad, and toss. Add the red wine vinegar and a few grindings of black pepper. Let marinate for 1 hour in refrigerator. Serve in a large shell or a pretty glass bowl with a sprig of parsley on top.

Pasta Salad with Roasted Eggplant, Green Peppers, and Pine Nuts
Serves 6

2 pounds eggplant (1 large eggplant)
3 tablespoons red wine vinegar
2 large green peppers, cut in half and seeded
4 or 5 plum tomatoes, chopped
6 ounces *farfalle* or large *cravatte,* cooked and drained
⅓ cup finely minced parsley
6 tablespoons olive oil
3 cloves garlic, finely minced
⅛ teaspoon hot pepper sauce
2 tablespoons toasted pine nuts
   black pepper to taste

Trim eggplant and cut in half lengthwise. Place on broiler pan lined with aluminum foil and broil 2 inches from heat, skin side up, for 5 minutes. Turn over and sprinkle with 1 tablespoon of vinegar. Add the green pepper halves, skin side up. Continue to broil for 15 minutes until the surfaces of both vegetables are charred and blistered. Remove eggplant and peppers and let cool.

Peel eggplant and cut into ¾-inch cubes. Rub off the skin of the peppers and cut into ½-inch pieces. Put in a large bowl along with the tomatoes, the cooked, drained pasta, and parsley. Toss gently.

In a small bowl, mix the remaining 2 tablespoons vinegar, the oil, garlic, and hot pepper sauce. Pour over salad and toss again. Sprinkle with pine nuts and a few grindings of black pepper. Serve at room temperature.

Pasta, Tuna Fish, Zucchini, and Tomato Salad
Serves 6

8 ounces *gemelli* twists, *mezzani, ziti,* or medium shells
2 cups zucchini (about 1 pound), cut into thin, 2-inch matchstick strips
18 to 20 cherry tomatoes, cut in half
1 small red onion, sliced paper thin (about ½ cup)
½ cup finely minced parsley (1 large bunch parsley)
¼ teaspoon red pepper flakes
4 tablespoons red wine vinegar
½ cup olive oil
1 6-ounce can water-packed tuna fish, drained
   freshly ground pepper to taste

Cook and drain pasta and place in a large bowl. Steam zucchini for 1 minute and refresh under cold water. Drain and add to bowl. Add the cherry tomatoes, red onion, parsley, and red pepper flakes and toss lightly to combine.

In a small bowl, beat vinegar and oil together with a wire whisk and then pour over salad. Before serving, crumble the tuna fish over the salad, add the pepper, and toss gently. Serve at room temperature.

Spinach Pasta Salad with Carrots, Turnips, and Leeks

Serves 6

¾ pound small turnips, peeled and cut into 1½-inch julienne strips

¾ pound carrots, cut into 1½-inch julienne strips

2 thin leeks, with ½ inch of green top, cut into very thin 1½-inch strips

¼ cup minced parsley

2 teaspoons minced dillweed

6 ounces green _penne_ or any green tubular short pasta, cooked and drained

1 cup mayonnaise

2 tablespoons lemon juice

2 tablespoons strong Dijon-style mustard

¼ teaspoon crushed green peppercorns

½ teaspoon hot powdered mustard

Place turnip, carrot, and leek strips in a steamer and steam for 1 minute. Refresh under cold water and drain well. Add to a large bowl. Then add the parsley, dillweed, and cooked, drained pasta.

In a separate bowl, mix all remaining ingredients and let stand for 5 minutes. Toss with pasta and vegetables and let stand at room temperature for at least 15 minutes before serving to develop the flavor of the mustard.

International Pastas

Horn and Hardart's American Macaroni, Cheese, and Tomato
Serves 4 to 6

As kids, our favorite treat was feeding 3 nickels into those little glass boxes at the Horn and Hardart Automat for this special pasta treat.

4   ounces tubular pasta
     (elbow macaroni, *ziti tagliati,* or *pennine*)
1½ tablespoons butter
1½ tablespoons whole wheat
     pastry flour
1½ cups milk
2   tablespoons cream
⅛   teaspoon each: white
     pepper, cayenne pepper,
     and onion powder
1   cup shredded sharp
     cheddar cheese
½   cup diced plum tomatoes

While pasta is cooking, make sauce and preheat oven to 400°F. Melt butter in top of a double boiler. Add flour and mix well with a wire whisk. Gradually add, whisking constantly, the milk and cream and then the white pepper, cayenne, and onion powder. Whisk for 10 to 15 minutes, or until sauce thickens. Add the cheese and continue to stir until it melts. Stir in the tomatoes and then the cooked, drained pasta.

Butter an 8-inch-square oven-to-table baking pan and add pasta mixture. Bake for 15 minutes and then slip under broiler until surface is dappled with a brown crust (about 4 to 5 minutes more). Serve at once.

Hungarian Noodles with Braised Cabbage and Poppy Seeds
Serves 6

3   tablespoons chicken fat or
     butter
1   large onion, finely chopped
     (about 1 cup)
1½ pounds cabbage, chopped
     (about 6 cups)
⅛   teaspoon ground cloves
2   teaspoons mild honey
½   teaspoon black pepper
¼   teaspoon sweet paprika
8   ounces wide egg noodles,
     broken
2   tablespoons butter
1   teaspoon poppy seeds

Heat chicken fat or butter in SilverStone-lined pot with tight-fitting lid. Add onion and cabbage and stir over high heat for 2 to 3 minutes. Stir in cloves, honey, pepper, and paprika and cook for 2 minutes more. Lower heat, cover pot, and simmer for 25 minutes, stirring occasionally, until cabbage is browned.

Meanwhile, cook noodles, drain, and toss with 2 tablespoons of butter. Stir in the cabbage mixture, sprinkle with poppy seeds, and serve hot.

Japanese Buckwheat Noodles with Shredded Chicken, Spinach, and Peanut Sauce
Serves 6

2 tablespoons peanut oil
2 cloves garlic, finely minced
⅓ cup finely chopped scallions
¼ teaspoon red pepper flakes, crushed
¾ cup water
⅓ cup tamari soy sauce
1 teaspoon mild honey
1 tablespoon peeled and grated ginger root
1½ teaspoon ground coriander
1 teaspoon grated lemon rind
¼ cup toasted peanuts
¼ cup lemon juice
1 teaspoon Oriental sesame oil
8 ounces medium-size buckwheat noodles *(soba)*
¾ pound cooked chicken breast, cut into slivers
4 cups spinach leaves, torn into pieces
2 tablespoons rice wine vinegar
1 teaspoon mild honey
1 teaspoon tamari soy sauce
1 teaspoon toasted sesame seeds
   pinch of Japanese chili powder
1 tablespoon shredded orange rind

Heat oil in a small skillet and saute garlic, scallions, and red pepper flakes. Cook, while stirring, for 1 minute. Set aside.

In a small saucepan, combine water, tamari, honey, ginger root, coriander, and lemon rind. Bring to a boil and add scallion mixture. Simmer for 1 minute and then remove from heat and cool.

Whirl peanuts in a blender until very fine and then combine with the sauce, lemon juice, and sesame oil.

Cook and drain noodles and toss with half the sauce. Place in center of large serving platter. Toss chicken with remaining sauce and scatter on top of noodles.

Place spinach in a bowl. Mix together the vinegar, honey, and tamari and toss this dressing with the spinach. Place spinach in a ring around the noodles. Mix the sesame seeds and Japanese chili powder together and scatter over all. Top the chicken with orange rind.

Jewish Apple and Cheese Noodle Kugel
Serves 6

6 ounces whole wheat egg noodles, medium width
2 tablespoons butter
1 3-ounce package cream cheese, cut into pieces
½ pound ricotta or cottage cheese
½ cup sour cream
½ cup mild honey
3 eggs, separated
1½ teaspoons vanilla extract
½ teaspoon cinnamon
1 tablespoon grated lemon rind
3 apples, thinly sliced (about 1½ cups)
⅓ cup raisins

Cook noodles, drain, and toss with butter while hot. Set aside.

Butter a 9-inch-square pan and preheat oven to 350°F. In a food processor, mix cream cheese and ricotta or cottage cheese together until blended. Add all remaining ingredients except the egg whites, apples, and raisins and process until smooth. Toss with noodles and then stir in apples and raisins.

Beat egg whites until stiff and fold into mixture. Spoon into prepared pan and bake for 40 to 45 minutes, or until surface is browned. Let stand for 20 minutes before cutting. Serve warm.

Katayef
Serves 6

8 ounces *vermicelli,* cooked and drained
3 tablespoons butter
½ teaspoon almond extract
1 teaspoon grated lemon rind
½ cup chopped almonds with skins
1 teaspoon wheat germ
¼ teaspoon cinnamon
⅔ cup mild honey

A classic Turkish noodle dessert baked with nests of *vermicelli,* honey, and almonds. It is sometimes made with shredded *phyllo* dough.

Butter an 8-inch-square baking pan and preheat oven to 375°F. When *vermicelli* is drained, mix with 1 tablespoon of the butter, the almond extract, and lemon rind. Spoon into prepared pan. Sprinkle top with chopped almonds, wheat germ, and cinnamon. Trickle honey over the surface, dot with the remaining 2 tablespoons of butter, and bake for about 40 minutes, or until top is browned slightly. Cool on a wire rack for 15 minutes before cutting into squares. Serve warm or cold. The Turks usually spoon clotted cream over the top of each portion.

Pastitsio
Serves 6

Pasta, a layer of tomato-flavored pork and beef nestled in a creamy cheese sauce. The Greeks have a word for it—*pastitsio*.

Meat Layer:

- 1 tablespoon butter
- ½ cup chopped onions
- 1 pound ground meat:
  - ½ pound ground beef plus ½ pound Homemade Pork Sausage (see Index)
- 1 teaspoon Syrian Mixed Spices (see Index)
- ¼ teaspoon crumbled dried oregano
- 3 tablespoons tomato paste
- 2 tablespoons Chicken Stock (see Index)

Melt butter in a medium-size skillet and saute onions until wilted. Crumble the meat and add to the skillet, stirring with a wooden spoon until pink color is lost. Add the spices and oregano and stir. Mix the tomato paste with chicken stock to dilute and then add to meat. Stir and set aside.

Pasta Layer:

- 8 ounces small elbow pasta cooked, drained, and cooled slightly
- 2 eggs
- ¼ cup grated Parmesan or Kefalotiri cheese
- 1 tablespoon soft butter

After pasta is cooled slightly, beat eggs in a small bowl with the cheese. Add the butter. Mix the egg mixture with the pasta and set aside. Preheat oven to 350°F. and butter a 9-inch-square baking pan. Set aside and prepare sauce.

Cream Sauce:

- 3 tablespoons butter
- 1½ tablespoons whole wheat pastry flour
- 2 cups light cream
- ½ cup Chicken Stock (see Index)
- ¼ cup grated Parmesan or Kefalotiri cheese

Melt butter in a saucepan. Stir in flour until well blended and bubbly. Slowly add cream and chicken stock and cook over low heat, stirring constantly, until thickened. Do not allow to boil. Stir in Parmesan cheese and set aside.

Topping:

- ¼ cup grated Parmesan cheese
- ¼ teaspoon paprika

Spoon half the pasta mixture evenly in the prepared pan. Then spoon a third of the cream sauce evenly over pasta. Spoon all the meat over the sauce. Then add a third of the sauce and another layer of pasta. Spread with the remaining sauce, sprinkle with Parmesan cheese, and dust with paprika. Bake for 30 to 35 minutes, or until bubbly. Remove and cool on a wire rack for 15 minutes before slicing into squares to serve.

International Pastas

Seven Vegetable Rice Stick Noodles with Cashews
Serves 6

Salad:

Slice each of the following into 1½-inch-long pieces and then very thin strips: 1 small cucumber, 2 small carrots, 1 small turnip, 1 sweet red pepper, 1 sweet green pepper

3 scallions, sliced diagonally into 1-inch pieces

6 red radishes, thinly sliced, stacked, and cut into strips or slivers

1 cup bean sprouts shredded rind of 1 lime

1 hot green chili pepper, finely chopped (optional)

2 tablespoons finely minced chives (preferably Chinese flat chives)

1 teaspoon grated ginger root

¾ cup coarsely chopped cashews

¼ cup leaf coriander (Chinese parsley, also called cilantro)

12 ounces of fine rice stick noodles, cooked, drained, and chilled (toss with a few drops of sesame oil to prevent sticking together)

Combine all above ingredients and spread out on a large oval platter. Pour dressing on top and toss well.

Dressing:

4 tablespoons fresh lime juice

2 tablespoons rice wine vinegar

¼ teaspoon mild honey

3 tablespoons Oriental sesame oil

1 tablespoon hot chili oil, or more to taste

Combine all the ingredients in a blender and process for about 5 seconds. Slivers of cold cooked chicken can be added to vegetables if desired.

Note: Hot chili oil and sesame oil can be purchased at Oriental markets.

Sino-Japanese Buckwheat Noodles with Chicken and Cucumber
Serves 6

4   ounces fine Japanese buckwheat noodles *(somen),* cooked and drained
1   teaspoon sesame oil
4   tablespoons tamari soy sauce
2   tablespoons peanut oil
1   large clove garlic, finely minced
6   scallions, sliced diagonally into 1-inch pieces
2   cucumbers, cut into very thin 2-inch strips
6   large mushrooms, thinly sliced
1   pound cooked chicken, thinly sliced into strips 2 inches long (about 4 cups)
1   teaspoon grated lemon rind
¼   teaspoon Japanese chili powder

Garnish:

1   teaspoon finely minced leaf coriander (Chinese parsley)
1   carrot, finely shredded

In a large serving bowl, toss cooked, drained noodles with sesame oil and 2 tablespoons of the tamari and set aside. In a wok or a skillet, heat peanut oil until hot but not smoking and saute garlic for a few seconds, stirring constantly. Then quickly add the scallions and cucumbers and cook, while stirring, for 1 minute. Add the mushrooms and cook, while stirring, for 1 minute more. Stir in remaining 2 tablespoons of tamari, the chicken, lemon rind, and chili powder. Cook briefly until chicken is hot. Toss with noodles and sprinkle surface with coriander and carrot shreds.

Note: Japanese chili powder is a mixture of sesame seeds, orange peel, pepper, and seaweed. It is totally different from Mexican chili powder.

Vietnamese Lettuce Bundles with Rice Stick Noodles and Pork
Serves 6

Sauce:

1	small dried hot red chili pepper
5	tablespoons rice wine vinegar
5	tablespoons tamari soy sauce
3 or 4	cloves garlic
4	tablespoons Oriental sesame oil
¼	teaspoon mild honey
2 or 3	drops hot chili oil
1	teaspoon grated lemon rind

Place chili pepper in blender (not food processor), and blend just enough to crush. Then add all remaining ingredients and blend. Transfer sauce to a bowl and set aside.

Stuffing:

2	center-cut lean pork chops (about 1½ pounds)
1½	cups water
8	ounces thin rice stick noodles
1	teaspoon Oriental sesame oil
8	large lettuce leaves
8	small sprigs mint
8	medium-size basil leaves

Remove pork from bone. Place bones in water and simmer. Trim fat from meat and slice meat into thin strips. Remove bones with tongs and add pork slivers. Simmer for 6 to 7 minutes. Lift pork out with a slotted spoon, add to the sauce, and marinate for 30 minutes. Reserve broth.

Meanwhile cook the noodles for 5 minutes and drain well. Add to a large bowl and toss with the sesame oil and ½ cup of the reserved pork broth. Set noodles aside.

When ready to assemble, lift pork slivers out of sauce into a bowl, reserving sauce for dipping. Lay out lettuce leaves, spoon 1 or 2 tablespoons each of noodles and pork (depending on the size of lettuce leaf) onto each leaf. Top with a sprig of mint and a basil leaf. Roll into a bundle, turning sides in to enclose, and lay seam-side-down on a serving plate. Repeat until all is used up. To serve this finger food, dip bundles in dipping sauce, then pour dipping sauce over any remaining noodles, and serve in separate bowls.

You Don't Have to Be Italian to Make Pasta (But It Helps to Know an Italian)

Jackie Hickey is a dear Fire Island friend, a stylist in the film industry, a superb and original cook, and a close friend of George Meluso, the Italian "baker" who provided the traditional Jewish *challah* recipe for Mel's *Bread Winners.* She spends many of her weekends making homemade pasta; so, naturally, we turned to this expert when we began to write this book. Over this past year, Jackie has been retesting her old recipes, devising new ones, and making notes for this chapter. What follows is entirely hers, for this marvelous woman, daughter of an Irish-French father and a Scottish-English mother, is the best Italian-pasta-maker on our island! Here's how she tells it.

I love making homemade noodles. It's not only fun, but it's rewarding—and it's easy. Once you get the feel for the dough consistency, the rest is limited only by your imagination.

I might mention that if you are a serious pasta lover, it is well worth investing in a pasta machine. Aside from the time and effort you save, the texture and consistency of the end product will be much better than if you hand roll it. Either a manual or an electric machine would be an improvement over the hand method.

Pasta Flours

Several flours, either alone or in combination, lend themselves nicely to making pasta at home.

- *Whole Wheat:* This is the basic flour to be used alone, combined with vegetable purees, or with other flours. Make sure, however, that you use a whole wheat that is ground very fine, such as pastry flour.

Do not try to use stone-ground flour, or you'll wind up with a paste that is impossible to roll out thin enough.
- *Triticale Flour:* This can be used in the same way as whole wheat.
- *Buckwheat Flour and Corn Flour* (not meal): These must be used in combination with whole wheat flour.

To Dry or Not to Dry

As the noodles are made, they should be placed on a clean towel or on lightly floured waxed paper. Let them rest for about 10 to 15 minutes before cooking, for they are at their tender best at that point.

However, if you want to keep them for future use, let them dry for about 30 minutes, put them in plastic bags or in waxed-paper-lined boxes or tins, and store them in the refrigerator for up to 2 days. They can be stored in your freezer for up to 30 days.

Another method of drying the noodles for future use is to separate them and hang them over a wooden dowel or pole, braced horizontally on the backs of two chairs. Let them hang there until thoroughly dry. The length of time will depend upon the circulation of air and the humidity in the room. When completely dry, store in waxed-paper-lined boxes or tins in the cupboard, where they will keep indefinitely.

Basic Dough Recipe

This is the basic pasta dough recipe using whole wheat flour. For variations using other flours, see the following section. Each recipe makes one pound of pasta—about eight servings.

Whole Wheat Pasta — Machine Method

Yields 1 pound

2 cups whole wheat pastry flour or triticale flour
2 large eggs
1 tablespoon corn oil
3 to 6 tablespoons warm water

Mound flour in a large mixing bowl or directly on work surface. Make a deep well in the center of the mound. Drop the eggs into the well and whip them with a fork, while slowly drawing flour into the mixture. Add oil and continue drawing the flour toward the center until the dough starts to form. At this point, you may have to add the water as necessary until dough becomes firm, shiny, and elastic. Then divide the ball of dough into 6 equal pieces and finish kneading through the machine. After each piece is kneaded thoroughly, put it under a bowl to keep from drying and let rest for about 1 hour. Flour dough well so it will not stick to rollers. Put one piece through the smooth roller set at the widest notch. Fold in thirds and run through again. Repeat this procedure, using the next smaller notch number each time, until you get to #2, which is the thinnest (¹⁄₁₆ inch) you will ever want to make your pasta. Lay sheet of dough out on floured board and let dry slightly (about 15 minutes depending on the humidity). You are then ready to roll out into noodles by machine, or to cut into whatever shape suits you.

Whole Wheat Pasta—Hand Method

Kneading and rolling by hand will, of course, take a little more time and muscle. Follow directions for Machine Method to the point of forming the dough until it becomes firm, shiny, and elastic. Knead for about 10 minutes in order to achieve the right consistency. Cut the dough into 4 sections and let rest for 1 hour. Then roll out on a floured board until it is about 1/16 inch thick, or until it will flutter when you blow under it softly. Let it rest and dry slightly. Then, starting on each end of the rolled-out pieces, roll toward the center until they meet, somewhat like a jelly roll. With a very sharp knife, cut into 1/4-inch-thick strips. Unroll and cut into desired lengths.

Seven Vegetable Rice Stick Noodles with Cashews   For this recipe, see page 268

Pesto Genovese—*A Fresh Basil and Nut Sauce*   For this recipe, see page 230

Vegetable Pastas

Some of the most interesting and tasty pasta is made from dough flavored with vegetables and herbs. By the addition of ¼ cup cooked, cooled, pureed vegetables, meals become both festive and nutritious.

When using vegetable purees, eliminate the water in the Whole Wheat Pasta recipe unless the dough is very crumbly. Some of the most suitable additions are:

- Carrot Puree: Steam carrots until soft and then puree.
- Beet Puree: Steam beets until soft and then puree.
- Tomato Puree: Peel and seed tomatoes and then puree.
- Spinach or Broccoli Puree: Chop spinach very fine and cook slowly in a bit of olive oil until all liquid has evaporated. To insure the fresh taste and brilliant green color of spinach pasta, do not blanch or cook in water.

A favorite of mine is what I call *Pesto* Pasta. This must be made with fresh basil only.

Homemade Pastas and Sauces

Pesto *Pasta*

½ cup basil leaves
1 tablespoon olive oil

Combine the basil and oil in a blender or food processor. Add this mixture to the basic pasta recipe, but eliminate the oil in the dough and use the water.

These noodles are best when served very simply, tossed with freshly chopped garlic, olive oil, and freshly grated Parmesan cheese. Garnish with fresh chopped basil.

Note: A dash of onion, garlic, oregano, or curry powder added to the dough adds zip to the pasta.

Barley Noodles

Yields 1 pound

½ cup finely ground barley
  flour
1½ cups whole wheat pastry
  flour
2 large eggs
1 tablespoon corn oil
3 to 6 tablespoons warm water

Follow basic dough recipe directions for Whole Wheat Pasta.

Buckwheat Noodles

Yields 1 pound

½ cup finely ground
  buckwheat flour
  (preferably light
  buckwheat)
1½ cups whole wheat pastry
  flour
2 large eggs
1 tablespoon corn oil
3 to 6 tablespoons warm water

Follow basic dough recipe directions for Whole Wheat Pasta.

Corn Noodles

Yields 1 pound

1 scant cup yellow corn flour
  (not corn*meal*)
1 heaping cup whole wheat
  pastry flour
2 eggs
1 tablespoon corn oil
3 to 4 tablespoons warm water

You will find a difference between working with this dough and working with the straight whole wheat. It will require more kneading by hand (about twice as much), but the flavor is worth it. Once you have it properly kneaded, the procedures for whole wheat pasta apply up to the point where it is ready to be rolled out. Corn dough cannot be rolled as thin as whole wheat, because it has a tendency to fall apart in cooking. Therefore, use the #3 setting on the pasta machine. If rolling by hand, roll out about ⅛ inch thick as opposed to ¹⁄₁₆ inch thick.

Pasta Forms for Homemade Pasta

After you have made the dough, you may wish to make shapes other than the traditional noodle. Let's explore some of the possibilities:

Ravioli: "Little cushions" can be made with a special ravioli tray, available in most gourmet shops, or they can be made by hand. I find the hand method quite easy. Roll out the dough on the #2 setting or to a thickness of 1/16 inch. Sheets should be approximately 3 × 15 inches.

You will need two of these sheets, one for the bottom and one to cover the top. On bottom sheet, drop filling of your choice by the teaspoonful, spacing two across and ten down. With wet finger, moisten (grid style) between filling mounds. Place cover sheet gently on top and press dough around filling mounds. With a pastry cutter, cut in half lengthwise, and in tenths across the width, giving you 20 1½-inch ravioli squares. If the edges do not seem properly sealed, press around all the edges with the tines of a fork. Allow them to dry one to two hours before cooking.

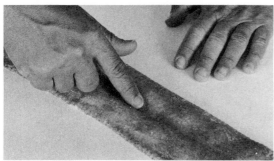

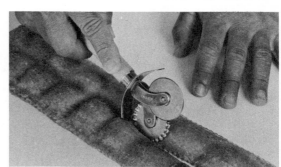

Tortellini: Use any of the pasta dough recipes except corn pasta. To form, divide dough into six equal pieces and follow the directions of the Whole Wheat Pasta recipe for rolling out dough. Cut out circles with a 2-inch round cookie cutter, one strip at a time, and place ½ teaspoon of filling (see recipes on next page) in the center of each circle. This must be done immediately since dough will dry and will be impossible to shape. Next, moisten edge of half the circle with a little water to insure a good seal. Fold over to form a half circle, pressing the edges together firmly. With seam side out, grab each corner with thumb and forefinger and bend the half circle to form a ring. Pinch the overlapping points firmly together. When this strip has been completed, repeat procedure until all dough is used, rerolling any scraps.

Filling #1: Chicken Filling

1¾ cups Chicken Stock (see Index)
1 small carrot
1 small onion pierced with 4 cloves
1 small stalk celery
1 whole skinned and boned chicken breast
1 egg, beaten
4 tablespoons grated Parmesan or Romano cheese
3 tablespoons minced parsley
¼ teaspoon nutmeg
freshly ground black or white pepper to taste

Combine chicken stock, carrot, onion with cloves, and celery and bring to a simmer. Add chicken breast and cook for about 15 to 20 minutes. Remove cooked chicken and set aside to cool. Reserve broth for another purpose.

Mince chicken finely (a food processor is helpful), add remaining ingredients, and blend.

Filling #2: Spinach Filling

1 cup cooked, chopped spinach, squeezed dry between palms of hands
¼ cup Parmesan cheese
1 cup drained ricotta cheese
2 tablespoons whole grain fine bread crumbs
1 egg, beaten
freshly ground pepper to taste
¼ teaspoon nutmeg

In a large bowl, combine all ingredients and blend well.

Tortellini can be served in broth or with a sauce. I like them prepared with the following Tomato Cream Sauce. Cook *tortellini* in boiling water for 6 to 8 minutes.

Tomato Cream Sauce

6 tablespoons butter
2½ cups warmed light cream or half-and-half
¾ cup fresh grated Parmesan cheese
6 drained, canned Italian plum tomatoes
¼ teaspoon nutmeg
2 basil leaves
1 egg yolk, beaten

Melt butter in a 12-inch skillet. Add warmed cream and Parmesan cheese. Stir well to combine. Crush the drained tomatoes with the back of a wooden spoon and add to the sauce, along with nutmeg and basil. Simmer for 8 to 10 minutes, stirring occasionally. Remove from heat, add egg yolk, and combine well. Add cooked *tortellini* and toss gently to coat the pasta with the sauce. Serve on a warm platter.

Note: For a variation of this sauce, omit the tomatoes and add ½ cup cooked fresh green peas.

Agnoletti: Tiny turnovers made with dough of the same thickness as ravioli. The sheets should be 4 × 16 inches. Use a cookie cutter (2-inch diameter) and cut out two circles across and eight circles down. Place filling by the teaspoonful on half of each circle, moisten edge with finger dipped in water, and fold dough over to make half-moon-shaped turnovers. Seal by pressing around edge with tines of a fork. Like ravioli, these should dry one to two hours before cooking.

Lasagna: For casseroles, lasagna noodles are rolled out on #2 setting or to a thickness of ¹⁄₁₆ inch by hand, cut in 1½ × 10- to 12-inch strips. The length depends upon the size of the baking dish you are going to use. Remember, the pasta will grow when it is cooked.

Acini di Pepe: "Little peppercorns" used in soup instead of rice or other grains. After kneading dough, roll out on #3 setting on pasta machine or to a thickness of ¹⁄₁₆ inch by hand. Next, run through standard noodle cutter (on #3 setting) or follow instructions for cutting by hand. After noodles have rested for 15 to 30 minutes, cut each strand into ¼-inch lengths

with a very sharp knife. Dry thoroughly and store in cupboard for future use.

Farfalle: "Bows or butterflies" for casseroles or sauces with vegetables or classic ragus. Roll out dough on #2 setting or to a thickness of ¹⁄₁₆ inch by hand. These bows must be cut by hand jelly-roll fashion as described in the Whole Wheat Pasta recipe. They can be large or very small but I have found a good size to be ¾ inch wide. After unrolling the ¾-inch noodles, use a pastry cutter to cut into 1½-inch lengths. Take each noodle strip and, holding both ends of strip between thumb and forefinger, make one full twist. Gently squeeze center of bow to secure. Let dry and store.

Easy Tomato Sauce
Yields 2½ cups

This sauce can be used for any recipe calling for tomato sauce or alone on noodles with grated cheese.

  3 tablespoons olive oil
  ¼ cup minced onions
  2 cloves garlic, finely minced
  1 20-ounce can imported
      Italian plum tomatoes
      with basil
2 or 3 leaves basil, or ½ teaspoon
      dried basil

In a saucepan, heat oil. Add onions, stir, and cook for 1 minute. Stir in garlic and cook for 1 minute more. Add tomatoes and basil, crushing tomatoes with back of wooden spoon. Simmer, stirring occasionally, for about 45 minutes or until liquid has been reduced by one-third.

Curried Chicken Sauce

Yields enough sauce for 1 pound pasta

- 3 cups Chicken Stock (see Index)
- 1 cup plain yogurt
- 1 tablespoon whole wheat flour (or chick-pea flour)
- 2 tablespoons corn oil
- 2 tablespoons butter
- ½ teaspoon cumin
- ½ teaspoon mustard seeds
- ½ teaspoon cinnamon
- ½ teaspoon ground cloves
- 1 teaspoon ground coriander
- 1 teaspoon turmeric
- ½ teaspoon cayenne pepper, or to taste
- 2 cups diced cooked chicken

Any of the vegetable or plain noodles can be used for this delectable dish.

In a large bowl, combine chicken stock, yogurt, and flour. Mix very well and set aside. In a 12-inch skillet, heat oil and butter. Add the cumin, mustard seeds, cinnamon, and cloves and stir until spices are heated. Add yogurt mixture to the spices, stir well, and lower heat. Stir in coriander, turmeric, and cayenne and simmer for about 20 minutes. Add chicken to the sauce and heat slowly. Serve on freshly cooked, drained noodles.

Peanut Butter and Ginger Sauce

Yields enough sauce for 1 pound pasta

- 3 tablespoons creamy peanut butter diluted with 4 tablespoons water
- 4 tablespoons tamari soy sauce
- 2 tablespoons Oriental sesame oil
- 2 teaspoons hot chili oil
- 1 clove garlic, finely minced
- ¼ cup minced scallions
- 1 ¼-inch slice ginger root, finely minced

Mix all ingredients in a small bowl with a wire whisk. Toss with cooked, drained buckwheat noodles (hot or cold).

Note: Chili oil is available in Oriental markets and groceries.

Corn Pasta Chili **Cannelloni**
Serves 6

Filling:

2 tablespoons corn oil
½ cup chopped onions
1 tablespoon chili powder, or to taste
3 cups cooked kidney beans

In a saucepan, heat corn oil and saute onions. When transparent, add chili powder and cooked kidney beans, toss, and set aside.

Sauce:

2 tablespoons corn oil
½ cup chopped green peppers
¼ cup minced onions
2 cloves garlic, finely minced
1 20-ounce can Italian plum tomatoes
pinch of oregano
4 ounces Monterey Jack cheese, grated

Heat corn oil in a medium-size saucepan and saute green peppers. When slightly cooked, add minced onions. Then add garlic, stir, and cook for 2 minutes. Add tomatoes, crushing them as they simmer. Stir in oregano and let simmer for 20 minutes. Set aside.

Preheat oven to 350°F. and spoon a light coating of sauce into an 11¾ × 7½ × 1¾-inch baking dish.

Pasta:

1 pound corn pasta, cut into 4-inch squares

Cook pasta squares, one at a time, in boiling water for 4 minutes and then drain. Place 2 tablespoons of filling in the center of each cooked pasta square. Roll squares, enclosing filling, and place seam side down in one layer in prepared pan. When dish is full, spoon sauce lightly over *cannelloni* rolls. Top with grated Jack cheese and bake, covered with foil, for 15 minutes. Uncover and continue baking for 10 to 15 minutes more, or until bubbly.

Pasta Party Rolls with a Variety of Fillings
Makes 36 party rolls

Different kinds of pasta doughs with different fillings make an interesting party food. Instructions are the same for each pasta and filling variation.

Spinach or Beet Pasta with Feta Cheese Filling:

1   pound spinach or beet pasta dough
1   cup crumbled feta cheese
2   scallions, chopped
1   tomato, seeded and chopped
1   teaspoon dried oregano
1   teaspoon lemon juice
1   teaspoon walnut oil

Roll out dough for noodles, but instead cut into 36 3 × 4-inch rectangles. Set aside to dry for 1 hour. Drop rectangles, a few at a time, into 5 quarts of boiling water (maintaining boil). Cook for about 3 minutes. They should be firm. Rinse in cold water and drain. Place on waxed paper and cover with another sheet of waxed paper and then a damp towel to keep them moist while you prepare filling.

In a medium-size bowl, combine all remaining ingredients, mixing well. Spread 1 tablespoonful of filling evenly on each cooked pasta rectangle and roll up. The cheese will seal them.

When all rolls are finished, heat 1 tablespoon oil and 1 tablespoon butter together in a large skillet and place rolls seam side down in one layer. Saute until lightly brown on each side. Serve hot or at room temperature.

Prepare the following variations, using same instructions.

Variation #1: Carrot or Buckwheat Pasta with Tuna Filling
Makes 36 party rolls

1   pound carrot or buckwheat pasta dough
1   6½-ounce can water-packed tuna fish
2   tablespoons mayonnaise (preferably homemade)
    dash of cayenne pepper
    twist of freshly ground pepper
1   tablespoon finely minced onions
1   tablespoon finely minced sweet red peppers

Variation #2: Broccoli or Basil Pasta with Cream Cheese Filling
Makes 36 party rolls

1   pound broccoli or basil pasta dough
6   ounces soft cream cheese (2 3-ounce packages)
1   tablespoon milk
1   tablespoon coarsely chopped pistachios or walnuts
2   tablespoons finely minced pimientos

Zucchini Stuffed with Pasta
Serves 6 to 8

Zucchini:

4 medium-size zucchini, cut in half lengthwise

Steam the 8 zucchini halves for about 8 to 10 minutes. Scoop out and reserve pulp, leaving a ¼-inch-thick shell. Set aside.

Filling:

2 tablespoons corn oil
½ cup minced onions
1 medium-size tomato, peeled, seeded, and diced
½ cup reserved zucchini pulp
¼ cup fully dried *acini di pepe*
1 cup Chicken Stock (see Index)
2 tablespoons Easy Tomato Sauce (see recipe in this section)
¼ teaspoon dried oregano
¼ teaspoon dried dillweed
¼ teaspoon dried mint

In a large skillet, heat oil, and saute onions and tomato. Add reserved zucchini pulp, *acini di pepe,* chicken stock, tomato sauce, and herbs. Simmer until liquid is absorbed (about 6 to 10 minutes). Set aside.

Sauce:

6 tablespoons Chicken Stock (see Index)
2 tablespoons Easy Tomato Sauce (see recipe in this section
4 tablespoons grated Fontina cheese for topping

Mix chicken stock and tomato sauce together in a bowl. Preheat oven to 350°F. Fill reserved zucchini shells with filling and place shells in a 2-quart, rectangular casserole. Pour sauce over stuffed zucchini, sprinkle with cheese, and bake 20 minutes. Serve hot.

Carrot Noodles and Mixed Vegetable Salad

Serves 6

Dressing:

2 tablespoons lemon juice
4 tablespoons apple cider vinegar
  freshly ground black pepper to taste
1 teaspoon fresh tarragon, or ½ teaspoon dried tarragon
1 teaspoon minced shallots or scallions
1 cup olive oil

In a small bowl, mix lemon juice, vinegar, pepper, tarragon, and shallots or scallions. In a thin stream, slowly add oil, whisking vigorously. Set aside to allow flavors to blend.

Salad:

1 pound carrot noodles, cut into 4-inch lengths, cooked, and drained
1 sweet red pepper, diced
1 cup broccoli florets steamed for 3 minutes (reserve stems for other use)
1 cup thinly sliced zucchini
½ cup thinly sliced celery
⅓ cup sunflower seeds
½ cup golden raisins
  Boston lettuce for garnish

Combine cooked, drained pasta with half of the prepared dressing and chill.

In a large bowl, combine chilled pasta with red pepper, broccoli, zucchini, and celery. Toss lightly with remaining dressing and sprinkle with sunflower seeds and raisins. Serve on a bed of Boston lettuce.

Buckwheat Noodle Salad
Serves 6

- 2 dried Chinese mushrooms
- ½ cup beef stock
- 2 tablespoons safflower oil
- 1 tablespoon Oriental sesame oil
- 2 tablespoons tamari soy sauce
- 2 tablespoons rice or cider vinegar
- 1 medium-size cucumber, seeded and shredded
- 1 cup mung bean sprouts
- 4 scallions, thinly sliced
- 4 water chestnuts, peeled and thinly sliced
- 1 pound buckwheat noodles, cooked not more than 3 minutes and drained

Garnish:

- ⅓ cup chopped walnuts
- ⅓ cup chopped coriander or parsley

In a bowl, soak dried mushrooms in beef stock for 30 minutes, or until soft. Squeeze mushrooms dry and slice thinly. Strain and reserve liquid; set aside.

Mix oils, mushroom liquid, tamari, and vinegar in a small bowl. In a large bowl, combine cucumber, sprouts, scallions, water chestnuts, and mushrooms. Add oil mixture to large bowl with vegetables and toss. Add noodles and toss again. Garnish with chopped walnuts and coriander or parsley.

Cold Oriental Chicken Salad

Serves 6

Dressing:

⅓ cup safflower oil

2 tablespoons Oriental
sesame oil

dash of cayenne pepper, or
½ teaspoon crushed red
pepper flakes

2 tablespoons rice vinegar or
apple cider vinegar

1 clove garlic, minced

Combine dressing ingredients and mix well. Set aside.

Salad:

1 cup shredded cooked
chicken

½ cup shredded sweet red
peppers

½ cup shredded green peppers

6 to 8 scallions, thinly sliced

½ pound vegetable or plain
pasta noodles, cooked
and drained

Combine all salad ingredients, except pasta, with dressing and toss. Add pasta and toss again. Serve chilled.

Part IV
Appendix

Fabulous Ways to Flavor Grains

Cooking without Salt

As we mentioned in the introduction to the recipes, we use no salt in cooking grains. For those of our readers who wish to do the same, either out of necessity or to wean themselves from sodium, here are some tips.

Dressing Up Your Breakfast Cereals

- Sprinkle wheat germ, corn germ, bran, or rice polishings on hot cereal.
- Cook hot grains in apple juice or apricot nectar.
- Drizzle honey, maple syrup, or molasses over surface.
- Add dates, raisins, dried apples, prunes, or apricots.
- Add fresh or frozen fruit.
- Add toasted nuts for crunch.
- Add cinnamon, powdered ginger, lemon peel, or cardamom.

For Pilafs

- Cook grains in stock instead of water.
- Add green or red peppers.

For Fish and Poultry

- Use vinegar, fresh green herbs, bay leaf, anise, or fennel.
- Add tamari soy sauce, mustard, or horseradish.

For Meat and Meat Soups

- Use peppercorns, hot pepper, root vegetables, celery, or most green herbs.

For Cream Soups and Sauces

- Add a few gratings of nutmeg, allspice, or ginger.

For Vegetables

- Citrus peel or dried or green herbs.

Some other quickie recipes for spicing up your grains without using salt follow.

Some Like It Sweet . . .

Whipped Honey-Cream
Yields 1½ cups

4	tablespoons mild honey
2	tablespoons orange juice
2	teaspoons lemon juice
1	cup heavy cream
1	teaspoon cinnamon

Pour honey into a medium-size bowl. Mix orange and lemon juice together; gradually add to the honey and beat well.

In a separate deep bowl, whisk the cream until slightly thickened. While whisking slowly, pour in honey mixture and continue to whisk until cream is soft but thickish. Stir in cinnamon. Refrigerate if not using at once. Before using, return mixture to room temperature and beat again. Excellent as a fruit topping.

Orange Date-Nut Butter
Yields 1½ cups

You can use this tasty spread for filling cookies, for bar cookies, for cakes, and for grain puddings, waffles, or pancakes.

1	cup pitted dates (½ pound), cut into pieces
½	cup orange juice
1	teaspoon grated orange rind
½	cup toasted chopped walnuts
½	cup soft butter (optional)

In a small saucepan, mix dates, orange juice, and orange rind together. Simmer, uncovered, until very thick and pasty, stirring occasionally. This should take about 5 to 10 minutes. Cool and stir in nuts. If you wish, you can beat this mixture with butter.

Maple-Walnut Syrup
Yields 2¼ cups

Real maple syrup can be expensive. Here's a way to stretch it for use on pancakes. If you like, spoon a bit over yogurt or ice cream.

1	cup apple juice
1	cup maple syrup
4	tablespoons butter
½	teaspoon ground cinnamon
¼	teaspoon freshly grated nutmeg
½	cup finely chopped walnuts

In a small saucepan, add and stir in all ingredients except the nuts. Bring to a boil slowly, stirring constantly. Remove from heat and stir in the walnuts. Serve warm.

Apricot-Pineapple Butter
Yields 2½ cups

1 1-pound, 4-ounce can of
  crushed, unsweetened
  pineapple
½ cup water
2 cups dried apricots
¼ cup mild honey

Drain pineapple and add the juice plus the water to the dried apricots. Let soak overnight. (Reserve the pineapple.)

Next morning, whirl apricots and liquid in a food processor or a blender. Put pureed apricots in a saucepan and add the pineapple and honey. Cook, covered, for 10 to 15 minutes, stirring occasionally. If the taste is too tart and you prefer it sweeter, add more honey while cooking.

Some Like It Hot . . .

For the readers who like to season their food on the hot side, here are some suggestions, several of which can be put right into your unused salt shaker.

Syrian Mixed Spices
Yields 1½ tablespoons

2 teaspoons powdered
  allspice
1 teaspoon fine black pepper
¾ teaspoon powdered
  cinnamon
½ teaspoon grated nutmeg
½ teaspoon powdered ginger
⅛ teaspoon ground cloves
⅛ teaspoon ground cardamom

This mixture can be bought already mixed in Middle Eastern groceries. You may want to adjust the proportions to your own taste and preference.

Combine all ingredients and mix together thoroughly.

Classic French Blend
(**Quatre Épices**—*Four Spices*)
Yields ¼ cup

1½ tablespoons ground ginger
1½ tablespoons ground black
  pepper
1½ tablespoons ground
  nutmeg
2½ tablespoons ground cloves

You can use this seasoning by adding a pinch of it to sauces, meats, poached fruits, soups, root vegetables, and, of course, grains.

Combine all ingredients and mix together thoroughly.

Fresh Summer Herb Bouquet Mix

Yields ½ cup

Use this fresh herb bouquet in or on almost anything (except ice cream!).

- 2 tablespoons finely minced parsley
- 2 tablespoons finely minced chives
- 1 tablespoon finely minced savory leaves
- 1 tablespoon finely minced basil leaves
- 1 teaspoon finely minced tarragon
- 1 teaspoon finely minced mint

Combine all the ingredients in a food processor or chop and blend by hand. Store in an airtight container in the refrigerator.

Dried Winter Herb Mix

Yields ½ cup

In the dead of winter (unless you have fresh herbs growing on a sunny windowsill), try this dried herb mix for a bit of snap on foods that seem too bland.

- 3 tablespoons dried oregano
- 2 teaspoons dried rosemary
- 2 teaspoons dried thyme
- 2 teaspoons paprika
- ½ teaspoon black pepper
- 1 teaspoon dried onion powder

Mix together and store in an airtight glass container—or use in a shaker with a pierced top.

Ethiopian Spiced Butter

Yields 1 cup

This is a tangy, "instant" spice butter that can be used in all your grains cooking, as well as pastas, vegetables, and soups. It will keep for several months.

- 2 cups butter, cut into pieces
- 1 small onion, finely chopped
- 1 tablespoon finely chopped garlic
- 2 teaspoons finely chopped ginger root
- ½ teaspoon turmeric
  seeds from 1 cardamom pod
- 1 ½-inch piece of cinnamon stick
- 1 whole clove
- 2 or 3 gratings nutmeg

Heat butter slowly. Do not brown. Then increase heat and allow to boil. When surface is foamy, add all remaining ingredients. Place pan over flame tamer and cook, without stirring, for 45 minutes, or until milk solids on bottom are brown and top butter is transparent. Pour top off, straining through 4 layers of damp cheesecloth. Discard spices. Pour into a jar and refrigerate. It will solidify.

Some Like It Fat, Some Like It Lean . . .

Ghee—*East Indian Clarified Butter*
Yields about 1½ cups

Ghee has marvelous keeping qualities and may be safely kept for 2 to 3 months without refrigeration, if properly prepared. Store it in a crock, where it will solidify, and when ready to use, let it melt slowly. *Ghee* also has a distinctive flavor.

2 cups unsalted butter, cut into pieces

In a heavy, 5-quart saucepan, melt butter over low heat, while stirring, without browning. Then raise the heat and bring the butter to a boil. When the surface is covered with white foam, reduce heat to the lowest possible temperature, using a flame tamer if necessary. Simmer, uncovered and without disturbing, for 30 minutes, or until the milk solids on the bottom of the pan are golden in color and the butter on top is transparent. This slow cooking allows the water to evaporate and adds a lovely nutlike flavor to the butter. Slowly pour off the clear liquid by straining it through a strainer lined with several layers of dampened cheesecloth. Discard remaining solids. Make certain there are no solids in the *ghee,* since they will turn rancid. (We use an acrylic gravy separator and pour off the clear top liquid, discarding the solids that remain on the bottom of the pot.) It is the clear mixture that keeps so well and tastes so good.

Homemade Pork Sausage
Makes 2 pounds or 8 patties

Tasty, easy homemade sausage without salt or preservatives and as lean as you like it.

2 pounds lean boneless pork shoulder, loin, or butt
1 tablespoon finely minced parsley
2 tablespoons finely minced sage, or 1 tablespoon dried sage
1 teaspoon anise seeds
1 teaspoon red pepper flakes
½ teaspoon black pepper

Use a meat grinder or food processor and chop pork finely. Mix all remaining ingredients into the chopped pork with a wooden spoon. Refrigerate for at least 1 hour to blend flavors.

Note: Shoulder of pork is the leanest cut. Butt has more fat and makes a somewhat juicier sausage.

Lower Cholesterol Spread
Yields 2½ cups

The taste is still of fresh, sweet butter, but this spread will cut your cholesterol intake in half. Safflower oil is light and almost neutral in taste.

2 cups soft unsalted butter
1 cup safflower oil

Blend by beating together with a wooden spoon, or use a few strokes in your food processor. Pour into a container and refrigerate. Use wherever you would use butter.

Investing in the "Stock Market"

In many cases we suggest the use of various stocks to flavor grain dishes and eliminate the use of salt. They can be made in large batches and then frozen or refrigerated for future use. One favorite trick of ours is to freeze the stock in ice cube trays, making it readily available in small portions anytime we need them in our recipes.

If you prefer to use the instant dehydrated stocks (without salt), try the soups made by Barth: Veg-Nutra, Chicken, or Beef. If you prefer "homemade," the following work well with any type of grain dish.

Vegetable Stock
Yields 6 to 8 cups

2	medium-size carrots, cubed
3	stalks celery, with leaves, diced
1	large onion, sliced
2	medium-size leeks, including 2 inches of green tops, coarsely sliced
6	white peppercorns
8	black peppercorns
3 or 4	large, unpeeled garlic cloves, crushed
1	bay leaf
1	sprig tarragon, or ¼ teaspoon dried tarragon
4 to 6	sprigs parsley
2	sprigs thyme, or ½ teaspoon dried thyme
2	large tomatoes, cut into pieces
8	cups water
2	tablespoons white wine vinegar

This stock can be kept in the refrigerator for about 3 weeks. To prevent it from turning sour, bring it to a boil every few days. It can also be frozen and then heated before using.

Place all the ingredients, except the vinegar, in a large stock pot (not aluminum), and bring to a boil. Cover pot, reduce heat, and simmer for 40 minutes. Add vinegar and simmer for 10 minutes more. Let cool.

Strain into a large container, forcing vegetables against the side of the strainer with a wooden spoon so that all the liquid is released. Cover and keep in the refrigerator.

Chicken Stock

Yields about 2 to 3 quarts

4	pounds chicken pieces (backs, necks, wings, or other parts)
12	cups water
2	large whole onions, punctured with a few whole cloves
1	leek, green part trimmed
2	carrots
3	stalks celery, with leaves
1	clove garlic, peeled
1	bay leaf
6 to 8	black peppercorns
1 each:	small turnip, parsnip, parsley root (optional)
2	sprigs dillweed
5 or 6	sprigs parsley
1	sprig thyme, or ½ teaspoon dried thyme

Place chicken in a large soup pot, add water, and bring to a boil. Skim surface and add all the remaining ingredients, except the dillweed, parsley, and thyme. Cover pot and simmer for 2 hours. Tie the fresh herbs with a string and add to the pot. Continue to simmer for 20 minutes more. Strain into a large container, pressing solids against strainer with a wooden spoon. Chill overnight and then remove surface fat, if you wish.

Variation: "Poor Boy" Bone Stock   This is an economical variation of the chicken stock. Instead of chicken parts, use 3 to 4 beef marrow bones, or 2 to 3 pounds lamb bones or veal bones. All the other ingredients remain the same, and the cooking directions are exactly alike. Some cooks like to combine 2 pounds short ribs of beef with beef marrow bones to make a richer beef stock—or, you may combine the beef bones with the chicken parts for a richer version of the stock.

Grains and Other Specialty Foods

Arrowhead Mills, Inc.
Box 866
Hereford, TX 79045
806-364-0730
Most whole grains (many organically grown). Large assortment of beans, seeds, nuts, cereals, and flakes. Source for 7-Grain Cereal. Catalog available for mail order.

Balducci
424 Avenue of the Americas
New York, NY 10011
Italian specialty foods. Imported cheeses, oils, pasta, and dried mushrooms. Retail and mail-order sales.

Barth's Vitamin Corporation
Valley Stream, NY 11582
800-645-2328
Natural foods and teas. Instant Nutra Soup in three flavors—chicken, beef, and vegetable. Catalog available for mail order.

Birkett Mills
P.O. Box 440-A
Penn Yan, NY 14527
Stone-ground flours, buckwheat groats and flours, including a light rye flour. Four grades of roasted buckwheat (kasha) from whole to fine grind. Price list available for mail order.

Calloway Gardens Country Store
Highway 27
Pine Mountain, GA 31822
404-663-2281, ext. 100
Stone-ground white hominy grits. Only source we know of that does mail order.

Casa Moneo Spanish Imports
210 W. 14th St.
New York, NY 10011
212-929-1644
Tortilla-making equipment and ingredients. *Pozole,* spices, and dried peppers. Mail-order catalog available for $2.00.

Mail-Order Sources

El Molino Mills
345 N. Baldwin Park Blvd.
City of Industry, CA 91746
Most whole grain flours and puffed corn, wheat, millet, and rice. Does not mail order, but is widely available in supermarkets and natural foods stores.

Erewhon Trading Company of Brookline, Inc.
236 Washington St.
Brookline, MA 02146
617-738-4516
Large variety of whole grains, beans, seeds, nuts, and tamari soy sauce. Catalog available for mail-order or retail sales.

Fearn Soya Foods
4520 James Place
Melrose Park, IL 60160
Only source we know for corn germ. Complete product catalog available for mail order.

Katagiri
224 E. 59th St.
New York, NY 10022
212-755-3566
Japanese specialty foods and equipment. Features sesame seed toaster and "kitchen helper" (My-Ace) for paring, grating, trimming, and garnishing vegetables. Retail and mail-order sales.

Moose Lake Wild Rice
Box 325
Deer River, MN 56636
Mail-order source for Minnesota wild rice. Free catalog available.

Oriental Pastry and Grocery Company
170-172 Atlantic Ave.
Brooklyn, NY 11201
Bulgur in four grades, assorted dried fruits and nuts, Syrian Mixed Spices, and legumes. Syrian, Greek, and Middle Eastern specialties. Retail sales or catalog available for mail order.

Pines Distributors International, Inc.
P.O. Box 1107
1040 E. 23rd St.
Lawrence, KS 66044
913-841-6016
Dehydrated wheat grass products, all-vegetable seasoning. Catalog available for mail order.

Shiloh Farms
Box 97, Highway 59
Sulphur Springs, AR 72768
501-298-3297
Branch office:
White Oak Road
Martindale, PA 17549
717-354-4936
Large variety of whole grains, meals, flours, date sugar, and dried fruits. Catalog available for mail order for $1.00 (refundable).

Star Market
3349 N. Clark St.
Chicago, IL 60657
312-472-0599
Chinese and Japanese specialty foods and equipment. Mail-order and retail sales.

Walnut Acres
Penns Creek, PA 17862
717-837-3874
Large selection of whole grains, cereals, and flours (many organic). To date this is our only source for sorghum (milo) flour and amaranth grain and flour. Complete product catalog available for mail order.

Kitchen Equipment Suppliers

Bazaar de la Cuisine
1003 2nd Ave.
New York, NY 10022
   Complete selection of items. Catalog available for mail order. Retail sales.

Dean & Deluca
121 Prince St.
New York, NY 10012
212-254-7774
   Specialty equipment, including flour mills. Specialty foods also. Retail sales. Call or write for mail-order information.

Hoffritz
515 W. 24th St.
New York, NY 10011
   Cutlery, serving pieces, and equipment. Retail and mail-order sales. Catalog available for nominal fee.

H. Roth & Son
1577 1st Ave.
New York, NY 10028
   Features large selection of grains and spices, as well as kitchen equipment. Retail and mail-order sales. Catalog available.

Sunkist Growers, Inc.
P.O. Box 7888
Van Nuys, CA 91409
   Lemon-Aid Kit: with grater, juicer, faucet, and two "snackers." Very handy for use with all citrus fruits. Write for information and current price.

Williams-Sonoma
P.O. Box 3792
San Francisco, CA 94119
   Large assortment of specialty food equipment, as well as standard equipment. Retail or mail-order sales. Catalog available.

Grain Mill Manufacturers and Distributors

Grover Company
Dept. 2 GGP
2111 S. Industrial Park Ave.
Tempe, AZ 85282
800-528-1406 or 602-967-8738
   Marathon grain mills, grain mill kits, and grain storage buckets, as well as a large selection of fresh ground grains. Retail and mail-order sales. Catalog available.

In-Tec Equipment Company
Box 123
D.V. Station
Dayton, OH 45406
513-276-4077
   Grain mills with flywheels for flour. Brochures and price lists available. Retail and mail-order sales.

Magic Mill
235 W. 200 S
Salt Lake City, UT 84101
   Magic Mill III, grain mill, and Bosch Kitchen machine available at retail, or through local distributors. See Yellow Pages. Catalog available.

Retsel Corporation
Box 47
McCammon, ID 83250
800-635-0970 or 208-254-3325
   Home grain milling machines and related items. Catalog available for retail and mail-order sales.

Sunset Marketing
8549 Sunset Ave.
Fair Oaks, CA 95268
916-961-2896
   Grain mills, mill kits, hand mills, and related equipment. Write or call for mail-order information.

Index